Lonely planet

ELECTRIC VEHICLE
ROAD TRIPS
— EUROPE —

Contents

Introduction

This book sets out to expand horizons across Europe for owners of electric vehicles. It's also for the try-before-you-buy experimenters, who can do so by hiring an EV to enjoy a road trip along any of the 60 routes our team of authors and cartographers have plotted in these pages. And it's for the not-quite-convinced-yet – read on to find how rapidly growing European charger infrastructure and the ever improving battery range of new EVs now makes an impressive mix of European nations, landscapes and experiences accessible.

WHAT EXACTLY IS AN EV?

An EV (electric vehicle) or BEV (battery electric vehicle) is a car, van or truck with a battery pack in place of a fuel tank, and an electric motor (or motors) in place of the internal combustion engine (ICE) in a vehicle fuelled by petrol or diesel. Most routes covered in this book are also suitable for plug-in hybrid electric vehicles (PHEVs) – these have a small electric motor with a battery pack that can be topped up by a charger, matched to an ICE to extend range.

In the EU and elsewhere in Europe, legislation brought in response to the climate crisis is driving the transition from ICE vehicles to EVs. Indeed, across much of Europe the sale of new ICE cars will likely soon be outlawed.

While the roll out of EVs is swiftly expanding and the technology used to propel them is also fast developing, the EV itself is not a recent invention. The first practical electric automobiles arrived way back in the 1890s and soon became as popular as the primitive petrol-fuelled contraptions of the time. Only with the immense expansion of road networks through the 1920s did the

longer range of ICE vehicles allow them to dominate. But now a second dawn for the EV has arrived.

ADVANTAGES TO EVS

Drive an EV and you'll have the happy experience of travelling in near silence, while releasing zero carbon dioxide and other emissions 'kerbside' from an exhaust. The greater the proportion of electricity produced from renewable sources that is used to charge an EV, the lower that EV's overall environmental impact becomes.

In Europe you'll often pay less to charge your EV than you would to fuel an ICE equivalent with petrol or diesel. Many large cities now have low emission zones that prohibit entry by ICE vehicles but not EVs. And in some countries, EVs are allowed to drive in bus or taxi lanes and have discounted tolls or parking, while some car parks have dedicated spaces for EVs.

CHOOSING AN EV

EVs come in greatly varied shapes and sizes, from the compact Mini Electric to the spacious Volkswagen ID. Buzz, via the well-established Nissan Leaf hatchback and the Tesla Model Y SUV. They vary in speed (and cost) from the city-focused Citroën Ami to the autobahn-focused Porsche Taycan.

While some small, older-generation EVs have a range limited to perhaps 100 miles (160km), most can now manage between 150 and 300 miles (240km to 480km) – with high-end models like the luxurious Mercedes EQS topping 450 miles (720km). We've made sure that even an EV with a modest range will be suitable for driving the majority of the road trips covered in this book.

Getting to know EVs

The transition to electric vehicles has brought radical change across Europe. There are new laws to promote their use, fast-growing charger infrastructure and ever-evolving technology to improve the experience of owning or hiring one. But still there's room for bafflement, especially if you're new to EVs and hope to travel abroad in one. This might be brought about by inconsistencies in regulations between European nations, in how EVs of different types are equipped, or in how they need charging. To follow are some essential tips to ease you in.

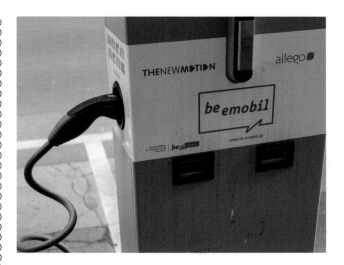

Connecting up EVs tend to have either a Type 1 or (typical for Europe) Type 2 socket that allows them to charge using AC (alternating current), 'slow' at around 3kW–3.7kW (kilowatts) or 'fast' up to a maximum of 22kW. Most EVs also have either a CHAdeMO or (typical now) CCS socket for 'rapid' charging using DC (direct current), from 50kW to 350kW.

AC charging The slowest way to charge an EV is to use a home-charging cable to connect to a regular electrical socket. This is a method car manufacturers tend to term as 'for emergency use only', given it's so slow (overnight won't be enough to fully charge many EVs) and you'll need to carefully check if the electrical circuit is safe to use for this purpose – if in doubt, don't. At overnight accommodation, offer to pay for any electricity used. A better and more usual way to charge your vehicle is to use the AC charging cable that comes with every EV and allows you to charge at an EV-specific AC charging station, such as might be fitted where you're staying. You plug one end of the cable into the vehicle's Type 1 or Type 2 socket and the other into the charger (unless it has a fixed cable), then pay to start the charge. While slow 3kW–3.7kW charge stations still exist, 7kW and 11kW versions are most prevalent across Europe. They're great to use for destination charging during a longer rest or overnight stay, as it can take several hours to charge the battery to 80–100%. 22kW stations are faster, but are only an option if your EV supports that AC charge rate – many vehicles have a maximum of 11kW.

DC charging Rapid DC charging stations (referred to as fast chargers in some countries) are less numerous than AC stations, but they're multiplying quickly and are fantastic to use while on the road. DC stations are most commonly found along motorways and always have a cable of their own, which you often activate by first paying, and then plug into the CCS or CHAdeMO port of your vehicle. DC stations offer speeds from 50kW to 350kW (soon to be even more), although the actual charging speed can fluctuate. It depends on the amount of kWs your vehicle can handle, as well as battery temperature and whether other EVs are charging at the same station. DC stations are best used for topping up on the go, as you'll find you rarely charge to more than 80% of battery capacity. Expect to be on the road again in 15 to 45 minutes, depending on your charging speed.

Finding a charger Flick through the entries in this book and you'll find some linking themes to charger locations mentioned in varied European countries. Along with at service stations and rest stops on motorways and other major roads, they tend to also appear in clusters at spots you'll likely enjoy pausing at for a while – environmentally-minded places to stay; national park offices; shopping centres; larger museums and restaurants; and public car parks at the edge of pedestrianised centres in towns and cities.

Apps for route planning One of the easiest ways to find charging stations on the road is to use Google Maps and search for 'EV charger/nearby' in your area. There are also many apps that make finding chargers easier by offering a filter on plug types and charging speeds: Chargemap (chargemap.com), Plugsurfing (plugsurfing.com) and ChargeFinder (chargefinder.com) are three examples. A Better Route Planner (ABRP; Android and iOS) is convenient if you want to plot a road trip with charging stops. Some charging station providers and car manufacturers offer similar apps, too. If your EV has a CCS socket, it's worth downloading the Tesla app (Android and iOS) and adding your credit card info. Many of Tesla's (extremely rapid) Superchargers in several European countries are now open to non-Teslas – find them via the Tesla app.

Paying for charging This isn't entirely as straightforward as getting out your (virtual) wallet. Although some charging stations will accept a credit card or have a QR code that you can use to easily pay online, most must be activated through a dedicated app, or RFID – a card or fob equipped with radio-frequency identification technology. That's why it's recommended to download some apps before your trip and to order at least one good, general charging card well in advance, such as Elli (elli.eco), Plugsurfing (plugsurfing.com) or Shell Recharge (shellrecharge.com), which will give you access to many stations throughout Europe. On your road trip, bring a credit card and make sure you have enough storage space and data on your smartphone to be able to download local apps.

Battery capacity The principle of charging the battery is not quite like filling up a fuel tank. EV drivers usually keep their battery charge in the zone between 20% and 80% full. The theory goes that it's always good to have a little battery charge left in case your expected charger of choice proves unavailable (think queues or technical malfunctions) – and in unfamiliar places, remember to keep your battery charged up to whatever level will cause no issue if the next charger station plotted on your route isn't working. On the other hand, a battery fills up more slowly when it's almost full, so the last 20% takes longer. Consider it like inflating a tyre: the last bit takes the most effort. To disconnect after charging, unlock your vehicle and remove the cable – sometimes you'll need to swipe your card again as well.

Charging etiquette If you leave your car charging, set a timer, such as on your phone, to remind you when it will be fully charged (you can see how long you have left to go on the vehicle's display). It's considered bad manners to leave your EV plugged in after completing a charge, and doing so can also cost you if the charging station has idle fees. And parking your vehicle in a dedicated EV parking space fitted with a charger but you then not using it to charge up is a big no-no. If you arrive at a charging station and there's a queue, be sure to patiently sit tight and wait for your turn.

Terrain and weather EVs can handle similar terrain and weather conditions to equivalent ICE vehicles, but it's good to be aware of circumstances that might reduce their range. When your vehicle's battery is cold, its performance is limited – so many EVs have systems to warm the battery up... but these drain power. Same goes for heating the vehicle's interior. Using air-conditioning or cooling the batteries also drains power, though less than is lost than by heating. Your EV will use more power when driving into a strong headwind or when driving up an incline – also, the faster you drive, of course the more energy you'll expend. If your EV has an eco-mode, this can be used to eke the most out of its range, but know that it can limit the vehicle's acceleration and the effectiveness of its air-conditioning. EVs have regenerative braking – in mountainous areas, when driving downhill stretches you can expect to get back around a third of the power that was lost on climbs. If there are enough chargers along the route, try not to charge up to 100% in the mountains or you'll wear your brakes faster, because you won't be able to use regenerative braking when the battery is full.

Renting an EV Most major car-hire companies across Europe now offer EVs. And Hertz and Sixt, for example, both include a charging key-fob with EV rentals. Rental electric campervans are becoming more commonly available, and are particularly useful for multi-country, multi-week trips. Always check with a rental company how to charge an EV you're booking from them, both in the country you'll pick it up from and any others that you're planning to drive to. If you're eager to save time throughout your road trip, consider renting an EV that supports at least 75kW of rapid DC charging.

How to use this book

Orange plug icons appear on every map in this book. These show where clusters of chargers can be found along each route covered, typically the fastest chargers available in the area. We've designed these routes so the places we recommend you stop for a charge (often overnight) are appealing in their own right. The gaps between clusters of chargers are paced so you won't feel pressure to always fully recharge at each, or you'll have options if one is closed. The tips for places to stay in 'plan & prepare' panels explain where you'll find chargers either on site or very close by, so you can top up overnight and banish range anxiety as you set out the next day. Many people contributed to this book (their names are listed on p304); they are a mix of experienced electric vehicle early adopters and newcomers, and bring with them first-hand knowledge of the greatly varied driving environments described here – from switchbacks in the mountains of Norway to secluded beach-side roads in Sardinia. They share their expertise on underlying themes, too; look for insights on history, art, culture, wildlife, outdoor activities, food and (we're assuming the help of a designated driver) drink. Each route's description includes the total distance you can expect to cover and the amount of time to allow for enjoying that road trip at an unhurried pace. You'll also find highlight experiences and directions mentioned throughout. The map with each entry gives an overview of the route to follow, along with suggested stopping off points. While you'll likely make use of your EV's satellite navigation system or a smartphone's mapping apps, the maps in this book will reassure of the manageable scale of routes and their suitability for EVs.

SOUTHERN EUROPE

➡️ **Distance: 294 miles (473km)**

➡️ **Duration: 3-4 days**

Athens to the Peloponnese

GREECE

Explore Greece's epic mythology and history as you road-trip via civilisations, legends and lore, from Athens through the Peloponnese, with halts to discover stellar local wines along the way.

Athens' Acropolis is a crowning icon of Western civilisation and serves as the perfect starting point to a Greek road-tripping odyssey. Walk this city layered with ruins, from the beautifully preserved Ancient Agora to Hadrian's Library, and visit its excellent exhibition spaces, such as the National Archaeological Museum. Refuel at its lively tavernas, cafes and bars to get a dose of city life, before driving out into the rural Peloponnese.

WEST TO THE PELOPONNESE

Take the A8 west, 48 miles (77km), to the Corinth Canal, an engineering marvel conceived at the end of the 7th century BCE by Periander of Ancient Corinth. Actually begun by Roman emperor Nero in 67 CE, and completed by the French in 1893, it's more than 3.7 miles (6km) long, cut through solid rock and linking the Ionian and Aegean seas.

Continue southwest on the A7 through the rolling hills of Nemea, known for its fine wines since vineyards supplied the royal court at Mycenae millennia ago. Designated driver excepted, sample the region's hallmark smooth, full-bodied reds – many produced from the local Protected Designation of Origin (PDO)

Plan & prepare

Tips for EV drivers

At the time of writing, outside Athens all of the chargers on this route are relatively slow (13–22kW), so factor in extra time. Chargers are not yet very common in the Peloponnese, so don't skip a charge. Also, remember that turning air-conditioning up to full in the middle of a steaming Greek summer reduces the maximum range claimed for your EV.

Where to stay

You're spoilt for choice with Nafplio's many boutique pensions. Pension Marianna's (hotelmarianna.gr) welcoming owners epitomise Greek *philoxenia* (hospitality) and serve delicious organic breakfasts. Monemvasia has delightful B&Bs, and cheaper options across the causeway in Gefyra: Moni Emvasis Luxury Suites' (moniemvasis. gr) three balconied rooms fill a renovated townhouse. Tidy Petrounis Hotel (facebook. com/petrounishotel), in Aeropoli's centre, is a beloved spot for tradition and comfort.

When to go

Athens and the Peloponnese are year-round destinations. Summer is, of course, hot, while in winter Peloponnesian mountains see snow. The pomp and ceremony of Carnival festivities (February) and Orthodox Easter (April or May) are unforgettable. The summer Athens Epidaurus Festival features music, dance and drama at the ancient Odeon of Herodes Atticus on Athens' Acropolis and the Theatre of Epidavros in the Peloponnese. September's Great Days of Nemea wine festival sees special tastings, concerts and more.

Further info

Signage can be limited along this route and other drivers may go at erratic speeds and have a loose sense of the rules of the road here – keep sharp. With your mapping app, download data for the general area in advance, so that when you need guidance you don't discover there's no phone signal and you become truly lost.

Hiking amongst the gods

The picturesque rural prefecture of Arkadia occupies much of the central Peloponnese. Its name evokes images of grassy meadows, forested mountains, gurgling streams and shady grottoes. According to mythology, it was a favourite haunt of Pan, the flute-playing, cloven-hooved god of flocks, shepherds and nature. Almost encircled by mountain ranges, Arkadia was remote enough in ancient times to remain largely untouched by the battles and intrigues of the rest of Greece, and was the only region of the Peloponnese that the Dorians did not enter. The area is dotted with crumbling medieval villages, remote monasteries and Frankish castles. The marked Menalon Trail explores some of Arkadia's prettiest mountain valleys, while the Peloponnese as a whole is crossed from north to south by the E4 long-distance trail. Greek nature is, of course, imbued with mythical creatures, so keep an eye out for dryads (tree nymphs), oreads (mountain nymphs), naiads (freshwater nymphs) and nereids (sea nymphs). The heart of Arkadia, to the west of the regional capital, Tripoli, comprises a tangle of precipitous ravines and narrow roads that wind their way through the valleys of the Menalon range, speckled with villages.

Clockwise from above:
Lagadia village, Arkadia region; charging-station signage; fresh-caught octopus hung out to dry, Gythio

Agiorgitiko grape – at Gaia Wines. It's a delicious place to begin sampling the 40-odd wineries signposted on an easy wine route.

A short 17-mile (27km) hop south through the green hills lies mighty Mycenae. Settled as early as the 6th millennium BCE, it was at its most powerful from 1600 to 1200 BCE. Spiral up the path to the grand entrance, the Lion Gate, Europe's oldest monumental sculpture. Its magnificent gold treasures, such as the Mask of Agamemnon, are now on display at Athens' National Archaeological Museum.

COASTAL CHARM & ANCIENT RUINS

A mere 14 miles (23km) further south, slip into enchanting Nafplio, where elegant Venetian houses and neoclassical mansions dripping with crimson bougainvillea cascade down the hillside to the azure sea. Crenulated Palamidi Fortress perches above it all. Charge up and sleep over at one of the many boutique hotels here, such as Pension Marianna. Just east lies Unesco World Heritage-listed Epidavros theatre and its ancient healing centre, the Sanctuary of Asclepius (god of medicine).

A couple of hours' drive southwest, Mystras was once the effective capital of the Byzantine Empire. Ruins of palaces, monasteries and churches, most of them dating from between 1271 and 1460, sit at the base of the Taÿgetos Mountains, surrounded by olive and orange groves. Charge up at nearby Sparta if you're running low.

Some 57 miles (92km) southeast, slip out along a narrow causeway, up around the edge of a towering rock rising from the sea and arrive at the exquisite walled village of Monemvasia. Enter the castle, which was separated from mainland Gefyra by an earthquake in 375 CE, through a narrow tunnel on foot, and emerge into a (car-free) warren of cobblestone streets and stone houses. Beat the day-trippers by staying over at one of myriad lovely guesthouses.

Break your journey west along the southern coast with a charge-up and a seafood lunch at Saga Fish Restaurant in Gythio, once the port of ancient Sparta. Now it's an earthy fishing town on the Lakonian Gulf and gateway to the rugged, beautiful Mani Peninsula.

Areopoli, 18 miles (29km) southwest of Gythio and named after Ares, the god of war, is a maze of stone lanes and ancient towers. Base yourself here to explore the Mani Peninsula, threaded with walking trails, tower settlements and dramatic juxtapositions of sea and mountains.

Patras

Erymanthos

Gulf of Corinth

Mount Parnitha
National Park

Marathon

GREECE

08

A1

Killini

Corinth

A8

2 Corinth Canal

1 Athens

Gaia Wines
3

A7

4 Mycenae

Lavrio

Argos

074

07

Artemisio

5 Nafplio, Pension Marianna

GREECE

Tripoli

Portochéli

Aegean Sea

039

Mystras

6 Sparta

Kalamata

Eurotas

Profitis Ilias

8 Gythio

Monemvasia, Moni Emvasis
7 Luxury Suites

*Mediterranean
Sea*

9 Aeropoli,
Petrounis Hotel

N ▲   30 km
─────
15 miles

➜ **Distance: 102 miles
(164km)**

➜ **Duration: 3-5 days**

Crete, Heraklion to Hania

GREECE

Cruise the north coast of Greece's biggest island for golden beaches, handsome fishing harbours and tempting tavernas, plus a good helping of big-city buzz and extremely ancient history.

Crete dances to its own rhythm. This southerly isle, at the crossroads of continents, has a distinctive dialect, unique customs and effusive hospitality. It also has some of the Mediterranean's best beaches, fringing a rugged interior of high peaks, deep gorges and traditional villages. The north coast is where you'll find Crete's two biggest cities, capital Heraklion and, to the west, Hania. The island's E75 highway links the two, via the Venetian port of Rethymno – and unlike in other parts of the island, several spots on the way have EV chargers.

HERAKLION TO RETHYMNO
Big, hectic Heraklion is lively year-round and, while not exactly beautiful, has an appealing historic centre, a promenadeable waterfront and a thriving cafe scene. The biggest draw is the modern Heraklion Archaeological Museum, jam-packed with treasures from Neolithic to Roman times, notably an unmatched Minoan collection. A joint ticket covers the museum and the Palace of Knossos, 3 miles (5km) south. Knossos was capital of the Minoans, the earliest Aegean civilisation; you can wander amid its excavated and recreated royal apartments, courtyards, baths and frescoes. Driving in Heraklion can be confusing, so park at the museum and catch the bus to Knossos.

© Jim E White / Getty Images

Tips for EV drivers

EVs can be hired in Heraklion. The charger network in Crete is limited, with the greatest number found along the island's north coast road. If detouring to the south coast or into the mountainous highlands, ensure you have a full charge before setting off, and factor in the draining effect that the steep, hairpinning terrain will have on battery reserves.

Where to stay

The minimalist-chic Sea Side Resort & Spa (seaside-hotel.gr) luxuriates in a jaw-dropping clifftop spot above Mononaftis Bay, near Agia Pelagia; as well as charging your car here, recharge yourself – there are pools, treatment rooms, yoga classes and more. The Rimondi Grand Hotel & Spa Resort (rimondigrandresort.gr) sits up in the village of Nea Magnisia, near Rethymno; it's a good midway charge stop, with views of the sea and the hills behind from its pool.

When to go

Summer is hot and busy – roads, car parks, bars and beaches will be crowded. The shoulder seasons are easier times to visit: Crete emerges from hibernation in April; May to June is warm and quiet; and in September and October, things wind down but seas are still balmy. Winters are mild but businesses shut; however, plenty stay open in the cities. Knossos is open year-round.

Further info

Book car hire (EVs are available here) and accommodation well in advance if travelling in high season – this is a popular island. Signage in more populated areas is good, with town names written in both Greek and Latin alphabets. Roads – even twisty mountain ones – are generally decent, but may present hazards such as falling rocks or meandering herds of sheep and goats.

Cretan cuisine

Just as Crete has a distinctive culture, it also has a distinctive cuisine, born from its wild, mountainous topography and unique location. This is most obvious in its cheeses. Each village seems to have its own speciality, found nowhere else and usually made from sheep or goat milk, or a mix of both. Some are used to make *kalitsounia* (small cheese-filled pastry pies), which are often served with herby Cretan honey. *Dakos* is the local salad of choice, a combination of softened barley rusks, fresh tomato, creamy *myzithra* cheese, virgin olive oil and oregano. *Kolokithoboureko*, a layered courgette-and-potato pastry dish from Hania, is a good veggie choice. Meat dishes to look out for include *gamopilafo*, a rich rice dish

prepared in meat broth and traditionally served at weddings; lamb with *stamnagathi* (an endemic wild green); and Cretan *stifado*, a slow-cooked stew centred on anything from beef to rabbit, with onions, garlic, tomatoes and maybe spices like cinnamon and cloves. *Chochlioi bourbouristi* (snails) are also popular, best fried in olive oil. If the car is safely parked for the night, finish your meal with a shot or two of raki, Crete's potent grape brandy.

Above: Greek salad, topped with sheep- or goat-milk cheese
Right: alleyway in Hania's atmospheric Old Town

Next, hit the beach: the lovely hill-hugged fishing village of Agia Pelagia, 18 miles (30km) west, offers a sweep of sand and cluster of rocky coves. For a bit of pampering, check in at the smart Sea Side Resort & Spa. More beaches await at Bali, 20 miles (32km) on, from family-friendly Varkotopos to pretty Karavostasi. Or plough on to the charming village of Panormo, which has retained its traditional, laidback air. The calm, turquoise bay here is blissful for cooling off; you can poke about amid the 5th-century ruins of the Basilica of Aghia Sophia, too.

The highway sticks close to the coast as you continue west. At Stavromenos, 8 miles (13km) on, spend the night – and recharge your car – at the Rimondi Grand Hotel & Spa Resort in Nea Magnisia village. It's not far to Rethymno, Crete's third-largest town. Park up and stroll the Venetian harbour to the old lighthouse, past alluring aromas of grilled fish wafting from the tavernas, or among the crumbling mosques and mansions of the labyrinthine

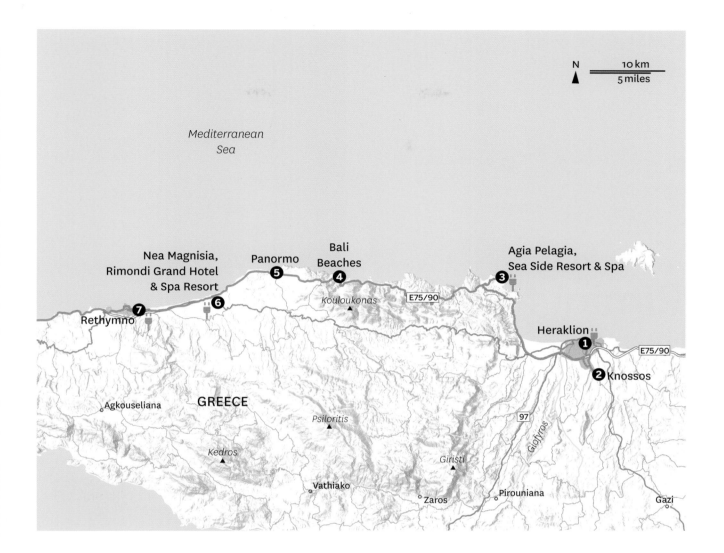

N

10 km
5 miles

Mediterranean
Sea

Nea Magnisia,
Rimondi Grand Hotel
& Spa Resort

Panormo ⑤

Bali
Beaches ④

Kouloukonas ▲

E75/90

Agia Pelagia,
Sea Side Resort & Spa

③

⑦ ⑥

Rethymno

Heraklion

① E75/90

② Knossos

Agkouseliana

GREECE

Psiloritis ▲

97

Giofyros

Kedros ▲

Giristi ▲

Vathiako

Zaros

Pirouniana

Gazi

Venetian-Ottoman quarter. Then, climb to the star-shaped 16th-century Fortezza citadel, an excellent vantage point.

OLD & OLDER

From Rethymno it's around an hour along the highway to Hania. But why rush? Stop at ancient Aptera, founded in the 7th century BCE and occupied continually until it was razed by an earthquake around 1400 years later. The ruins spill across the hills above Souda Bay – a spectacular spot.

End the trip 9 miles (14km) away, in Hania. Several resorts around the city have chargers; leave the car and walk, bus or taxi into the handsome old centre. This is a follow-your-nose sort of place, with alleyways leading to leatherwork shops, pastel townhouses and bakeries filled with flaky *bougatsa* pastries, as well as maritime and archaeological museums and the island's last remaining synagogue. Then join the locals on the Venetian harbour walls to finish with the most Cretan of sunsets.

Below: parmesan
production at
Emilia-Romagna's
Fattoria Marchesini
Right: sunset drive in
San Leo, near Rimini

➡ **Distance: 200 miles
(320km)**   ➡ **Duration: 3-4 days**

Rimini to Parma

ITALY

Emilia-Romagna has some of Italy's stateliest cities, fastest cars, arguably its most delicious food and even a slice of the Adriatic. Its mix of arrow-straight roads and challenging twists are ripe for an EV road trip.

The question of where to find the best food in Italy is a deeply sensitive matter – acrimonious arguments can erupt over the relative merits of Sicilian *arancini* versus Genoese pesto, or Neapolitan pizza versus Venetian seafood. Most Italians will grudgingly admit though that, beyond their own allegiances, the nation's gastronomic heart lies in Emilia-Romagna – a region encompassing the Adriatic coastline, the plains of the Po Valley and the foothills of the Apennines. Emilia-Romagna's hams, cheeses, wines and pasta have seen it become regarded as a larder for the nation. Making a road trip through this corner of northern Italy is a temptingly tasty prospect.

MOVIE MAKERS & MOSAICS
Start out by the sea in Rimini. The hometown of film director Federico Fellini is appropriately blessed with a cinematic smattering of ancient ruins and local restaurants specialising in mackerel, sardines and anchovies. Most Italians who come here, however, do so for the beaches – Rimini fringes some 10 miles (16km) of parasol-shaded sands, lapped by Adriatic waves. It's got a reputation as a party city, with bars and nightclubs at their busiest and most boisterous in high summer.

Plan & prepare

Tips for EV drivers

Italy's major nationwide charger provider is Enel X – download their app (via enelx.com). Emilia-Romagna has one of the most comprehensive charging networks in the country, with a good number of fast chargers in all the main towns. Be aware that once you leave the old Via Emilia route (modern day E45, E35 and SS9) options become a lot more limited, especially in the Apennines, where steep gradients and cooler temperatures can sap charge, reducing your range.

Where to stay

Casa Maria Luigia (casamarialuigia.com) has a dozen individually designed rooms in an 18th-century farmhouse outside Modena. It's a short drive to the nearest charging point. Hotel Palazzo Bezzi (palazzobezzi.it) has smart, compact rooms just outside the historic centre of Ravenna, with charging points in the surrounding streets.

When to go

Emilia-Romagna is a year-round destination, though you might want to avoid Rimini and the coast during crowded July and August. The cooler temperatures of spring can be a great time for touring the cities, as can autumn, when there's a flurry of food festivals variously devoted to the likes of olive oil, truffles, balsamic vinegar and Parma ham. Parma's Verdi Festival also sees arias ringing out through September and October.

Further info

Luxury travel companies can lease you a variety of Italian sports cars for touring the region, such as locally-built Maseratis, Lamborghinis and even a Ferrari SF90 Stradale, which features cutting-edge plug-in hybrid technology. Note that having winter tyres fitted, or carrying snow chains on board, are requirements between November and April on certain stretches of road in Emilia-Romagna.

Motoring in Motor Valley

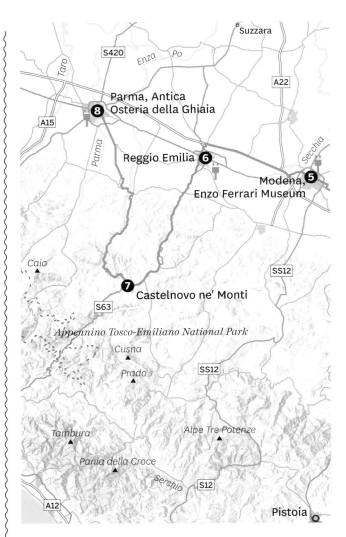

Some say it's the straight roads, others claim an inheritance from a flourishing carriage-making industry in the 19th century – either way, the Italian automotive industry has its heartland in Emilia-Romagna, aka 'Motor Valley'. Ferrari often gets top billing: as well as Enzo Ferrari's birthplace museum in Modena, there's a second museum adjoining the car factory in nearby Maranello, where pride of place is given to Michael Schumacher's F1 cars. An early pioneer here was Maserati, founded in 1914 by brothers in Bologna; the three-pronged Trident logo was borrowed from the Fountain of Neptune in the town square (treacherously, the company has now shifted production to Modena, where it offers factory tours). A relative latecomer, in the 1960s, was Lamborghini – there's a swish museum in Sant'Agata Bolognese just outside Bologna and, a little east, a smaller museum devoted to founder Ferruccio Lamborghini, showing how he started out making tractors (variants of which still till the local fields). Other industry names include Pagani and the motorbike producer Ducati. Emilia-Romagna specialises in sports cars that can reach top speeds of over 200mph (320kph) – just remember, though, that the speed limit is very much 130kph (80mph) on the fastest highways here.

Above: at Lamborghini's Sant'Agata Bolognese museum
Right: market stalls on Via Pescherie Vecchie, in Bologna's Quadrilatero

Drive the coast road north for an hour, skirting forests and coastal lagoons, and you'll see a very different face of Emilia-Romagna in Ravenna. The capital of the Western Roman Empire in its twilight years as Rome slipped into decline, this pretty town is best known for its glittering Byzantine mosaics – some of the most sublime religious art in all Italy. The 6th-century CE Basilica di San Vitale is the crowning glory, its surfaces awash with gold, green and blue tilework, their lustre undimmed by the passing of the centuries. Rest for the night at Ravenna's Hotel Palazzo Bezzi, a contemporary establishment with a terrace overlooking terracotta rooftops, before veering south to connect to European route E45, which travels the generally unblemished landscapes of Emilia-Romagna.

INLAND TOWARDS 'THE FAT ONE'
This arrow-straight highway is a sort of modern day successor to the Roman road Via Emilia, first built in

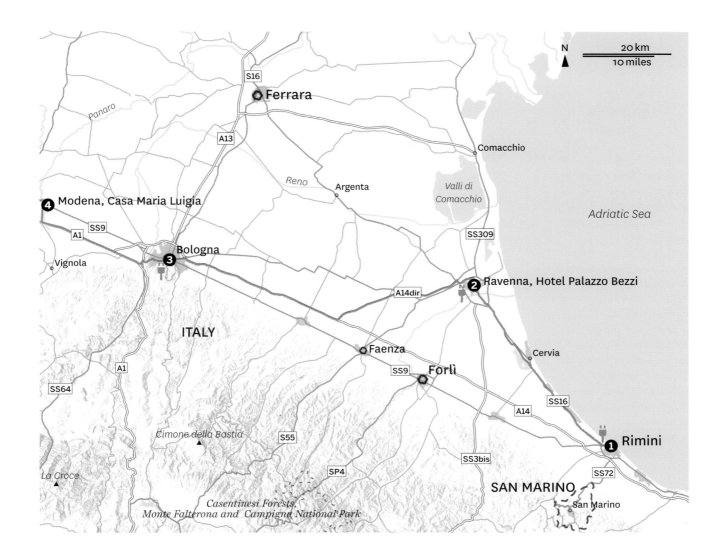

187 BCE to transform these fertile plains into a bread-basket for the empire. Here and there, remnants of old mile markers and bridges can still be found by the wayside, as can a string of colonies that legionaries established along the route. Among them was Bononia – modern Bologna, now the capital of Emilia-Romagna and possibly the most underrated city in Italy.

Steering among its leafy boulevards, you'll find Bologna has both brains – it claims the world's oldest university – and beauty: long, shady colonnades ramble beneath medieval towers. And yet its most famous moniker is *la grassa* (the fat one) on account of its love of food. Join locals shopping in the Quadrilatero, a grid of alleyways atop the old Roman town, amid which you'll find stalls selling fresh vegetables, butchers' shops noisy with the thwack of cleavers, and old-world delis crammed with hanging hams and pyramids of stacked jars brimming with delicacies.

Tagliatelle in a tangle

Spaghetti bolognese ostensibly ranks among the most famous Italian dishes in the world, devoured in the UK, North America and beyond. There's just one problem: it doesn't exist in Italy, and it's debatable whether the dish is actually Italian at all. 'Spag bol' takes its name from the city of Bologna, and its inspiration from *tagliatelle al ragù*, which involves a ground veal-and-pork sauce slathered over flat tagliatelle pasta. The dish is practically sacred in Bologna, with a recipe symbolically kept in the city's Chamber of Commerce. Spaghetti bolognese is a different proposition – using thin spaghetti, and often with myriad more ingredients muddling the sauce. It's hypothesised that spag bol was popularised in the Anglophone world by soldiers returning from WWII service in Italy – real Italian chefs often turn their nose up at this foreign interloper, insisting something has been lost in translation.

From left: Bologna's *tagliatelle al ragù*; the Battistero on Parma's Piazza del Duomo; wheels of Emilia-Romagna's signature Parmigiano Reggiano

If you're shopping for balsamic vinegar, however, hold fire and drive the 20 miles (32km) to its spiritual hometown, Modena, the next stop up the Via Emilia. Along with vinegar, fast travel by road has long been a preoccupation in Modena. This was the birthplace of Enzo Ferrari, and visitors can explore his home, now converted into a museum, complete with a sleek car-design gallery and a GT simulator on which to burn virtual rubber. You'll need to move at supersonic speed to bag a room at the much-sought after Casa Maria Luigia, an idyllic country house hotel on the outskirts of town, with mint-green shutters and cypress-studded grounds. This hotel also lays claim to one of Emilia-Romagna's most celebrated restaurants, with olive oil and honey pressed on site.

INTO THE APENNINES

The next day, head on west – you may need to briefly charge your car in likeable but little-visited Reggio Emilia (birthplace of the Italian flag) before leaving the Via Emilia and detouring into the Apennine Mountains. Bearing south, the road begins to wiggle as the verdant ridges of the Parco Nazionale dell'Appennino Tosco-Emiliano crest the horizon. Stop just short of the Tuscan border in Castelnovo ne' Monti, a springboard for walks beneath the Pietra di Bismantova, a limestone outcrop rising Table-Mountain-like over the landscape.

Finally, loop north into pancake-flat Po Valley, and end your adventure back on the western edge of the Via Emilia in pretty, prosperous Parma. Toast your arrival with a meal at Antica Osteria della Ghiaia, a neighbourhood eatery in business since the aftermath of WWII, serving up the city's signature flavours: Parma ham, *cappelletti* pasta in fragrant broth, and other dishes dusted with Parmesan. Emerge feeling happier (and perhaps heavier) and take an evening *passeggiata* around Parma's piazzas – a fitting final course in the great tasting menu of Emilia-Romagna.

Below: gazing
out across Verona's
fair cityscape
Right: Franciacorta
vineyards, Lake Iseo

➡ **Distance: 258 miles
(416km)**

➡ **Duration: 4-5 days**

The Italian Lakes

ITALY

For the James Bond of road trips, visit the Italian Lakes. From beautiful Garda to fashionable Como via mountains and some marvellous meals, explore the endless diversity of Italy's watery north.

I t is in fair Verona where we lay our scene. The city is famed for its associations with Shakespeare, though the Bard never actually set foot here – but those who do tend to fall for Verona for different reasons. Start by exploring the well-preserved Roman amphitheatre at its heart – impossibly romantic even if you don't visit during its summer opera festival. Wander on for your own *Romeo and Juliet* moment on the banks of the River Adige, or among the tangled web of lanes that connect Verona's many picturesque piazzas.

LEAVING VERONA

A mere half-hour drive west of the city is the spot Shakespeare's star-crossed lovers would undoubtedly have chosen for a spa break, had their relationship ever made it that far. Spread across an enormous glasshouse and winter garden, the thermal park at Villa dei Cedri Spa Hotel offers endless ways to bask in the warmth of health-giving sulphurous waters, all the while surrounded by rolling parkland and rare trees and plants.

Sufficiently relaxed, you'll savour the lovely onward drive. Hug Lake Garda's eastern shoreline for an hour, passing through its namesake resort and charming Campo di Brenzone before reaching Malcesine.

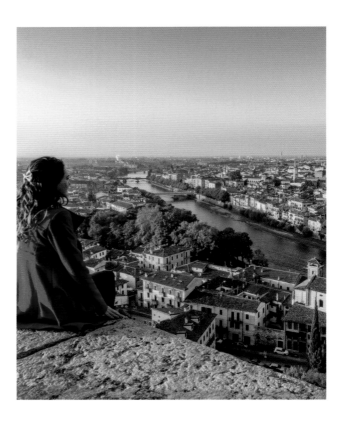

Plan & prepare

Tips for EV drivers

Verona has two airports and Milan three; all have companies offering EV hire. Most fast chargers are in urban centres, but there are a few at the Lakes' high-end hotels; download the app of nationwide charger provider Enel X (enelx.com). EVs are exempt from Milan's 'Area C' congestion charge. Villa Melzi d'Eril belongs to the Grandi Giardini Italiani, a network of Italy's most beautiful public gardens which also promotes Lake Como as Italy's first 'electric' destination. Check out their suggested route at grandigiardini.it

Where to stay

Expect impeccable service at Verona's art-filled Hotel Indigo (ihg.com); Salò's Hotel Villa Arcadio occupies a handsome former convent (hotelvillaarcadio.it). Vintage-styled Hotel Aethos is close to Milan's Navigli nightlife (aethoshotels. com/milan). Grand Hotel Tremezzo on Lake Como (grandhoteltremezzo. com) is the epitome of old European elegance, with a floating pool and an on-site charger; more affordable is Como's boutique Palazzo Albricci Peregrini (palazzoalbricciperegrini.it).

When to go

Verona's Opera Festival (arena.it/en) runs from June to September each year, but avoid July and August if you want to see the Italian Lakes at their least crowded. April and May are also lovely, with warm weather and flowers in full bloom. The Lakes are as popular with weekenders from Milan as they are with everyone else: if possible, it pays to visit midweek.

Further info

Be aware of local road regulations such as drivers being legally obliged to carry a warning triangle, and that the blood alcohol limit is a comparatively low 0.05%. Pack a couple of smarter outfits – you'll be especially glad of them in glamorous Lake Como and fashion-forward Milan. The official tourist board website (italia.it) has pages devoted to each of the Italian lakes.

Movie detours in the lakes

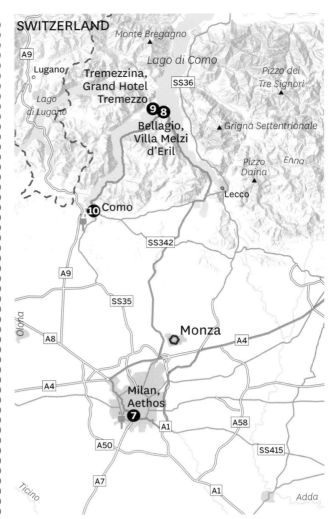

With its abundance of cinematic scenery, this part of Italy has had no shortage of starring appearances as a blockbuster-movie backdrop. Lake Como stood in for the Lake Country of planet Naboo in *Star Wars* prequel *Attack of the Clones*, with Natalie Portman shooting scenes both at the Grand Hotel Tremezzo and at nearby Villa del Balbianello. This 18th-century building has trifold dramatic appeal, its romantic architecture a perfect complement to terraced gardens and peerless lake views – the ideal setting for a tender moment between James Bond and Vesper Lynd in the 2006 remake of *Casino Royale*. Daniel Craig's next Bond movie,

Quantum of Solace, opens with villains chasing 007's Aston Martin around Lake Garda's west bank. You can replicate part of the route (at a more sedate pace) by taking a short detour up to Tremosine, a village perched on a natural upland. Famously fond of the Italian Lakes, actor George Clooney is thought to own a house on Lake Como. Clooney apparently put the cast of *Ocean's Twelve* up at Como's Villa Erba while filming scenes for the second instalment of Steven Soderbergh's heist franchise.

Above: Varenna, Lake Como
Right: the view from Hotel Villa Arcadio, Salò

The main town on Garda's upper shore, Malcesine is also one of the prettiest, sitting on a promontory in the shadow of Monte Baldo. From here the mountain can be easily reached by cable car; the cabins rotate 360 degrees as they swiftly ascend 5774ft (1760m). At the top are various well-maintained trails, and some of the best views for miles around.

GARDA TO ISEAO

Once you've descended, it's back in the car for Garda's northern loop, passing through Riva del Garda before pausing in Gargnano. This unassuming port town is home to one of the Italian Lakes' best places to eat, La Tortuga. All white linens and dark wood walls, the intimate dining room is teeny-tiny, so be sure to book ahead to try dishes such as lake fish or *cannoli* pastries filled with local cheese, Alpine butter and caramelised pears. It's a mere 25 minutes' drive on to your bed for the night at Hotel

Trento

Sarca

SS42

Bondone▲

Brembo

Alben▲

Serio

SS237

Oglio

Clombine▲

Lago d'Idro

Capione▲

Guglielmo▲

❸ Malcesine

Serio

Lago d'Iseo

**Gargnano,
Restaurante La Tortuga**

Monte Baldo▲

ITALY

Bergamo

❻ Sulzano

❹

*Monte
Pizzocolo*▲

A22

SP42

Garda°

Salò, Villa Arcadio Hotel

❺

Lago di Garda

Brescia

A4

SP498

SS11

❷

**Colà di Lazise,
Villa dei Cedri Spa Hotel**

Verona

ITALY

❶

A21

Oglio

Chiese

Mincio

N
▲

20 km
10 miles

Villa Arcadio, set on an olive-tree-strewn hillside just
above Salò. After breakfast drive the 3.5 miles (5.6km) into
Salò for a charging point, then set out on foot to explore
this intriguing town. It was once fleetingly the capital of
Mussolini's doomed fascist republic, and its museum –
housed in an old monastery – gives a good overview of this
extraordinary period in its history.

Next, head from Salò to Sulzano. Though driving time
between the two is only an hour, the Roman ruins of
Brescia make a delightful halfway stop: take a stroll among
the Corinthian columns. Sulzano sits on the eastern shore
of Lago Iseo, perhaps the wildest of the Italian Lakes and
all the more lovely for it, its fortress-like ring of mountains
making it seem mysteriously shut off. Get even further
away from it all by boating out to Monte Isola, Europe's
largest lake-island. Walk or cycle its perimeter along a
meandering 6-mile (10km) route through traditional
fishing villages like Carzano.

Local produce in the Italian Lakes

Unsurprisingly, freshwater fish features prominently on local restaurant menus – sometimes as a starter of *antipasto di lago*, a tasting plate that might include trout, pike, crayfish, perch and rudd, served variously salted, marinaded or smoked and with a side order of polenta. Mountain cheeses are also popular, including *tombea*, made with raw cow's milk; or *bitto*, from the Lombardy Alps, which is aged for up to 10 years. Franciacorta, south of Lake Iseo, is famed for producing some of Italy's finest sparkling wines; vineyards are also found along the shores of Lake Garda, and the pale and dry local rosé, Bardolino Chiaretto, is particularly lovely – especially on a summer's day. Lake Garda also has a long history of lemon cultivation – visit the Limonaia La Malora in Gargnano to learn more and to try homemade products including alcoholic liqueurs and jams.

From left: dinner at Hotel Aethos, Milan; drying the catch at Lake Iseo; beautiful Bellagio, Lake Como

EXPLORING MILAN

Get ready for a change of gear – both literally and metaphorically – as it's the *autostrade* almost all the way into Milan, an hour and 20 minutes away. After checking in at Hotel Aethos, set out to explore the many excellent bars sitting alongside the Navigli Canal. A favourite place to spend aperitivo hour is MAG Café, where an inventive cocktail list and endless good vibes are served up among intriguing ephemera, from a wall-mounted bicycle to a vintage birdcage.

Leave the car at one of the city's many charging points and begin the next morning with a stroll through the Galleria Vittorio Emanuele II, a temple to shopping lined with designer outlets such as Prada and Versace. Equally beautiful but infinitely more affordable are the pastries at Marchesi 1824, perfect with a mid-morning espresso. Five minutes' walk away is the Duomo di Milano, the city's cathedral, a Gothic vision in pink marble.

THE HOME STRETCH TO COMO

Next, it's back on the road for the scenic drive north to Lake Como, skirting its southern shore before stopping in waterfront Bellagio. With a maze of stone staircases intersecting buildings the colour of sunset, the town is so undeniably charming it's inspired pretenders as far away as Las Vegas. Sitting alongside the small boats that ply the waters is the magnificent Villa Melzi d'Eril, its flower-strewn grounds gradually unfolding to reveal a grotto, an orangery and a sprinkling of Roman-era busts. Equally magical is the accidentally Wes Anderson-esque Grand Hotel Tremezzo, which sits on the opposite shore, easily reached by ferry. Even if you can't stretch to one of their rooms, the T Bar overlooking the lake is an unparalleled spot for a sundowner. Tear your eyes away from the view for the final leg south. Como is the Lakes' hippest hub, offering cool hotels, restaurants and bars that draw a fun, young crowd to the town; join them for a final night out.

➡ **Distance: 98 miles (157km)**

➡ **Duration: 4-6 days**

The Amalfi Coast

ITALY

Combining picturesque villages that tumble down the cliffsides, epic coastal views and some heavyweight Italian culture, this has got to be one of the most alluring drives in the country.

No matter how many times you visit, the Amalfi Coast takes the breath away. Driving around a succession of sharp curves, the steep, ribbon-like cliffs plunge into turquoise waters, colourful villages clinging to their slopes. It's every bit as lovely as the photos suggest.

Start your journey in the resort town of Sorrento on the Bay of Naples, wandering the narrow streets to take in the 18th-century palazzos and pastel-coloured townhouses. Stop for coffee on the leafy Piazza Tasso, and visit the ornate cathedral and the tranquil church and cloisters of San Francesco, before soaking up the views from the Villa Comunale Park.

THE CENTRAL AMALFI COAST

From Sorrento, it's a 40-minute drive across the peninsula to Positano, a stunner of a town sliding down the coastal cliffs to the sea below. The steep streets link rows of charming houses, swanky boutiques and narrow laneways shaded by blankets of bougainvillaea. Have lunch on the gorgeous terrace at La Zagara; pop into the elaborate Chiesa di Santa Maria Assunta, with its majolica-tiled dome; or laze on the pebble beach. If you're feeling overwhelmed by the crowds, hike up to nearby Nocelle, a tiny village with panoramic views of the coast. Better still,

Plan & prepare

Tips for EV drivers

The nearest airport to the Amalfi Coast is in Naples, where you can rent an electric car. Classic-car alert: Hertz's EV fleet (hertz. com/p/european-fleet-guide/ selezione-italia) includes the Fiat 500 Jolly, converted into what's known as the 'Icon-e'. EVs are exempt from Naples' urban access regulations for low emission zones. There are plenty of EV chargers along the Amalfi Coast; download the Enel X app (enelx.com) for the latest locations.

Where to stay

Hotel Lorelei Londres (loreleisorrento.com) has on-site parking and one of Sorrento's best locations. In Positano, Villa Yiara (villayiara. it) offers rooms in an 18th-century home; in Amalfi, you can stay in a 13th-century monastery at the Grand Hotel Convento di Amalfi (www. ghconventodiamalfi.com). The simple rooms at Hotel Parsifal in Ravello (hotelparsifal.it) offer respite from the coastal bustle; in Vietri sul Mare, Palazzo Suriano Heritage Hotel (palazzosuriano.it) has spacious rooms in a 17th-century palazzo.

When to go

Spring and autumn are by far the best times to see the Amalfi Coast; not only is the weather generally warm and the days long but you'll avoid the summer crowds, which can often cause long tailbacks on the roads and make finding parking impossible. Between June and September, Ravello hosts its annual arts festival (ravellofestival.info), with performances all over town.

Further info

Sorrento's seasonal ZTL (Zona a Traffico Limitato) is in place from June to October from 7.30pm until midnight and from 10am-1pm on Sundays and holidays. At peak times – over Easter and at weekends 15 June–30 September (daily in August) – an alternate number-plate system is in force between Positano and Vietri sul Mare; plates ending in even numbers are allowed on even-numbered days only, plates ending in odd numbers on odd-numbered days only.

Eat your way around the coast

Along with alluring views and picturesque towns, the Amalfi Coast is home to deep-rooted food traditions that guarantee you'll leave a little heavier than when you arrived. Lemons are the most obvious local speciality, and in Sorrento you'll see them in every shape and variety. They make their way into dishes such as the simple but stunning *pasta al limone*, the ubiquitous limoncello liqueur and numerous sweet treats. The protected *mozzarella di bufala* is produced near Salerno; *ndunderi*, a ricotta or pecorino gnocchi that's recognised by Unesco as one of the world's oldest pastas, comes from Minori. Most of all though, the region is known for its seafood, which dominates every menu. In Amalfi look out for *scialatielli*, a shorter, fatter version of spaghetti served with a mixture of mussels, shrimp and clams. Other local favourites include *paccheri con la rana pescatrice*, a short hollow pasta teamed with tomato and monkfish; and *polpette di alici*, sardine meatballs. And if anchovies are your thing, make your way to the little fishing village of Cetara, where the local speciality is *colatura di alici*, an extract of fermented anchovies adapted from the classical Roman recipe for *garum* (fermented fish sauce).

Above: find pasta perfection along the Amalfi Coast
Right: seaside Salerno from above

walk the Sentiero degli Dei (Path of the Gods): high above the coast and one of Europe's most scenic walking trails.

Back in your EV, wind your way around the tight bends between Positano and Praiano. Smaller, quieter and more relaxed, Praiano is a good spot to stroll the narrow streets, explore forgotten churches or have shoreside drinks at a beach bar. Continue on for another 20 minutes and you'll arrive in the former naval powerhouse of Amalfi. Up a sweeping flight of stairs you'll find the imposing Cattedrale di Sant'Andrea, a handsome Arabic-Norman confection with a baroque interior. Almost next door is the historic Pasticceria Pansa: sit with a coffee and *delizia al limone* (lemon cake) overlooking the Piazza del Duomo.

ON TO RAVELLO & SALERNO

Settle in for the evening in Amalfi or continue on to clifftop Ravello, about 15 minutes' drive away, a cultural heavyweight with a history of wooing writers, musicians

© Mark Read / Lonely Planet

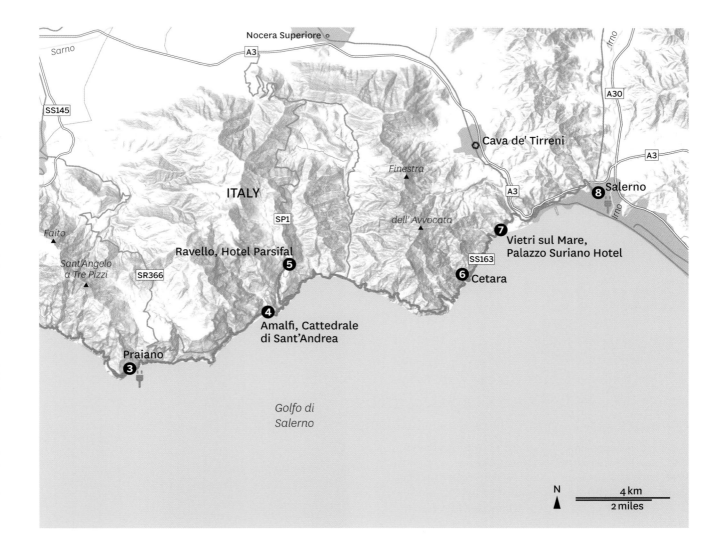

and filmmakers with its gorgeous gardens and views. Explore its streets the next morning and you'll instantly understand why. Along with the town's 11th-century cathedral, plush hotels and fine dining, the magnificent gardens at Villa Rufolo and Villa Cimbrone melt hearts with their clifftop terraces and heavenly vistas. Once home to Wagner, Ravello is renowned for its music festivals, so you may be able to catch a performance before descending to the coast and winding your way east through a series of small towns towards Salerno. If you have time, stop at traditional Cetara, the route's only remaining fishing village; and Vietri sul Mare, known for its ceramics.

Hectic Salerno comes as a bit of a shock after the beauty of the coastline, but persevere beyond the industrial suburbs and head for the historic core to see the Moorish cathedral, with its ridiculously ornate crypt; the medieval Giardino della Minerva; and the clifftop Castello di Arechi, with heady views back along that glorious coast.

➡ **Distance: 200 miles
(320km)**   ➡ **Duration: 5-7 days**

Bari to Lecce

ITALY

While the hordes head for Tuscany and Rome, plot a road trip instead around Italy's heel. With hilltop villages, clifftop towns, ancient chapels and endless olive groves, Puglia offers essential Italy, minus the crowds.

Puglia isn't the undiscovered secret it once was, but with far lighter tourist traffic than many Italian regions, it's ideal for an EV drive off the beaten track. Big-city Bari is Puglia's powerhouse, a busy port and university town with much grand architecture – not least the splendid 12th-century Basilica di San Nicola, which houses the bones of one St Nicholas (aka Santa Claus). It's a fine city for food lovers, with trattorias serving simple seafood and classic Bari dishes. At the seafood market, you can try the Puglian version of sushi: raw oysters, squid and sea urchins, served with crusty bread and cold beer.

INLAND TO THE MURGIA

After Bari, drive west into the Murgia, a sprawling limestone plateau carpeted with some of Puglia's oldest vineyards and olive groves. At the top of one escarpment looms the 13th-century Castel del Monte, possibly the strangest castle in all Italy. Perfectly octagonal, with a squat eight-sided tower marking each of the eight corners, it's quite unlike any other medieval fortress. Adding to the eccentricity, nobody really knows why it was built – it's miles from anywhere and seems to serve no strategic purpose. On the south side of the Murgia stands another archaeological oddity: the *sassi* (cave dwellings) of

Plan & prepare

Tips for EV drivers

Puglia remains a rural area and, at the time of writing, EV infrastructure rollout hasn't yet reached all of it – so plan your recharging carefully. Hilly, winding roads and searing-hot days (hard work for the air-con) are taxing on battery charge, too. When visiting hilltop towns it's nearly always better to park on the outskirts, where you may well find a public car park with a charge point.

Where to stay

Puglia's most characterful places to stay are its *masserie*, or manor farms. Modern and minimalist, the Nicolaus (thenicolaushotel.com) makes a fancy Bari base, with a handy location in Poggiofranco and private parking. Borgo dei Lecci (ilborgodeilecci. com), near Fasano, is a former nobleman's mansion with its own *trulli* (traditional conical-roofed houses) within its grounds. The Hotel delle Palme (hoteldellepalmelecce. it) is one of the few Lecce hotels with private parking. All the above hotels have charging facilities.

When to go

It's no surprise that peak summer in Puglia can prove to be unpleasantly hot. July and August are worth avoiding, not just for the excessive temperatures, but also for the excessive crowds. September and October are the ideal months, as they fall after the harvest, allowing you to taste the pick of that season's grapes, vegetables and olives.

Further info

Puglia offers the potential for onward travel to Greece, Croatia and Albania. The two main ports are Bari and Brindisi, from where you can catch ferries to Vlorë and Durrës (Albania), Bar (Montenegro), and Cephalonia, Corfu, Igoumenitsa and Patras (Greece). Fares from Bari to Greece are more expensive than those from Brindisi.

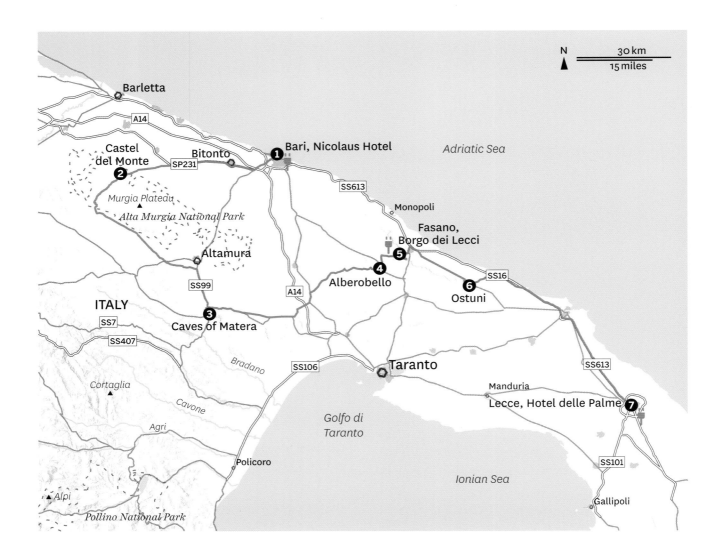

Matera. Deep hollows and caverns in the limestone here made perfect pre-made homes in prehistoric times. The caves were expanded and built upon over the centuries – many were still lived in as recently as the 1950s. It's said that Matera is the world's third-oldest human settlement, with an inhabited history stretching back 7000 years.

FROM HILLTOP TOWNS TO THE SEA

East of Matera lies the picturesque, green Valle d'Itria, characterised by drystone walls, narrow lanes, old vineyards and almond and olive groves. It's also home to a string of hilltop towns, as well as Puglia's most prestigious Unesco World Heritage Site: the *trulli* of Alberobello. These curious, beehive-shaped houses pepper the hillsides around the town. Bright-white and built from limestone, they're a fascinating sight, but it can become hectic with visitors here in summer, so plan accordingly. If you only have time to explore one of the area's hilltop

towns, Ostuni is a fine choice: white as marble and set around a sparkling cathedral, it's best-known to Italians for its premium olive oil, DOC Collina di Brindisi.

After exploring the *zona trulli*, follow the road along the coast, admiring blue Adriatic views en route to the port of Brindisi. It's not the prettiest city, so skip it and head on to lovely Lecce, 'the Florence of the South'. Brimming with ostentatious buildings – cathedrals, townhouses, chapels and basilicas – it even has its own architectural style, *barocco leccese* (Lecce baroque), exemplified by the fabulously over-the-top Basilica di Santa Croce, where a menagerie of gargoyles, cherubs, dragons and dodos cavort across the facade. Lecce is a beguiling town, with lots of buzzy cafes and traditional trattorias serving *cucina povera* (cuisine of the poor) dishes. Once you've exhausted the sights, explore the coastline and seaside towns en route to Otranto and the headland at Santa Maria di Leuca – the spiky tip of Italy's heel.

Cucina povera

If you want to taste Italian food like mamma (or nonna) makes it, Puglia's the place. Italy's 'foot' was once dominated by agriculture and fishing, and most people survived off the fruits of the land and the sea. Simple, rustic dishes still predominate, with traditional recipes passed down through many generations. Today, *cucina povera*, the 'cuisine of the poor', is a term used by TV chefs and Michelin-starred restaurants, but it's a practical, unpretentious style of cooking born out of necessity. Vegetables and seafood feature heavily, with meat used more sparingly. Classic Pugliese *primi* (first courses) include *orecchiette con cime di rapa*, which combines green, leafy vegetables with anchovies, olive oil, chilli peppers, garlic and Pecorino cheese. It's served with *orecchiette* (little ears), the region's signature pasta. Another popular *orecchiette* dish is *ragù di carne di cavallo* (horsemeat), sometimes known as *ragù alla barese*. In Bari, look out for *riso, patate e cozze* (rice, potatoes and mussels baked in the oven). Staple cheeses are *burrata* and *pecorino di filiano*, a sheep's-milk cheese from Basilicata. And in Matera, look out for *pane di Matera*, the crusty, horn-shaped loaves sold in every bakery.

Clockwise from top left:
The elaborate Basilica di Santa Croce, Lecce; making *orecchiette* pasta; freshly opened sea urchins, Bari

Below: reach scenic spots like Grotta del Bue Marino on a boat-trip from Cala Gonone
Right: pastel perfection in the Bosa backstreets

→ **Distance: 357 miles (575km)**

→ **Duration: 3-4 days**

Sardinia, south to north

ITALY

Wind your way up the length of gorgeous Sardinia, visiting mysterious ancient ruins, jewel-toned waterfront towns, mountain hamlets and soft white beaches, all the while sampling creative Sardinian cuisine.

Sardinia's capital, Cagliari, twists from modern roads up into the narrow walking lanes of its *castello* district, perched on a rocky peak. Circled by imposing ramparts, this hilltop citadel is crammed with palazzi and towers glowing gold in the sun. Capture the moment at one of the laidback terrace bars on the parapets, with dress-circle views of the city below.

DRIVING NORTH INTO PREHISTORY

An hour's drive north through fertile countryside brings you to the intriguing ruins at Barumini. Nuraghe Su Nuraxi is Sardinia's sole Unesco World Heritage Site, rising from between knolls and valleys as you head along the undulating country road. This grand black tower of massive stones is surrounded by an entire hamlet of ruins. While you charge your EV, take a guided tour to actually climb inside.

It's beautifully paired with the Nuraghe di Santa Cristina, an hour north, another mind-boggling remnant of the Bronze Age (11th–9th century BCE). The extraordinary *tempio a pozzo* (well temple) is one of the best preserved in Sardinia. If you're feeling peckish en route, stop for lunch in Oristano's charming old centre and top up your car's charge.

© Kite_rin / Shutterstock

Plan & prepare

Tips for EV drivers

Rapid chargers are almost exclusively located in Sardinia's larger cities, although slower chargers abound across the island – with the exception of the mountains, where they don't exist at all. Be sure to plan your charging stops carefully. Expect infrastructure to improve, along with more widespread availability of EVs for rent from hubs such as Cagliari.

Where to stay

In Bosa, several rooms at restored 1890s Palazzo Sa Pischedda Hotel (palazzosapischedda.it) retain their frescoed ceilings; some have river-facing terraces. Set in gardens on the cliffs above Cala Gonone, Hotel L'Oasi (loasihotel.com) offers sea views from many of its breezy rooms. In Olbia, the upper-floor rooms at Hotel Panorama (hotelpanoramaolbia. it) brilliantly live up to the name. Family-run Residenza Mordini, in La Maddalena (residenzamordini.com), provides delicious breakfasts, parking and a pool.

When to go

May to October is the best time to travel, with warmer weather and plenty of sunshine, but a trip in February could include Carnival, when *mamuthones* wear shaggy sheepskins and beastly wooden masks in Mamoiada. March/April brings Holy Week, with solemn processions and Passion plays around the island. Festa di Sant'Efisio, on 1 May, explodes with an enormous and colourful parade from Cagliari to Nora.

Further info

Local drivers are generally courteous, and driving in Sardinia is reasonably stress-free. Traffic is only really a concern in the main towns (Cagliari, Sassari and Olbia) and in high summer. The chief hazards are flocks of sheep. A fabulous alternative to the expressways is the system of smaller *strade provinciali* (provincial roads), marked as P or SP on maps. These are sometimes little more than country lanes, but provide access to beautiful scenery and small towns and villages.

Clockwise from top left: traditional *mamuthones* costume at Mamoiada Carnival; Cagliari Old Town; Cala Fuili, a short drive south of Cala Gonone

Sardinia's larder

'Organic' and 'slow food' are modern-day buzzwords for what Sardinia has been doing for centuries. Trawl the countryside for farms selling their own cheeses, salami and full-bodied Cannonau red wines. Buy artistic-looking loaves and almondy sweets from bakeries and confectioners in Cagliari and Nuoro. Dive into a smorgasbord of seafood. Or sample the lot at a rustic *agriturismo*, where your hosts will ply you with course after course of antipasti, potato-and-mint-filled *culurgiones* (ravioli), slow-roasted suckling pig and honey-drenched *seadas* (fritters). Unique pastas here include *malloreddus*, dense, shell-shaped and made of semolina flavoured with saffron; they're usually served with *salsa alla campidanese* (sausage and tomato sauce). Another uniquely Sardinian creation is *fregola*, a granular pasta similar to couscous, which is often served in soups and broths. Sardinia is an island of shepherds, so it's hardly surprising that cheese-making is a fine art here. Cheese has been produced on the island for nearly 5000 years, and Sardinia makes about 80 per cent of Italy's Pecorino (sheep's milk cheese). Gourmands will delight in flavours and textures, from tangy *pecorino sardo* to smoked varieties, creamy goat cheeses (such as *ircano* and *caprino*), *ricotta* and speciality cheeses like *canestrato*, with peppercorns and herbs.

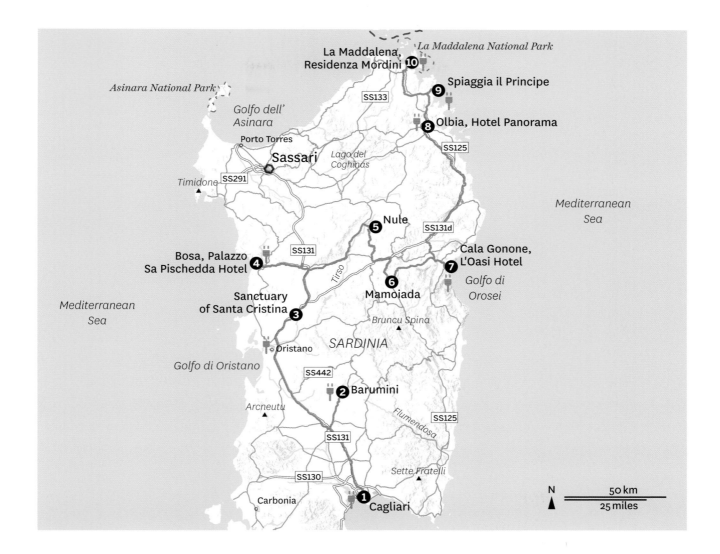

It's worth getting to the next stop, Bosa, for sunset, when the elegant houses in a fresco-painter's colour palette are alight. Fishing boats bob on the Temo River and the medieval Castello Malaspina perches on a steep hillside above. Sample fresh fish at Bosa's family-run restaurants or explore ruined coastal towers, then spend the night.

Drive east for an hour and a half to reach tiny Nule, a hamlet in high plains patchworked with oak groves. There, virtuoso designer and weaver Eugenia Pinna and her team make and sell intricate, hand-dyed tapestries. Call ahead for an appointment to see the looms and finished works.

An hour south, Mamoiada is part of the rugged, fascinating mountain terrain called Barbagia. Sitting at this region's northern tip, the town gives a taste of ancient culture and ritual, passed down through the ages but very much alive today. The Museo delle Maschere Mediterranee's excellent exhibits include a multimedia presentation and the area's renowned Carnival costumes.

ON TO THE SEA

If you need a charge, top up in Nuoro during lunch, then descend east to the scintillating scoop of Cala Gonone, where brilliant-blue waters twinkle along sheer white cliffs and rock pinnacles. Overnight to enjoy a leisurely dip and take a boat to hidden coves and white-sand beaches. An hour-and-a-half north over a mountain pass, Olbia returns you to city life. Lunch at one of its many superb osterias and stay at scenically-located Hotel Panorama.

Finally, continue on to the storied Costa Smeralda, playground of the wealthy. Leave the car charging at Spiaggia il Principe while you swim in the warm, cerulean waters. Then wind north along undulating inlets to reach the ferry to the Maddalena Islands –you can bring your EV and charge it in the main town. This protected archipelago offers days of exploration or R&R, from boating around its islets to exploring the home of Garibaldi amidst wild boar and mouflon clambering over rocks.

Below: Mġarr, arrival
point of Gozo-bound
ferries from Ċirkewwa
Right: fortified Senglea,
across the Grand
Harbour from Valletta

→ **Distance: 48 miles
(78km)**

→ **Duration: 2-4 days**

Valletta to Gozo

MALTA

This brief, easy-paced driving tour of Malta explores elegant cities built by
the Knights of St John, cathedral-topped warrens of medieval streets, and
impeccably-preserved prehistoric sites, all surrounded by beautiful blue waters.

Glorious honey-coloured Valletta, Malta's capital,
is the setting for the start of this tour, if not any
driving just yet. The Unesco World Heritage-listed
city's narrow streets are a nightmare to navigate by car, so
park your EV up before exploring on foot. There's a park-
and-ride facility just south of the capital near Floriana,
with charge points close by.

Highlights of this broadly 16th-century city include
the monumental St John's Co-Cathedral, whose baroque
interior is adorned by Caravaggios, and the Grand
Master's Palace, the richly decorated former residence of
the Grand Masters of the Knights of St John.

You can cross from Valletta's Grand Harbour to the
Three Cities (Vittoriosa, Senglea and Cospicua) by
dgħajsa – Malta's traditional hand-rowed water taxi
service – or by ferry. Pre-dating Valletta and lending
beautiful views, Vittoriosa's alleys and waterfront
are ideal for a stroll. A ferry service also runs from
Marsamxett Harbour on the northern edge of Valletta to
Sliema's harbourside bars and restaurants.

LEAVING VALLETTA
From Valletta, it's a short 15-minute drive south to
the Ħal Saflieni Hypogeum (from the Greek, meaning

Plan & prepare

Tips for EV drivers

Despite the Maltese government's push for widespread adoption of EVs, the airport is still your best bet for renting one. To get a good deal, reserve well in advance. Smarter Car Rentals in Valletta has two-seater electric Twizys, suitable for day trips. While there is a healthy spread of chargers throughout Malta, most tend to be slower 22kW types, so build time into your schedule for charging. EVs can enter Valletta without paying the city's emissions charge.

Where to stay

In Valletta, 19 Rooms (19rooms.com.mt) offers contemporary design in a handsome 300-year-old townhouse, while the classic Grand Harbour Hotel (grandharbourhotel.com) has unbeatable views. The Point De Vue (pointdevue-mdina. com) is an affordable family-run guesthouse in Mdina; choose a large room for a balcony. At ThirtySeven Gozo (thirtysevengozo.com) the owners' fashion backgrounds are put to good use, with converted farmhouses providing a stylish base.

When to go

Be aware that the summer months of June, July and August are by far the most popular for visitors, including the many circling the Mediterranean by cruise ship. Head to Malta off-season and you'll avoid the most intense heat and those crowds; the shoulder-season months of April, May and September strike an ideal balance.

Further info

Malta is a compact destination, with only short distances to cover between the major sites to visit. However, traffic can be heavy, particularly around more built-up areas. A leftover of this island nation having once been part of the British Empire, you still drive on the left and traffic signs are mostly the same as those in the UK.

Keeping ancient traditions alive

An aerial view of Malta reveals a chequerboard of fields, each a stone-bordered square devoted to the cultivation of crops such as tomatoes and strawberries, many of which are farmed with traditional methods. It's hard work and a world away from the beach resorts most people know the islands for. Malta's natural beauty and history have attracted visitors for centuries, but mass tourism has threatened to homogenise much of what made the islands so unique. Over the past decade a local organisation, The Merill Rural Network (merill.com. mt), has sought to find ways to revive pride in Malta's heritage, by working with farmers, ecologists and local artisans to promote ancient traditions like salt panning and olive oil production to visitors. The island's salt panning industry has been led by a handful of families for over two hundred years, and you can visit them near Xwejni Bay on Gozo (facebook.com/ xwejnisaltpans) and at the Darmanin Salt Pans on the main island, at Marsaskala. Check maltaruraltours.com for details of rural tours, and support local producers by choosing to buy panned salt, cheese and olive oil as gifts to bring home.

From left: salt pans near Marsalforn, Gozo; a dip at the Blue Hole, stellar snorkel and scuba spot on Gozo's northwest coast

'underground'), an astounding subterranean necropolis, discovered during building work in 1902 and dating from the 4th century BCE. From here, follow the road southeast to Marsaxlokk, a pretty fishing village with a lively Sunday market and, close by, St Peter's Pool – a natural lido in the rocks, popular with swimmers.

Drive south to the megalithic temples of Ħaġar Qim ('standing stones') and Mnajdra. Positioned on a hilltop, these late-Neolithic temples are Malta's best-preserved prehistoric sites. There are photo opportunities en route too at the Blue Grotto, sea caves set among cliffs just to the east of the seaside hamlet of Wied iż-Żurrieq.

From here the route takes you past vineyards and farmland back round to the coast and Malta's highest point – the Dingli Cliffs, a sharp slice off the bottom of the island extending around 800ft (250m) to the sea below. It's then a short hop to lovely Mdina.

MDINA & ON TO GOZO

Mdina's cathedral-topped city rises up ahead of you as you approach, its fortified walls enclosing hidden lanes and sunlit squares. 'The silent city' is car-free, so leave your EV at one of the car parks outside and explore the atmospheric streets on foot. Much here appears unchanged since medieval times.

Adjoining Mdina, Rabat's sand-coloured architecture dates back to when it was a suburb of its neighbour, but as a working city it has a more local feel. This is where you'll find St Paul's Catacombs, a labyrinth of chiselled tombs dating to at least the 3rd century BCE.

Next stop is Gozo, Malta's second island. To explore it, you'll first need to head north to Ċirkewwa, where car ferries depart every hour and take 30 minutes for the crossing.

Despite its diminutive size, Gozo is home to some of Malta's most impressive sights. Among them is the restored Il-Kastell fortress, towering above the island's compact capital, Victoria. East of here, the hilltop megalithic temples at Ġgantija are the largest on the islands – the walls stand 20ft (6m) high, and the two temples span 130ft (40m). There's 28 miles (45km) of exquisite coastline to kayak, mountain-bike or trek, before dipping down to crowd-free beaches.

Base yourself in one of Thirtyseven's converted farmhouses in Muxar for a luxurious end to this experience-packed mini road trip.

N
6 km
3 miles

Ta' Dbieġi ▲
3 Ġgantija
Victoria ○
Daħlet Qorrot ○
Santa Luċija ○
2
10
Thirtyseven
1
GOZO

Ċirkewwa ○

Mediterranean Sea

1
Burmarrad ○
Wardija ○
16
Iż-Żebbiegħ ○

Valletta, 19 Rooms
1
Three Cities
2
3 Sliema

Mdina, Point De Vue
Rabat
9
8
7
21 MALTA
Ħal Saflieni Hypogeum
4
26

Mediterranean Sea

Dingli Cliffs
7
Ta' Dmejrek ▲
29 5 Marsaxlokk

Ħaġar Qim and Mnajdra
6
Għar Lapsi ○
Wied iż-Żurrieq
1

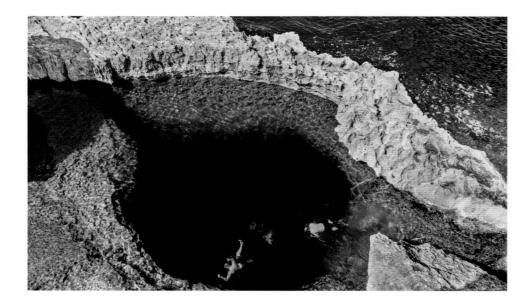

Below: grapes on
the vine, Jerez
Right: Córdoba's
Mézquita overlooked by
the San Rafael statue,
Puente Romano

➡ **Distance: 300 miles (483km)**   ➡ **Duration: 7-10 days**

Cádiz to Granada

SPAIN

The most Moorish of drives? Hop between a handful of A-list Andalucían cities for a heady mix of sherry, flamenco, tapas, glittering seascapes, soaring mountains and Europe's finest Islamic architecture.

Andalucía sizzles, and not just on those incendiary days of peak summer when the mercury can rise to 40°C (104°F). No, this southern Spanish province is fiery year-round: a place of passionate flamenco, exuberant fiestas and a history of conquest and conflict that's left a rich cultural legacy. You could spend a month exploring by EV (well, if the fast charger network were more extensive) and still not scratch the surface. But a road trip between the major cities – where chargers are most reliably found – is an excellent start.

SEA TO SHERRY

Many an epic journey has started in Cádiz. Founded by the Phoenicians around 1100 BCE, it's been one of Spain's main ports ever since. And what a port it is, with a golden-domed cathedral, a maze-like ancient centre, a relaxed vibe and incredible, undeveloped Costa de la Luz beaches nearby. Don't hurry away.

When you are ready to leave, head 18 miles (29km) north, across the San Pedro and Guadalete rivers, to Jerez de la Frontera. Compact Jerez crams in all that's typical of Andalucía: the roots of the region's equestrian culture, flamenco music and sherry are found here. To really soak up the latter, check in to Hotel Bodega Tío Pepe, which

Plan & prepare

Tips for EV drivers

At present Spain has a relatively limited network of public charging points, with most found along the coast and in larger cities such as Granada, Sevilla and Malaga. If you're tempted to detour into the Sierra Nevada mountains, where there are some very scenic drives, research locations of charging facilities and top up to the max beforehand.

Where to stay

In the heart of Jerez de la Frontera, the Hotel Bodega Tío Pepe (tiopepe. com) has no on-site chargers or parking, but it's close to public chargers. Hotel Occidental Sevilla Viapol (barcelo.com) is a comfortable, convenient option in Seville that doesn't require navigating the hectic centre, and has a charger on site. Córdoba's Ayre Hotel (ayrehoteles.com) also has chargers, along with a garden and pool.

When to go

July and August are crowded and fiercely hot. Visit April to May or September to October for pleasantly warm weather and fewer people. November to March is very mild, so a low-season city-hopping road trip would be a good way to mix winter sunshine with seeing Andalucía at its most authentic, without the crowds of visitors (though it can be chilly in the mountains).

Further info

Seville, Malaga and Almería airports are the main gateways to Andalucía; there are also airports at Granada and Jerez. Spain's motorways and A-roads are generally in good condition. There are no tolls on this route – the Seville–Cadiz motorway was made toll-free in 2020. Avoid hiring a large car if possible, to make it easier to park in cities and to negotiate narrow roads.

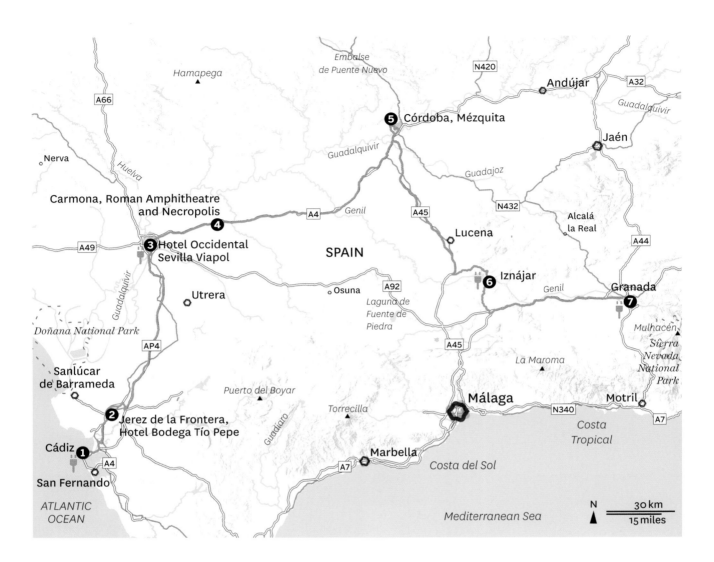

lies within the grounds of a 200-year-old sherry bodega, opposite the cathedral and close to the Moorish Alcázar and the city's historic core. That means you're well-placed for hitting Jerez's *peñas* (social clubs) and *tabancos* (bars), which over-spill with earthy live music, inexpensive tapas and, of course, sherry.

MOORISH MASTERY

Take the swift AP-4 highway and you can reach Seville in under an hour and a half. There are numerous potential detours – the fortified clifftop town of Arcos de la Frontera, the sherry port of Sanlúcar de Barrameda – but you'll want to maximise your time in the biggies. And Seville is big. Big, beautiful, brassy and as flamboyant as a frilled flamenco dress. Allow time to take it all in from the Hotel Occidental Sevilla Viapol, close to the ostentatious Plaza de España and the tree-shaded Parque de María Luisa beyond. Don't miss the city's magnificent Moorish Real

Alcázar; the cathedral and its Giralda bell tower; the colourful *barrio* of Santa Cruz; and independent-spirited Triana, traditionally the neighbourhood of potters, Gitanos (Roma people) and sailors.

Allow at least two days in Seville. Then hit the road: it takes about an hour and a half to get to Córdoba on the A-4, via parched plains and endless olive groves, though it's worth detouring 20 miles (32km) into the journey to Carmona. One of Spain's oldest towns, it's brimful of historic interest – not least a Roman necropolis where hundreds of tombs are hewn into the rock; you can clamber down into some of them.

Arriving in Córdoba, check-in at the Ayre Hotel (in an easy-to-drive-to residential neighbourhood just outside the centre). Then make for the Mézquita, a multifaith masterpiece and one of the finest buildings in Spain. It's essentially an exquisite 8th-century mosque with a 16th-century cathedral wedged inside, the original

Top tipple

Sherry is only made in Andalucía. In fact, it's only made in a very specific part of the region. This fortified wine – one of the oldest types of wine in the world – has protected PDO (Denominación de Origen Protegida) status, and must come from the 'golden triangle' between the towns of Jerez de la Frontera, El Puerto de Santa María and Sanlúcar de Barrameda. It's made from three traditional white-grape varieties: Palomino, Pedro Ximénez and Moscatel. These are used to create different styles of sherry, from pale, dry Fino and Manzanilla (made around coastal Sanlúcar) to crisp Amontillado and darker, richer Oloroso. Visit a bodega or two in Jerez for insight and tastings. González-Byass (gonzalezbyass.com), producer of big-brand Tio Pepe sherries, has one of the slickest operations; for a more boutique experience, take a tour of the atmospheric old cellars at Lustau (lustau.es).

Clockwise from top left:
Barrio de Santa Cruz, Seville; sherry and *jamón ibérico*, Jerez; Seville's Metropol Parasol, aka Las Setas ('the Mushrooms')

Moor of the same

The occupation of the Iberian Peninsula by the Moors began in 711 CE, when Ṭāriq ibn Ziyād led his army across the Strait of Gibraltar from North Africa. The Moors, descended from Amazigh (Berber) and Arab tribes, would go on to rule parts of the region for 800 years, until their last stand in Granada in 1492. They left quite the legacy, influencing everything from Spain's guitar music to its national dish (they brought the saffron that lends paella its yellow colour). The Moors also bequeathed a distinctive architectural style, known for its arches, courtyards and ornate geometric motifs. You can see excellent examples in Andalucía's main cities – and beyond. The vast Unesco-listed Medina Azahara palace-city complex, 5 miles (8km) west of Córdoba, was founded in 940 CE but sacked just 70 years later, then forgotten about for centuries. Only a fraction has been excavated so far, but what you can see hints at the former scale and sumptuousness of the place.

From left: guitarists, Cádiz; Granada's Alhambra and the snowcapped Sierra Nevada; looking up within the Catedral de Granada

minaret ensconced in a (climbable) bell tower. Admire the hypnotising lattice of red-and-white striped double arches, supported by over 800 columns, and breathe in the fragrant, citrusy air of the Patio de los Naranjos outside. In fact, this is a city of flower-festooned patios and courtyards, built to combat the excessive summer heat – after leaving the Mézquita, seek them out before ambling the narrow lanes of the atmospheric Jewish Quarter.

GRANADA BOUND

After a day or two in Córdoba, it's time to steer your EV to Granada. You could head straight there – it's a two-hour drive southeast. But for a little bit of big-city respite, go via Iznájar instead. About 65 miles (105km) from Córdoba, the site of this white-walled, red-roofed hilltop village in the Genil Valley has been inhabited since prehistoric times, but was transformed in the 8th century when Arab settlers built a castle here, the ruins of which can still be seen. The creation of an enormous reservoir in 1969 turned the ancient village into a lakeside retreat, giving Iznájar a laidback air – as well as strolling the maze-like lanes, you can kick back on the small, sandy beach.

From here, Granada is a little over an hour away, via Loja. The Sierra Nevada looms large on the approach: the city sits in the foothills of these massive mountains, and this final stronghold of the Spanish Moors is a fitting finale to an Andalucían road trip. Unmissable sights include the awesome fortified palace of the Alhambra, an unmatched flourish of Moorish craft, decor, design and garden landscaping; and the old Albayzín quarter, a slope-tumbling jumble of slender streets, Arab bathhouses, tapas bars and old *teterías* (teahouses). It's here that you'll find the Mirador San Nicolás lookout, which affords the classic view of the mighty Alhambra with the Sierra Nevada stretching out behind – the ultimate spot to take your last holiday snap.

Below: calm seas at
Cadaqués harbour
Right: Antoni Gaudí's
Park Güell, Barcelona

➡ **Distance: 150 miles
(240km)**   ➡ **Duration: 4-5 days**

Barcelona to Cadaqués

SPAIN

Blending Catalonia's creative and cultural highlights with seaside halts and some exceptional food, this route twists north from Barcelona, covering minimal driving miles but more than 2000 years of history.

Where better to begin your tour of Catalonia than the region's capital, Barcelona? Check out the progress on Antoni Gaudí's La Sagrada Família – despite having remained unfinished for 140 years, the cathedral is deservedly one of Spain's most-visited monuments. Conduct your own walking tour of the L'Eixample neighbourhood's many modernist marvels before landing up at Tapas 24 for a leisurely lunch of dishes including tortilla omelette and zesty *boquerones* (anchovies). Stroll straight into cocktails at renowned bar Dry Martini, which offers exactly what it says on the tin.

Next morning, drive north through Gràcia to Park Güell – another Gaudí masterpiece that feels like a party in architectural form. Get there early, while it's relatively crowd-free, to explore the myriad mosaics and the Casa-Museu Gaudí, devoted to the artist's life.

NORTH TO GIRONA

It's only just over an hour's drive onwards to Girona, but if you're in need of a lunch stop, divert to the charmingly low-key seaside town of Sant Pol de Mar.

Girona gets a fraction of Barcelona's visitors, and is all the more lovely for it. Leave the car to charge while you explore on foot – begin by getting your bearings at the

Plan & prepare

Tips for EV drivers

Barcelona's main international airport, El Prat, has several companies offering electric vehicle hire. The city's low emission zone (ZBE) excludes vehicles that don't meet minimum environmental standards – electric cars are exempt but foreign-owned vehicles still need to be pre-registered (at barcelona.cat). Iberdrola (ibil.es) has Spain's most extensive network of EV chargers – their app has a reservation feature which can be activated before you reach a charge station.

Where to stay

Hotel Praktik Garden (hotelpraktikgarden.com) is an urban oasis in a less touristy part of Barcelona's L'Eixample district. Hotel Nord (www.nord1901.com) in Girona has just 18 well-priced rooms and a lovely outdoor pool. Hotel Marítim in Roses (hotelmaritim.es) has charming sea-facing terrace – and two 22kW chargers. Hotel Restaurant Bon Retorn (bonretorn.com) is a five-minute drive outside Figueres, but compensates with gardens, an EV charger and pool.

When to go

As July and August can be very hot, making sightseeing on foot difficult to endure, the shoulder seasons of May to June and September to October are ideal windows in which to visit. The sea off the costas Brava and Daurada is still a good swimming temperature either side of high season. Visit in autumn to catch Girona's biggest festival, the Fires de Sant Narcís (web.girona.cat).

Further info

Road tolls can be paid using credit or debit cards, but it's worth having more than one card to hand as machines can be temperamental. Consider getting to Barcelona via flight-free travel – for instance, it's a six- or seven-hour drive from the major north coast ferry ports at Bilbao and Santander.

Catalonian culture

Perhaps the most distinct of all the regions of Spain, Catalonia has a strong independence movement and its own unique language and heritage. Local people really appreciate a few words spoken in Catalan – even if you're more confident in Spanish, try opening with *'bon dia'* (good day) and peppering your conversation with the odd *'si us play'* (please) and *'merci'* (thank-you). The most distinctive expression of Catalonian culture is the building of *castells* – literally 'castles' – human towers, at least six but sometimes 10 storeys high. These extraordinary feats of strength and teamwork can be seen at festivals throughout the area, including Barcelona's September celebration for its patron saint, the Festes de la Mercè. Easier to work into a year-round itinerary is the regular sampling of *pa amb tomàquet*, toasted bread rubbed with tomato, olive oil, garlic and salt; and *butifarra,* a classically-seasoned local sausage. The region even has its own distinctive sparkling mineral water, Vichy Catalan, with its bottle an homage to the mosaics of beloved son Antoni Gaudí. The drink's high sodium content gives it a salty flavour which you'll either love or hate.

From left: a Catalonian *castell* in construction; Plaça d'Espanya, Barcelona; Greco-Roman ruins at Empúries

top of Torre Gironella, an old stone tower with a peerless position over the city. This is Girona's most *Game of Thrones*-esque view: the medieval walls and cobbled lanes that featured in the series spread out before you like a living TV set. Almost as famous is resident superstar restaurant, El Celler de Can Roca – book your table right now, as the waiting list is over a year long.

After an overnight (and a swim) at Hotel Nord, head north out of Girona on the motorway before peeling off east for the clifftop ruins at Empúries. This seaside archaeological site was once a Greek, then Roman, trading port – the audioguide does a brilliant job of bringing the place to life as you wander among its reconstructed 1st-century-BCE forum and insightful museum. Your bed for the night is a half-hour drive away through a wetland area rich in birdlife: Parc Natural dels Aiguamolls de l'Empordà. Just beyond is Hotel Marítim in Roses, which has sea-facing rooms, a pool and a great position opposite Santa Margarita beach – as well as an on-site EV charger.

ON THE DALÍ TRAIL

With vehicle and spirits replenished, continue along the GI-614 for half an hour until you reach Cadaqués, a whitewashed village at Catalonia's most easterly edge. Its pebbled shores and pretty port are part of the draw, but Cadaqués' real claim to fame is its connection with Salvador Dalí. The artist's former home here is now a museum, the Casa Museu Dalí – you can't miss the giant surrealist egg, balanced precariously on one of its terracotta-roofed turrets.

The motif recurs at the even more fascinating Teatre-Museu Dalí, an hour inland in Figueres. This red, castle-like structure is a temple to oddness, curated by the artist himself. Highlights include the famous Mae West Room and a series of progressively more bizarre installations – allow plenty of time to explore them all. Day-trippers besiege Figueres, although stay overnight and you'll see the small but lively city's considerable charms slowly reveal themselves. Start with the diverting shopping spots around tiled Carrer de Peralada and end in one of its lovely low-key restaurants.

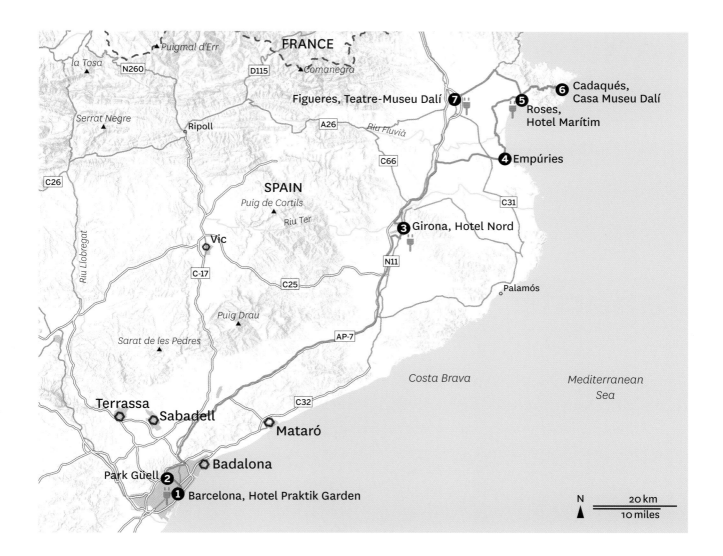

Below: Puerto
de la Cruz
Right: volcano-bound
in Teide National Park

➡ **Distance: 110 miles
(177km)**

➡ **Duration: 3-4 days**

Tenerife, north to south

SPAIN

Forget the popular image of Tenerife – the largest Canary Island is much more than a winter-sun destination, with road-trip-ready landscapes, distinctive cuisine and a cultured capital city.

Tenerife may be famous for its beaches, but your tour of the island begins in its terrific capital. Iberian at its heart but geographically closer to Africa than Spain, the dual heritage of Santa Cruz de Tenerife is most apparent at the Mercado de Nuestra Señora de África, with Moorish-style arches and patios, and a Latin American feel. This is the place to pick up foodie souvenirs including Canarian *mojo salsa* (chilli sauce) and the islands' famous banana wine. At the other end of the architectural spectrum is Tenerife Espacio de las Artes, its avant-garde design entirely in keeping with the contemporary exhibitions inside.

After staying overnight, drive 40 minutes west along the TF-5, ogling the Costa de Acentejo before parking up at the Jardín Botánico in Puerto de la Cruz. Established in 1788, its gardens of palms, tropical plants and fragrant herbs are made for meandering. Afterwards head to Puerto de la Cruz proper, where you can put the car on charge and settle down for a leisurely lunch – lots of lovely spots line its coastal boardwalk and leafy central plaza. After an appropriate post-prandial interlude, head to Lago Martiánez for a dip. An artificial lake designed by Canarian architect César Manrique, this is the town's star attraction.

© ronstik / Getty Images

© Marco Bottigelli / Getty Images

Plan & prepare

Tips for EV drivers

Rental EVs are available for pick up from both of the island's major airports. Websites like ChargeFinder aren't that up to date when it comes to Tenerife – to get a clearer picture of local charger availability, use the 'search nearby' function on Google Maps; there are plenty of 50kW options along this route. Driving to the base of Pico del Teide is a bit of a climb – be sure you have enough charge to tackle the twisting, mountainous roads.

Where to stay

AC Hotel Tenerife, in the historic part of Santa Cruz (marriott.co.uk), has great views from its rooftop bar and free bikes for guests. Part of a state-run chain offering luxurious stays in historic buildings, Parador de las Cañadas del Teide (parador.es) has an extraordinary location in the middle of Teide National Park. For sea views and all-inclusive good value, head to Meliá Jardines del Teide (melia.com), on the westerly edge of the Costa Adeje.

When to go

Tenerife's subtropical climate means you've got a decent chance of good weather whenever you visit. Even if you're in town for Santa Cruz's annual carnival, during its coolest month of February, daily averages are still 15-22°C (59-72°F). Because the Canaries are such a popular winter-sun destination, high season is January to Easter. September is particularly lovely: warm but typically not too hot.

Further info

Although Tenerife is the biggest of the Canary Islands, it's not enormous – with an early start, you could drive its entire perimeter before lunch. It's served by two airports: Tenerife Norte is less than a 15-minute drive from Santa Cruz, but Reina Sofía, which offers more flights, is still only 45 minutes' drive from the start of this route. The island's official tourist board has bags of useful info online (webtenerife.co.uk).

Canarian wildlife

The islands' most symbolically significant bird, the wild canary (cousin to the canaries kept as pets) is endemic to Tenerife – keep your eyes peeled for a flash of its yellowish feathers and an ear out for its distinctive, warbling tune. Lizards are also a common sight, especially geckos which cling to buildings with their grippy feet. More distinctive is the large and blue-smattered spotted lizard, an endangered species which lives in the cliffs of Parque Rural de Teno. The waters surrounding the island are equally rich with life. A 770-sq-mile (2000-sq-km) area between Tenerife and La Gomera was recently designated Europe's first Whale Heritage Site, recognising the Canary Islands' efforts to promote responsible cetacean observation. Run by a team of marine biologists, Biosean (biosean.com) offers small-boat expeditions of no more than 10 passengers from the port of Las Galletas. These trips contribute to local research efforts, as well as offering guests the chance to glimpse short-finned pilot whales and bottlenose dolphins, which can be spotted off the south coast year-round. During the summer months, loggerhead sea turtles can be seen in Tenerife's waters and even, occasionally, on the beaches.

Clockwise from top left:
Roques de García, Teide National Park; Tenerife canary; palms and painted facades in Puerto de la Cruz

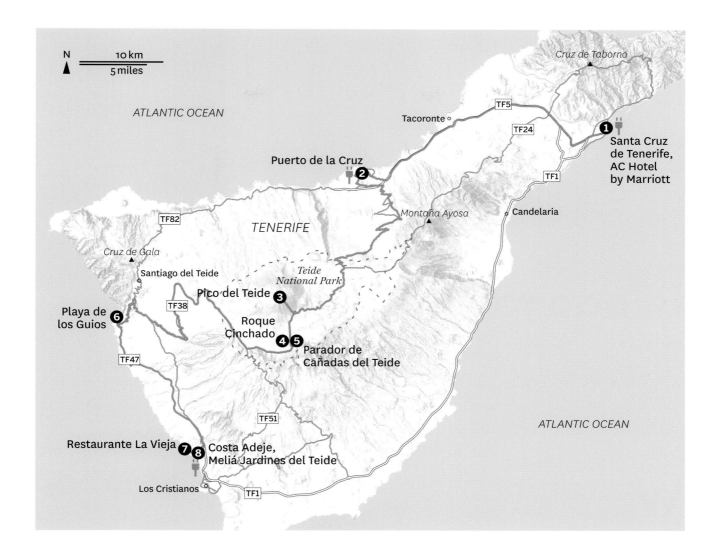

TEIDE NATIONAL PARK TO THE COAST

Next it's inland towards the volcanic peak of el Teide, a drive of one and a half hours that takes you through the Mars-like landscapes of its namesake national park. Check in first at Parador de las Cañadas del Teide, then set out on foot to explore the volcanic landscape of Roques de García. It's a four-minute walk from your hotel to the Roque Cinchado, a giant thumb of rock which once graced the old thousand-peseta note, but complete the hour-and-a-half circular hike for a fuller experience of this geological playground. Then head back to your hotel – clear skies make this one of the best spots in the world for stargazing, and the Parador has a telescope for guests' use.

As car parks serving this area are notoriously busy, leverage your local advantage and pre-book an early seat on the cable car up Pico del Teide; the lower station is a seven-minute drive from your hotel. It ascends 3900ft (1200m) in mere minutes, whisking you up to knockout views over the valley – the neighbouring island of La Gomera is also visible on a clear day. Pack an extra layer, though, as it's chilly up in the clouds – this is, after all, the highest point in Spain.

Back on the road, zigzag west for an hour, stopping at *miradors* (lookouts) to take pictures along the way. The tiny scrap of sand at Playa de Los Guios (also known as Playa de los Gigantes) has a stellar view of the Acantilados de los Gigantes to the north. Soaring 1950ft (600m) from the Atlantic Ocean, these sheer dark cliffs look even better seen from the sea: local companies offer trips out by boat.

Continuing on, skirt the shores south for half an hour until you reach the fishing village of La Caleta, home to elegant La Vieja, a restaurant serving seriously good *arroz caldoso de bogavante* (lobster rice) right on the water. Get used to those sea views – your final overnight, Meliá Jardines del Teide, is just five minutes' drive along the coast, and a great base for some well-deserved beach time.

➡ **Distance: 213 miles (343km)**   ➡ **Duration: 7 days**

Bilbao to Oviedo

SPAIN

Welcome to the 'other' costa. Take a drive from the regenerated Basque port of Bilbao to lively Asturian capital Oviedo, inching betwixt mountains and sea to discover some of Spain's most unspoiled shores.

With only a slender plain between the Bay of Biscay and the steeply rising Cantabrian Mountains, the roads that trace Spain's north-central coast face quite the challenge – there's barely room to squeeze in a country lane. What that does mean is dramatic driving, often with views both of summits and sea, plus fishing ports and beach resorts that have escaped the over-development that blights other Spanish shores.

BEYOND BASQUE

Begin in Bilbao, the once down-at-heel Basque port that's become Europe's most successful regeneration story, speckled with star-architect structures like Frank Gehry's groundbreaking Guggenheim Museum, Santiago Calatrava's Zubizuri Bridge and Philippe Starck's Azkuna Zentroa culture centre. Allow a couple of days, including an evening of *pintxos*-grazing in Plaza Neuva.

Then head west. Within 15 miles (24km), you've left the spirited Basque lands and entered blissfully undeveloped Cantabria. Wild coves (some only reachable on foot) might beckon you to park up and detour. Otherwise, continue to the Santoña, Noja and Joyel Marshes Nature Reserve, 45 miles (72km) beyond Bilbao, which is brilliant for birding. Then noodle along the 30-mile (48km) Costa Trasmiera,

© Ramón Espelt Photography / Getty Images

Tips for EV drivers

Spain has a low per-capita density of EV chargers, and relatively few fast chargers. The network by this route is largely concentrated along the coast – diverting inland, to rural areas, requires careful planning. Bilbao, Santander and Gijón are good charging hubs. It's possible to arrive in Bilbao and Santander by ferry, though bear in mind many ferry operators don't offer EV charging points on board.

Where to stay

The Center Suite in Santander (centersuitesantander. com.es) is a set of five studios with kitchenettes in a restored 19th-century building, located in the heart of the city and close to public EV chargers. Hotel La Palma de Llanes (lapalmadellanes. com) is well-placed for exploring the coast and the Picos de Europa National Park, with EV chargers on site. The Numa Boutique Hotel in central Gijón (bluehoteles.es/numa) has smart rooms and access to charging.

When to go

The Bay of Biscay coast is cooler than southern Spain, making June to September (when temperatures hover around 25°C/77°F) the loveliest time to visit. Keep in mind that the region has a maritime climate, so rain, cloud and fog are possible at any time – but, then, that's what keeps the countryside green. The Cantabrian Mountains are snow-cloaked from December to March.

Further info

If driving your own car into Spain, you must request a temporary circulation permit at customs when entering the country; this will be valid for six months. The Basque language (Euskara) is completely unlike Spanish (Castilian); you may notice that places in the Basque region have two quite different-sounding names.

Asturian sidra

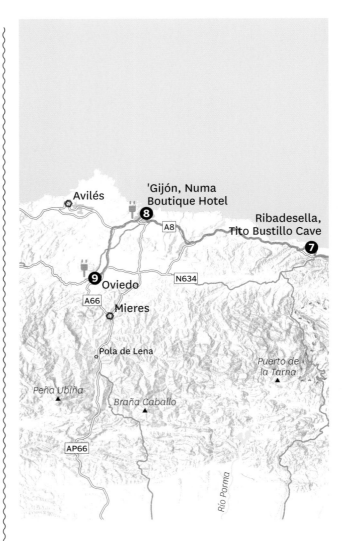

Whether with the help of a designated driver or via overnight halts in your EV, you can't pass through Asturias without sampling its legendary *sidra* (cider). Apples have been grown in this fertile region since pre-Roman times and around 500 varieties are cultivated here. However, only 22 types may be used (in any combination) for the end product to qualify as DO Sidra de Asturias, the traditional Asturian cider that has Protected Designation of Origin (PDO) status. The *sidra* is fermented in wooden barrels for several months; once it has an alcohol content of 5–6%, it's bottled without filtering, and is best drunk within a year. The premier places to sample it are at *sidrerías* (cider houses), also known locally as *chigres*. Here, it will be served by expert *escanciadores*, who hold the glass low with one hand and pour from on high with the other, aerating the brew, unlocking the flavours and releasing the aromas. Tasty, and fabulously theatrical too. *Sidra* is traditionally made within the area known as the Comarca de la Sidra, between Gijón and Ribadesella. You'll find *sidrerías* in both places, where it is delicious served alongside tortillas, cheese, chorizo and cod dishes.

Above: Asturian *sidrería*
Right: San Vicente de la Barquera, overlooked by mountainous Picos de Europa National Park

practically unknown outside Spain but lauded for its sublime seafood and succulent anchovies. The Trasmiera ends in Santander, the Cantabrian capital, where you'll find a revamped waterfront, Renzo Piano's futuristic Centro Botín cultural centre and a strong *pintxos*/tapas game. It deserves a day at least.

More wild Cantabrian coast awaits. Top pick is little Comillas, 30 miles (48km) from Santander, which has a small harbour, an historic centre and a cluster of striking Catalan Modernista buildings – not least El Capricho, Antoni Gaudí's exuberant minaret-topped summerhouse. A few miles further west, amid the dunes and estuaries of Oyambre Nature Reserve, lies the comely fishing village of San Vicente de la Barquera. Here, the Gothic church of Santa María de los Ángeles lords it over the harbour, while the jaw-dropping Picos de Europa National Park looms just behind. Seek out a restaurant serving *sorropotún*, a local stew of tuna and potatoes, and enjoy the views.

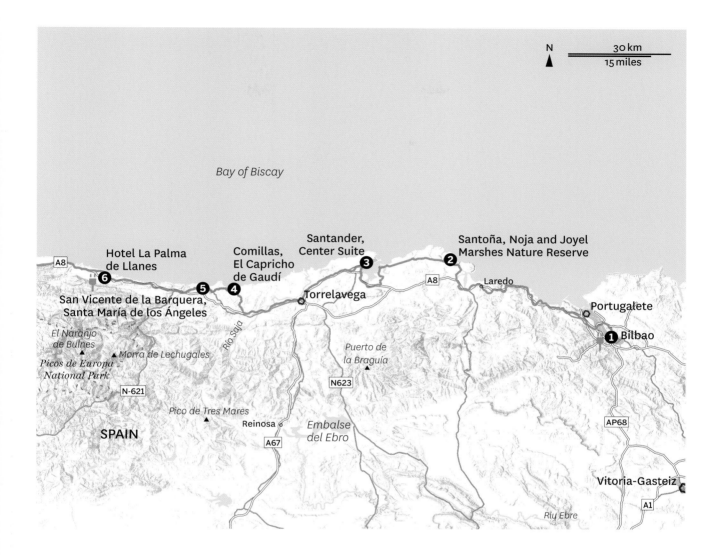

N
30 km
15 miles

Bay of Biscay

A8

Hotel La Palma
de Llanes **6**

Comillas,
El Capricho
de Gaudí **4**

Santander,
Center Suite **3**

Santoña, Noja and Joyel
Marshes Nature Reserve **2**

A8

Laredo

5 San Vicente de la Barquera,
Santa María de los Ángeles

Torrelavega

Portugalete

Río Saja

1 Bilbao

El Naranjo
de Bulnes

Morra de Lechugales

Puerto de
la Braguía

Picos de Europa
National Park

N-621

N623

Pico de Tres Mares

AP68

SPAIN

Reinosa

Embalse
del Ebro

A67

Vitoria-Gasteiz

A1

Riu Ebre

ASTURIAN ENDINGS

The rugged Picos still dominate as you drive into Asturias.
From Hotel La Palma de Llanes (20 miles/32km on),
delve into the national park or head into medieval Llanes
itself, to walk amid the remnants of the old city walls
and along the cliffs to Playa de Toró's golden sands and
rock formations. Indeed, there's plenty of fascinating
geology hereabouts. Drive Asturias' Costa Verde for
around 18 miles (29km) to Ribadesella, where the superb
paintings inside Unesco-listed Tito Bustillo Cave were
made between 15,000 and 10,000 BCE. Continuing on for
40-odd miles (64km), you'll hit the big, gritty port of Gijón,
recently rejuvenated with pedestrianised streets and
public parks. Park your EV at the central Numa Boutique
Hotel to wander into the old Cimadevilla fishing quarter.

Continuing south, end your adventure in compact,
student-filled regional capital Oviedo, with a striking
cathedral, a crop of good museums and tapas bars aplenty.

WESTERN EUROPE

Below: apple strudel,
staple of Vienna's
coffeehouses
Right: Berchtesgaden,
en route to the
Eagle's Nest

➡ **Distance: 350 miles
(563km)**

➡ **Duration: 7-8 days**

Vienna to Innsbruck

AUSTRIA

Some of Europe's grandest cities and most glorious landscapes reveal themselves on this road trip, along with wine tasting, lake swims, mountain hikes and the chance to sample some seriously good apple strudel.

It's a known fact that every great journey begins with cake, so start yours at Café Frauenhuber. This classic Viennese coffeehouse once served strudel to Mozart and Beethoven, so you're in fine company. You'll find yourself spending a lot of time in the city's grand cafes, fuelling up for attractions such as Mozarthaus, where the composer lived in the 18th century. Other must-see sights include the spectacular Gothic cathedral, Stephansdom, and the Hofburg Palace complex, now home to museums and the Spanish Riding School.

INTO WINE COUNTRY

When you've exhausted all that Vienna has to offer – or you're worried about your BMI – head west out of the city. An hour's drive away, the Wachau Wine Road leads you along the Danube and through Austria's wine country, with terraced vineyards running up and down valleys either side of the tarmac. Many of the wineries you pass offer tours and tastings. Josef Jamek is a good pit stop – the family-run winery has a lovely restaurant terrace, perfect for enjoying traditional Austrian dishes based on pike and veal, and a glass of Grüner Veltliner.

With a designated driver on board, take time in your EV to explore some of the region's pretty wine villages,

© Sina Ettmer Photography / Shutterstock

Tips for EV drivers

Austria has one of Europe's best charging infrastructures, but bear in mind that away from main roads, cities, towns and popular tourist spots, chargers can be relatively sparse – make sure you plan ahead. The 'A Better Routeplanner' (ABRP) app is useful for route-mapping and tracking down charging stations. The main rental companies hire out EVs.

Where to stay

Vienna's central Wien Messe Prater (bassenahotels.com) has bright, cheerful rooms; just outside Melk, Hotel Donauhof (pichler-wachau. com) has modern decor and EV charging. Rooms at Hotel Esplanade, Gmunden (hotelesplanade.info), give lakeside views. In central Salzburg, Hotel & Villa Auersperg (auersperg.at) has a bar, garden and spa. Up in the mountains, Lebenberg Schlosshotel-Kitzbühel (daslebenberg.com) has trad and modern rooms. Hotel Grauer Bär (grauer-baer.at) is an über-stylish Innsbruck stay.

When to go

Austria's cities are lovely to visit any time of year – with coffeehouses and beer halls keeping things cosy in winter, and terraces, parks and numerous events to enjoy in summer. The mountains are traditionally associated with winter and skiing, but the summer months are equally appealing, with plentiful options for hiking. Note that tourist sites are busiest during the Austrian school holidays, which fall from 1 July to 12 September.

Further info

You must have winter tyres fitted between 1 November and 15 April; all car rental companies can be expected to ensure they're fitted. Pay attention to road signs – fines for speeding can be steep, starting at €150 and rising to a maximum of €5000; the speed limit on motorways is 80mph (130kph). ASFiNAG (routenplaner.asfinag.at) has live traffic reports and route planning. The tourist board's site (austria.info) is full of tips and info.

Salzburg's Sound of Music

Since Julie Andrews, Christopher Plummer and assorted child actors first skipped and warbled their way into cinematic immortality in 1965, Salzburg has been pulling in *Sound of Music* fans from around the world. The city plays a starring role in the musical and there are myriad tours and performances on offer that add colour and context to visitors' pilgrimages. The film is based on the true story of the von Trapps, and much of the plot is drawn from events covered in the real Maria's 1949 autobiography, *The Story of the Trapp Family Singers*. Notable departures are Maria's actual occupation as a teacher (not a nun), and the family's escape from the Nazis – in the film, they

fled over the mountains into Switzerland; in reality, they caught the train to Italy. To learn more about the story and visit locations that feature in the film, download Trudy Rollo's audio tour (salzburg-tour-guide.com); her self-guided *Sound of Music* walk comes complete with singing. For an unusual rendition, check the calendar at the Marionettentheater, Salzburg's beautiful puppet theatre, which stages monthly performances of the Oscar-winning Rodgers & Hammerstein musical.

Above: singing the praises of Schafberg Mountain, Salzburg
Right: Austria's EV chargers await

among them Dürnstein, Spitz and Weissenkirchen in der Wachau, before trundling into Melk. The medieval town is topped by an impressive Benedictine abbey; the Unesco-listed site, founded nearly 1000 years ago, is still a working monastery.

You might be able to see the abbey from your digs for the night: the Hotel Donauhof, facing it from the other side of the Danube.

FROM LINZ TO LAKESIDE

Around 60 miles (100km) on, Linz propels you into the 21st century. While the city isn't short of heritage, not least in its handsome Old Town, it's a good spot to take the pulse of Austria's contemporary cultural life. Its Ars Electronica Center, dubbed the 'Museum of the Future', hosts interactive exhibits on science and technology; the Lentos Kunstmuseum displays modern art in a striking riverside gallery.

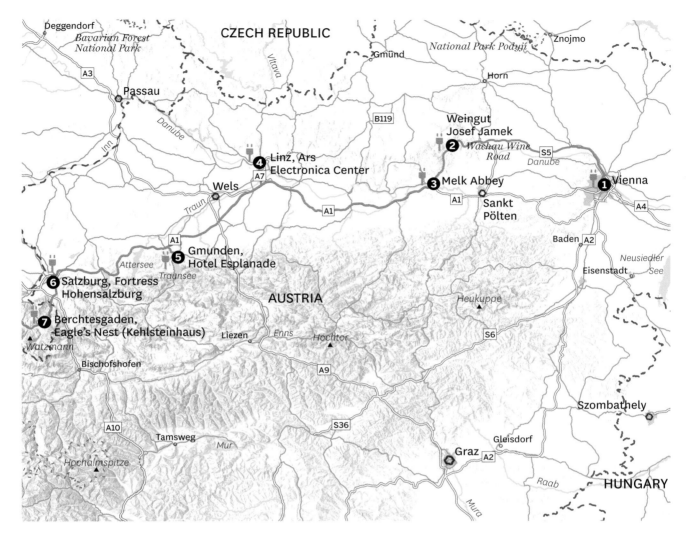

As soon as you're ready to swap man-made wonders for natural ones, hop back in the car and drive southwest. You're heading into a region where Austria starts to look like the country you've likely held in your imagination, with wildflower-strewn meadows edging vast lakes, and mountains dotted with wooden huts rising beyond.

Traunsee, Austria's deepest lake, is the perfect introduction. It's a place to kick back and fully embrace the great outdoors: swimming, hiking, cycling, climbing, via ferrata, boat trips and watersports are all options here. Make the Hotel Esplanade in Gmunden your base – it's right on the waterfront and staff can advise on local activities.

For stonking views, catch the cable car from town into the mountains, or head to the unusual spiral-shaped observation deck, Baumwipfelpfad Salzkammergut.

Vienna's coffeehouses

Wolfgang Amadeus Mozart, Ludwig van Beethoven, Gustav Klimt and Sigmund Freud... Vienna has gifted many things to the world, but perhaps its most welcome contribution lies in the combination of pastry, apples, cinnamon and sugar. Apple strudel (*Apfelstrudel*) is believed to have originated in Vienna in the 17th century; it's one of two desserts, along with the chocolate cake *Sachertorte*, that you mustn't leave without trying. The best places to indulge are Vienna's coffeehouses. No mere pit stops for a cuppa and a cake, they have served as meeting places for poets, philosophers, musicians and artists for centuries. They're so important to the city that they've been listed as places of 'Intangible Cultural Heritage' by Unesco since 2011. Head to wien.info to understand why; there's a section devoted to Viennese cafes, with tours, listings and history all covered.

From left: Café Sperl, just one of Vienna's many historic coffeehouses; Kitzbühel; the immersive Deep Space gallery at Ars Electronica, Linz

SALZBURG

If the scenery has you warbling 'the hills are alive', you'll be pleased to reach the next stop – Salzburg, a Unesco-listed city forever connected with *The Sound of Music*. Various tours take you to shoot locations, as well as spots associated with the real-life von Trapp family famed for inspiring the film. Their status almost eclipses that of another Salzburg icon – Wolfgang Amadeus Mozart. The composer was born in the town in 1756, and is celebrated every which way you can think of: in museums, recitals and walking tours, and in souvenirs ranging from chocolates to rubber ducks.

Salzburg is a city made for wandering, getting pleasantly lost down narrow cobbled alleys and stumbling across ancient taverns and storied old coffeehouses. You'll no doubt spy Hohensalzburg Fortress on your travels – you can ride a funicular up to explore the colossal hilltop castle. The stylish rooms at Hotel & Villa Auersperg provide a good place to sleep off the day's exertions.

ON TOWARD INNSBRUCK

There's a brief diversion into Germany as you wind towards journey's end. Twelve miles from Salzburg, and just outside Berchtesgaden, is Hitler's former retreat, the Eagle's Nest (Kehlsteinhaus). The mountaintop lodge is open for historical tours from May to October, though many come simply to eat in the restaurant and take in the panoramic views over the Bavarian Alps.

Austria's Alps are your penultimate stop. Kitzbühel is most famous as a ski resort but is equally appealing in summer, with numerous hiking trails radiating out into the mountains. If pushed for time (or reluctant to expend too much energy), take the Hahnenkammbahn cable car to its final stop and access the easy circular walking trail that links four viewing platforms from here. Active or not, you'll likely appreciate the spa and pool at your hotel for the night, the Lebenberg Schlosshotel-Kitzbühel.

An hour's drive west (and down) takes you to Innsbruck. Viewed by many visitors as a jumping-off point for mountain adventures, it's well worth devoting some proper time to the city, which has a charming Old Town lined with baroque mansions and a palace stuffed with *objets d'art* and Old Masters. End this road trip as you began: with strudel. Strudel-Café Kröll has too many varieties for just one visit – you'll just have to keep coming back.

➡ **Distance: 170 miles (274km)** ➡ **Duration: 6-7 days**

Salzburg to Lienz

AUSTRIA

The snow-topped Austrian Alps offer many challenging drives, but none compare to the Grossglockner Hochalpenstrasse: a legendary adventure, accessible by EV, awaits.

This mountain road trip ventures into the heights of the Austrian Alps, with lakes, castles, caves and, of course, some *Sound of Music* sightseeing along the way – not to mention the curves of the Grossglockner Hochalpenstrasse (Grossglockner High Alpine Road).

The adventure begins in Salzburg, home of both Mozart and Maria, a city that combines traditional alpine atmosphere with baroque architecture and incredible mountain views. You'll need at least a couple of days to appreciate it properly: visit Mozart's birthplace, marvel at the palaces of Mirabell and Hellbrunn, explore the DomQuartier museum and ride the cable car up to the clifftop Hohensalzburg Fortress (and whatever you do, don't miss a slice of sinful *Sachertorte* from the Hotel Sacher). Driving around the city isn't much fun at all, so it's best to park up your EV and rent an e-bike – just beware Salzburg's cobbles, which can play havoc with your suspension (and your spine).

THE SALZKAMMERGUT
Leaving Salzburg, it's southwest along the B158, better known as the Österreichische Romantikstrasse (Austrian Romantic Road), a famously picturesque route that meanders into the Salzkammergut, a land

Plan & prepare

Tips for EV drivers

Austria's urban charger network is generally excellent, but outside the cities and larger towns – and, here, along one of its most famous roads – it's a little patchy. There are only a couple of public chargers available on the Grossglockner, and its twisting, steep inclines and potentially cool temperatures will challenge your range – to make sure you don't run out, this route includes a stop at a hotel with chargers.

Where to stay

In Salzburg, Modern Hotel Arte (arte-salzburg.at) has its own car park with chargers; the more traditional Hotel Auersperg (auersperg.at) also has EV charging. There are many hotels around Halstatt, but few with EV charging facilities: charge just before the Grossglockner at roadtrippers' favourite Hotel Lampenhäusl in Fusch (lampenhaeusl.at), which has its own charging points. The Grandhotel Lienz (grandhotel-lienz.com) makes a luxurious last stop.

When to go

Despite the decent weather, summer isn't the best time to tackle this route: popular areas like Salzburg, Hallstatt and the Grossglockner will be at their busiest. Better to come in autumn, when the crowds have departed and the mountains are at their most ravishing: blue skies and golden foliage galore. Spring is another good season, but check the mountain roads are accessible: the Grossglockner is usually only open from May to November, depending on seasonal snowfall.

Further info

The Grossglockner Hochalpenstrasse has its own website (grossglockner. at), which provides a comprehensive overview of the whole route, along with handy planning information including opening times, maps and key places to stop. Most usefully of all, you can also buy a voucher to cover the fee for driving the road in advance online – a real boon during the busy summer season.

Hohe Tauern National Park

Covering 717 sq miles (1856 sq km), and straddling the Austrian states of Carinthia, Salzburgerland and Tyrol, Hohe Tauern National Park (hohetauern. at) encompasses an Alpine wonderland of lakes, peaks, valleys, waterfalls and glaciers. This is by far the largest of Austria's six national parks, and forms an important wildlife refuge: ibex, marmots, goat-like chamois, golden eagles, and griffon and bearded vultures can all be seen here. It's also home to many of Austria's biggest glaciers: 332 in all, covering 6 per cent of the national park, including the longest of them all, the great Pasterze, at around 5 miles (8km). Like other Alpine glaciers, however, it's shrinking fast

as a direct consequence of climate change: it's currently receding at a rate of around 160ft (50m) a year, and has lost almost half of its total volume since measurements were first officially recorded in 1851. Elsewhere in the park, don't miss the trek up to the thunderous waterfalls of Krimmler and Gastein, which make memorable spots for a mountain picnic. You can learn more about Hohe Tauern at the National Park Worlds visitor centre in Mittersill.

Left to right, from above: Krimmler Waterfall, Hohe Tauern National Park; Hallstatt, on the shores of Hallstätter See; Schloss Mirabell, Salzburg

of lofty mountains and alpine lakes. Among them are mirror-like Wolfgangsee and Hallstätter See, where one of Austria's most famously postcard-perfect villages, Hallstatt, stands beside the lakeshore (in fact it's so pretty, Chinese architects have made their own identikit copy in Guangdong Province, accurate down to the very last inch). The Salzkammergut region is known for its fantastic hiking, and was once a centre for salt mining – historically, salt was a vital commodity, used in everything from food preservation to gunpowder manufacture.

The surrounding limestone mountains are also pockmarked by deep cave systems such as Dachstein, a short detour from Hallstatt, where guided tours lead you deep underground into vast chambers decorated with ice formations, stalagmites and stalactites: a frozen wonderland that seems to be straight out of a Brothers Grimm fairy tale.

DRIVING THE GROSSGLOCKNER

Southwest of the Salzkammergut, mountains stack up along the horizon as you drive west towards the start of the Grossglockner Hochalpenstrasse, named after the Grossglockner, Austria's tallest peak at 12,461ft (3798m). More rollercoaster than road, this renowned stretch of tarmac runs for 30 miles (48km) between Fusch (where you can overnight and charge up at Hotel Lampenhäusl) and Heiligenblut, traversing 36 hairpin turns and crossing the Edelweissspitze – at 8435ft (2571m), the highest point navigable by road in the Alps. Constructed in the 1930s to capitalise on the newfangled pastime of motor touring, the road cost more than 25 million Austrian schillings – the equivalent to roughly €55 million today – to build. For many, it seemed like a completely madcap venture at the time, but around 900,000 people now pass through the Grossglockner's toll-gates every year, earning its shareholders a pretty euro or two. Mountain goats, ice patches and impenetrable cloud are all potential hazards for Grossglockner roadtrippers, but if you're lucky, the skies will stay china-blue, and you'll be treated to pan-mountain panoramas as impressive as any in Austria. It's easily driveable in a day, but this is definitely one road where it's worth dawdling.

The medieval town of Lienz stands at the southern end of the Grossglockner, and makes an exceedingly pleasant conclusion to your Austrian expedition, with an impressive castle to visit and easy access to the many trails of Hohe Tauern National Park.

Chiemsee

A8

GERMANY

Salzburg, Arte City Hotel ❶

Österreichische Romantikstrasse

A1

Attersee

A8

❷ Wolfgangsee

Traun

Bad Ischl

Woising

Untersberg

20

Katrin ▲

A9

Berchtesgaden

Watzmann ▲

166

❸ Hallstatt & the Dachstein Caves

Liezen

A12

Kitzbühel

Hoher Dachstein ▲

Hahnenkamm ▲

A10

Enns

B320

161

Zell am See

AUSTRIA

Schmittenhöhe ▲

311

Mittersill

168

Salzach

❹ Fusch, Hotel Lampenhäusl

B99

Grossvenediger ▲

Edelweissspitze ▲

A10

Grossglockner ▲

Tamsweg

❺ Grossglockner Hochalpenstrasse

Mur

Kreischberg ▲

Hohe Tauern National Park

Isel

107

Schwarzach

106

A10

ITALY

100

❻ Lienz, Grandhotel

Millstätter See

N

20 km
10 miles

Drau

Drau

→ **Distance: 120 miles (194km)**

→ **Duration: 3-4 days**

Bruges to Namur

BELGIUM

Explore some of Belgium's most inviting cities on this north-to-south route, taking in magnificent medieval architecture and the country's cultural heroes – with pit stops for beer, too.

Surely a hands-down winner in any beauty contest between Europe's medieval cities, Bruges' fairy-tale good-looks are no secret – but don't let that fame put you off. Spend the day wandering canals and cobbled lanes, stopping for beer at brown cafes (beerhouses) like 't Brugs Beertje and for art at intriguing museums like the Sint-Janshospitaal. At dusk the daytrippers depart and you'll bear witness to a transformation, with gabled squares like the Markt and Burg now quiet and serene.

GHENT TO BRUSSELS

After an overnight charge, set out for Ghent, around an hour southeast via the E40. The city is one of Belgium's oldest, but filled with fun bars and great-value restaurants that serve its younger-than-average population. On a sunny day you'll find a large proportion of them hanging out at Graslei, an area on the east bank of the River Leie, replete with striking architecture and scenic spots to eat and drink. Pakhuis is a perfect choice for lunch: a reclaimed warehouse with a contemporary menu and its own house beer, Principale. (Flip a coin before you order, to decide who's the designated driver.)

Next, it's on to Brussels, 35 miles (56km) away. Get there in time to park up and catch the last rays of daylight on

Plan & prepare

Tips for EV drivers

Several companies offer EV hire in Bruges; or you can fly into Brussels and rent an EV there. Shell (shellrecharge. com) and Plug Surfing (plugsurfing.com) have the largest EV networks in Belgium, covering several operators. Electric vehicles are exempt from Low Emission Zone (LEZ) restrictions in both Ghent (stad.gent) and Brussels (lez. brussels), but check local websites to see if you're required to pre-register.

Where to stay

A medieval house overlooking a canal, the Guesthouse Bonifacius (bonifacius.be) is one of Bruges' best addresses – but book early to bag one of its three rooms. Contemporary boutique Hotel des Galeries (hoteldesgaleries.be) is a few steps from Brussels' Grand-Place. Spend your final overnight at the Hotel les Tanneurs de Namur (tanneurs.com), its 37 rooms spread across several 17th-century houses in the heart of the city.

When to go

May to September is the season for outdoor eating and drinking, but avoid the July peak, when most Belgians take their summer holiday. The Walloon festivals, celebrating the region's unique local identity, take place in Namur each September. Christmas markets make Bruges especially lovely in December – but visit during the post-festive lull in January to see the city at its quietest.

Further info

Belgium is one of Europe's most accessible destinations to reach flight-free. You could travel from London to Brussels by Eurostar (eurostar. com), then catch a local train to reach the start of this itinerary in Bruges in a little over three hours. The country has strong regional identities with distinct languages, from Dutch-speaking Flanders (which includes the cities of Bruges and Ghent) to French-speaking Wallonia, and bilingual national capital Brussels. Each is served by its own tourist board (found via visitbelgium.com).

Belgian beer

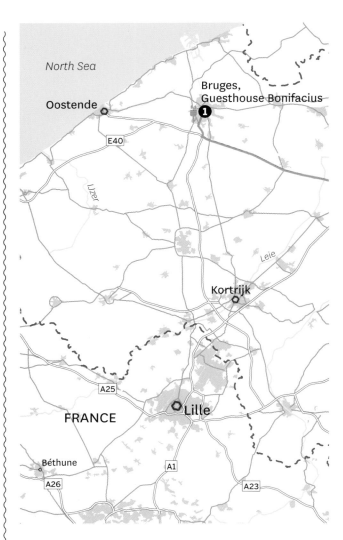

This is probably the only destination in the world where a sip of amber nectar can genuinely be chalked up as a cultural experience – Unesco's Representative List of the Intangible Cultural Heritage of Humanity has only one entry for beer, and it belongs to Belgium. The range available here is bewilderingly diverse. With around 1500 types produced nationally, each region offers up multiple variants – from the hoppy Saison ales hailing from southern Wallonia to the six Trappist breweries where production is supervised by Cistercian monks. You can get a good overview, and try a few examples, at the Bruges Beer Experience (mybeerexperience.com); in Brussels, bottle-shop De Biertempel has an

extraordinary range of both beers and bespoke glassware. Keep your eyes peeled, too, for culinary offshoots of the brewing industry, such as beer-washed cheese and restaurants offering tasting menus with beer pairings. Beer festivals are also scattered liberally across the national social calendar – from relatively obscure events to the enormous Belgian Beer Weekend in Brussels' Grand-Place (www. belgianbeerweekend.be). But save enthusiastic sampling for your overnight stops: any blood alcohol content above 0.05% is illegal for drivers.

Above: sampling Belgian beers in Bruges
Right: Musée Hergé, Louvain-la-Neuve

the Grand-Place, approaching the square on foot from Rue des Harengs for maximum impact. Once you've done a circuit of the ornate guildhalls and the spired 15th-century city hall, head up to the Warwick Hotel's rooftop bar for a sundowner. Suitably lubricated, head back to your hotel via the *Manneken Pis* on Rue Charles Buls – this famous fountain-statue of a urinating boy, surreal symbol of both Brussels and Belgium, is funnier after a couple of drinks.

After a night's rest at the Hotel des Galeries it's time for an actual gallery – in fact, several, all under the umbrella of the Musées Royaux des Beaux-Arts. Top picks here include the portraits by 15th-century master Hans Memling, and the museum celebrating the work of Belgian surrealist René Magritte. Forty minutes down the road in Louvain-la-Neuve is another artist-museum, the Musée Hergé, which honours the creator of comic-book hero Tintin. The building itself is extraordinary, an abstract concrete-and-glass construction that's as

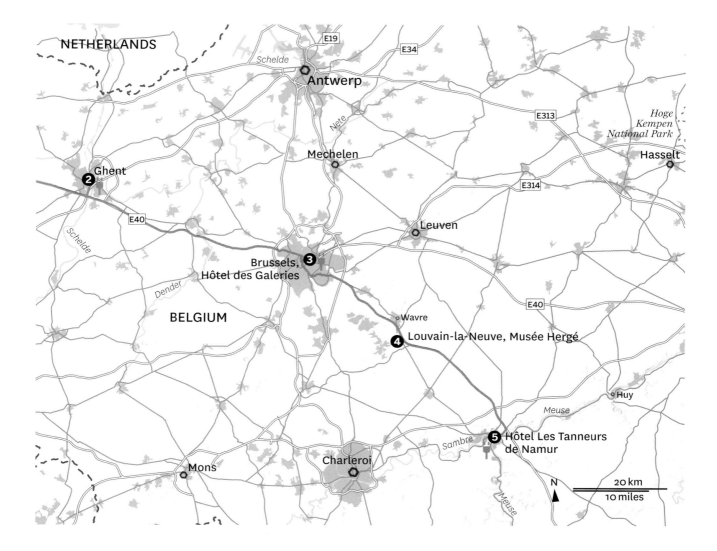

inventive as the man it commemorates. Don't miss Andy Warhol's triptych portrait of the cartoonist and be sure to exit through the gift shop, which is unusually good.

INTO WALLONIA

It's a half-hour drive on to the final stop, Namur, one of Belgium's lesser-known cities and capital of the Wallonia region. Its Old Town is a picturesque place for a wander, the lanes lined with bookshops and cosy cafes, but star attraction is the Citadelle de Namur, which looms over all from its strategic hilltop position. It was formerly one of the continent's mightiest fortresses, and walking its grey walls and ramparts is like exploring an especially convincing medieval film set. The tunnels beneath led Napoleon to dub Namur 'Europe's termite mound', and can be accessed via an immersive guided tour. Finish up with a boat ride along the Meuse to enjoy an uninterrupted view of the city's sights from the river.

Below: fossil exposed on the red-rock shore at Lyme Regis
Right: Durdle Door, near Lulworth Cove

➡ **Distance: 116 miles (186km)**

➡ **Duration: 3-5 days**

The Jurassic Coast

ENGLAND

Explore the ancient edges of East Devon and Dorset to discover fossils, rock stacks and cliffs in all colours, plus the pretty villages and craggy castles set in the hills behind.

The Unesco-listed Jurassic Coast stretches from Exmouth, in East Devon, to Old Harry Rocks, near Swanage in Dorset. Along the way it exposes 185 million years of Earth-in-the-making, with evidence of the Triassic, Jurassic and Cretaceous eras stacked like library books in the rockfaces, telling the story of this spectacular shore. Driving here is less road trip, more time travel.

DONKEYS & PIGS

A settlement long before its stint as a Roman fortress and town, Exeter has an impressive cathedral, a lively quayside and an exceptional collection of antiquities, art and natural history in its Royal Albert Memorial Museum and Art Gallery. It's also the biggest gateway to the Jurassic Coast, which begins 10 miles (16km) south at Exmouth. There's no coast road but you can weave along lanes in the hinterland, occasionally dipping down to the sea.

Some 12 miles (19km) from Exmouth is Sidmouth, where you'll get a good first look at Devon's imposing red cliffs. There's also plenty of good browsing in this elegant Regency resort. Then divert inland – potentially via the Sidmouth Donkey Sanctuary (home to hundreds of rescued animals and free EV charging). You're aiming for The Pig at Combe, 8 miles (13km) away near Gittisham,

© Andrew Pym / Getty Images

© Billy Stock / Shutterstock

Plan & prepare

Tips for EV drivers

Exeter has numerous charging points, but options are limited along the Jurassic Coast itself. Look for facilities at supermarkets; also, some hotels offer chargers for guests. The towns of Poole and Bournemouth, east of Swanage, have plenty of charging points, though getting to them from Swanage requires either a short journey across on the Sandbanks chain ferry or a longer drive around Poole Harbour.

Where to stay

The Pig at Combe (thepighotel.com) sits in the Otter Valley near Gittisham, with homely-luxe rooms, views of rolling hills and three walled gardens that supply fresh goodies for the excellent restaurant; there are also EV chargers for guests. Family-friendly Moonfleet Manor (moonfleetmanorhotel.co.uk), hidden away by a lagoon in the village of Fleet, has chargers, plus three heated pools.

When to go

Certain spots, notably Lulworth Cove, are horrendously busy on hot summer days: parking can be a big issue, and peak summer is not the time for a relaxing drive. Spring and autumn, especially outside half-term holidays, are the best choices, when wildflowers are out and the crowds diminished; visit Abbotsbury Swannery mid-May to June to see fluffy cygnets hatching. Some facilities close over winter, but there's plenty of potential for blustery coast walks.

Further info

The chunk of land between Lulworth and Kimmeridge Bay, known as the Lulworth Ranges, is owned by the British Army. Firing practice limits public access to the area, including the coast path and sometimes surrounding roads, including the B3070 (East Lulworth to West Holme), Grange Hill and the scenic Whiteways Rd. Search in gov.uk for up-to-date information.

Drive to walk

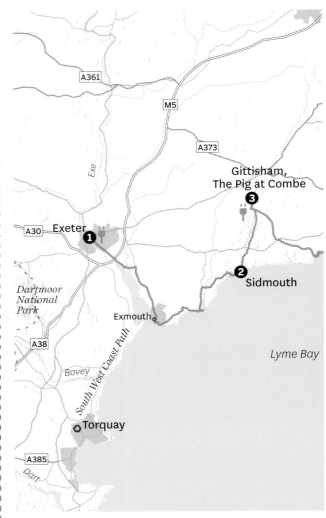

The South West Coast Path, a National Trail which runs for 630 miles (1014km) from Minehead to Poole, traces the entire 115 miles (185km) of the Jurassic Coast. In many places, it's the only way to get near to the sea – roads can't get close. So, to best appreciate this venerable shore, be sure to stretch your legs every now and then. You could make a 5-mile (8km) circuit from Sidmouth up Salcombe Hill, which traces the River Sid inland and affords great views of the rich-red cliffs. Alternatively, stop at the crumbly yellow cliffs of West Bay, east of Golden Cap, for an historic 5-mile (8km) hike via Burton Bradstock and Hive Beach, where training exercises were held for the D-Day landings. Or detour en route to Swanage for a 5-mile (8km) loop across the chalk grasslands to St Aldhelm's Head, finishing in Worth Matravers' excellent old Square & Compass village pub. For a satisfying challenge, make the 13-mile (21km) circuit of Portland, a limestone isle leashed to the mainland by Chesil Beach. A trail leads right around its perimeter, passing cliffs quarried since Roman times and the red-and-white-striped Portland Bill Lighthouse.

Above: Chesil Beach from the Isle of Portland cliffs
Right: farm-to-table fare from The Pig at Combe

an Elizabethan manor with gorgeous grounds, a superb restaurant and a kitchen garden.

FOSSILS & RAVISHING ROCKS
Return coastwards, through quaint fishing village Beer, cliff-flanked Seaton and over the River Axe; after 18 miles (29km) you'll enter Dorset, with Lyme Bay spreading out ahead. Here you'll find Lyme Regis, with its curling Cob (the man-made harbour, great to stroll), pubs aplenty and fossil-full cliffs, beloved of Victorian collectors. Visit the museum to learn about teenager Mary Anning who, in 1814, found the first full ichthyosaur skeleton nearby.

East of Lyme looms Golden Cap, a 627ft-high (191m) mass of glowing greensand rock. Drive on to the National Trust car park to walk its flanks – the views are outstanding. Then continue for 13 miles (21km) to chocolate-box Abbotsbury, with its medieval abbey ruins, swannery and 14th-century hilltop chapel offering

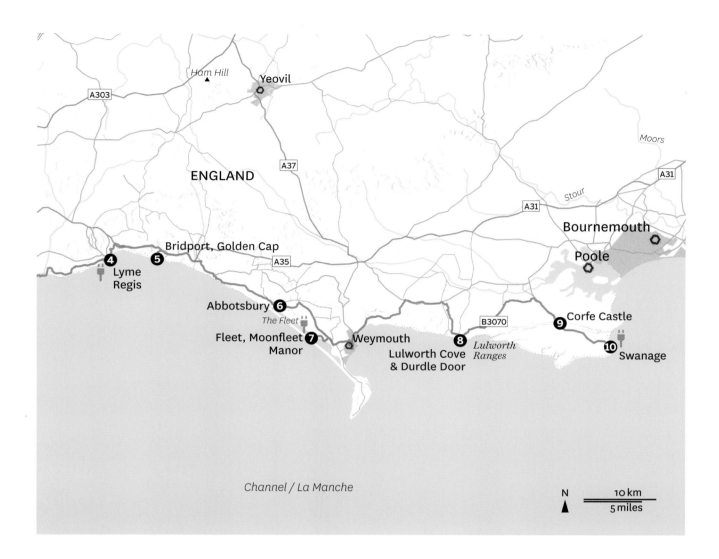

magnificent views. From here to Weymouth, the sea is shielded by the 49ft-high (15m) shingle bank of Chesil Beach, the strangeness of which is best appreciated by overnighting at Moonfleet Manor, tucked just behind.

The next day, yachty Weymouth is fun for traditional British seaside vibes. But for downright beauty, steer to Lulworth Cove, 15 miles (24km) on, where a hamlet hides behind a bay so perfectly circular it might have been drawn by a protractor and compass; the photogenic rock-arch of Durdle Door is a short walk west. No less photogenic is Corfe Castle, 12 miles (19km) up and around the Purbeck Hills. This 1000-year-old ruin looms over a fetching village: explore the old stones and order a cream tea in the cafe. The most romantic way on to Swanage is the steam railway, but there are wonderful country views on the 6-mile (10km) drive. In Swanage, amble the Victorian pier and head to Handfast Point for your final Jurassic Coast view: the chalk stacks of Old Harry Rocks.

➡ **Distance: 171 miles
(276km)**

➡ **Duration: 5 days**

York to Newcastle

ENGLAND

Moor, coast, dales and dells: this northeastern adventure travels from medieval York across the wilds of the North York Moors, then skirts the coast via Whitby en route to Newcastle-upon-Tyne.

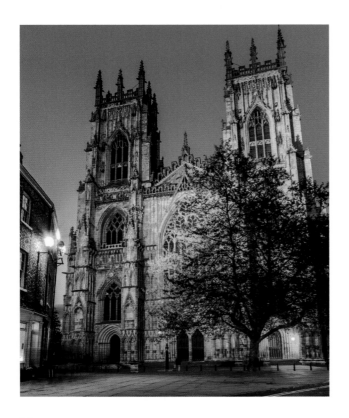

God's Own Country: famously, that's what the locals call Yorkshire, and to be frank, it's hard to quibble with their claim. A peak-packed landscape of stony hills, deep dales, patchwork fields and drystone walls, this expansive region of the north offers some of the grandest, greenest views in all of England.

Our journey begins in York, a city where history lurks around every corner: two millennia's worth of the stuff, in fact. Wander the original Roman walls; soak up the sights (and smells) of York's Viking past at the Jorvik Centre; explore the cobbled medieval streets around The Shambles (the nearest thing to a real-life Potter-esque Diagon Alley); and travel back to the golden age of steam at the National Railway Museum. And, of course, don't miss the view from the top of mighty York Minster – the largest medieval cathedral in northern Europe, and one of the world's most serene Gothic buildings.

STATELY SPLENDOUR

Beyond York, the views open up as you drive towards the Howardian Hills, a humpbacked range that marks the southern foothills of the North York Moors. The central sight here is Castle Howard, a country pile which puts the stately in stately home. Built for the Earl of Carlisle

© Barnes Ian / Shutterstock

Plan & prepare

Tips for EV drivers

The northeast has a reasonably good network of fast chargers, with all the big players – BP Pulse, ChargePlace, GeniePoint, InstaVolt, POD Point – represented. The cities have ample coverage; many supermarkets, shopping centres, public car parks and service stations also offer EV charging. Charge points are much scarcer along the Yorkshire coast and in the middle of the North York Moors – make sure you're fully charged before setting out to explore these areas.

Where to stay

Yorkshire has plenty of fine country hotels and cosy inns; we've picked out three which also offer EV charging. Middlethorpe Hall (middlethorpe.com), just outside York, is a 17th-century manor house encircled by extensive grounds. Equally aristocratic is Middleton Lodge (middletonlodge. co.uk), a Georgian pile near Richmond, with swish rooms, cottages and timber cabins. In Newcastle-upon-Tyne, Jesmond Dene House (jesmonddenehouse.co.uk) brims with Arts and Crafts elegance.

When to go

Winters can be harsh up north: expect snow, fog, hail and pretty much everything in between from November to February. Spring comes late: May and June can be good months to visit, before the holiday crowds. Late summer is the best time to see the heather on the North York Moors – the hilltops are an endless purple haze – while autumn brings its own displays of colour.

Further info

There are some useful Yorkshire-focused websites to check out when you're planning your drive. Visit Yorkshire (visityorkshire. co.uk) is the main portal, but also check Visit York (visityork.org), the North York Moors National Park site (northyorkmoors.org.uk) and 'NewcastleGateshead' (newcastlegateshead. com) for specific info on accommodation, sights, eating out and events in each area.

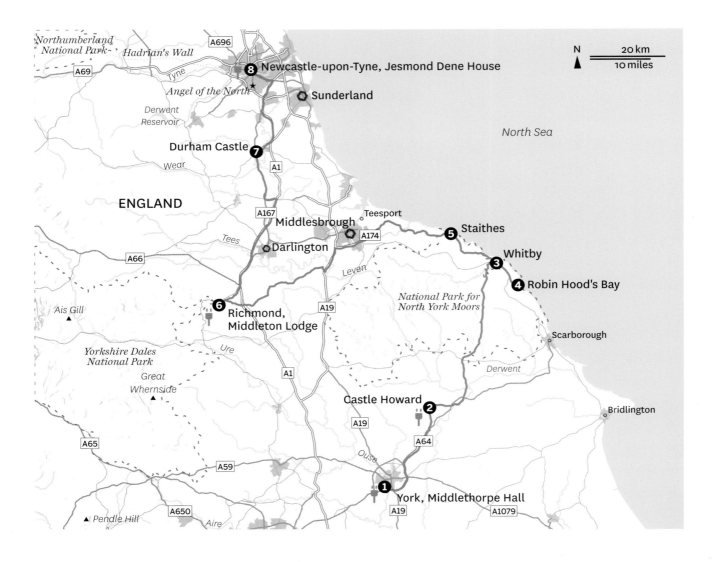

by the dynamic duo of Sir John Vanbrugh and Nicholas Hawksmoor, it's one of England's most outlandish and ostentatious pieces of architecture – part-baroque, part-Palladian, glittering with antiquities and boasting a monumental Great Hall and a central cupola modelled on the original in London's St Paul's Cathedral. It really is a sight to behold: you'll need a whole day to uncover its treasures and explore the extensive, folly-filled grounds. The house featured as a ready-made backdrop in the 1981 TV adaptation of *Brideshead Revisited*, starring Jeremy Irons, Anthony Andrews and, famously, Aloysius the teddy bear.

THE MOORS TO THE NORTH SEA COAST

North of the market towns of Maldon and Pickering, the stark, wind-scoured vistas of the North York Moors National Park unfurl splendidly through your windscreen. While it's almost entirely devoid of trees, this is very far

from a barren landscape: more than three-quarters of the world's heather habitat is found here, a vital haven for many songbirds, butterflies, other insects and birds of prey. The moors are also a good place to take a break from driving and lace up your hiking boots: countless trails wind through the hills and heathland, and you'll pass far fewer walkers here than in the busy Dales out to the west.

Further northeast, heather-clad moor fades into craggy coast as you near the North Sea, where the town of Whitby and its ruined abbey (as featured in Bram Stoker's *Dracula*) stand out moodily against the slate-grey horizon. Alongside its Gothic kudos, this stretch of the English coast is celebrated for its connections with local lad Captain Cook, who lived in Whitby as a young seaman. His old lodging house is now the Captain Cook Memorial Museum, and you can step aboard a replica of his ship, HMS *Endeavour*. Whitby is also a renowned spot for fossil hunting: fascinating guided walks head off in search

Hadrian's Wall

China might have its Great Wall, but northern England has its own world famous barrier: the 73-mile-long (117km) sweep of Hadrian's Wall, one of the great engineering feats of the ancient world. Named in honour of the eponymous emperor who ordered its construction, the wall was built between 122 and 128 CE to separate the 'civilised' Romanized south of Britannia from the lawless lands of the Picts to the north. When completed, this immense structure girdled the island from west to east, stretching from the Solway Firth all the way to the mouth of the Tyne. At its strongest points, the wall was up to 20ft (6m) high and 10ft (3m) deep. Though many sections have now disappeared – their stones mostly plundered for building materials – others remain impressively intact. Many watchtowers, milecastles and forts were built along the wall, and some can still be seen – including Segedunum, on the east side of Newcastle at Wallsend. Tracing the wall's route makes for a fantastic road trip – and if you feel like stretching your legs, the Hadrian's Wall Path National Trail (nationaltrail.co.uk) runs right along its length.

Clockwise from top left: EV road-tripping near Durham; Hadrian's Wall; ammonite in a Whitby fossil shop

The Angel of the North

At 67ft (20m) high and with a wingspan of 177ft (54m) – roughly the same as a jumbo jet – the *Angel of the North* is a soaring monument to metal, and one of Britain's most iconic modern artworks. Built from raw steel, spotted rust-red by the weather, it commemorates the northeast's illustrious industrial past but also, perhaps, hints at hope for the future, too – an important message in an area that's struggled to find its post-industrial mojo. It's the work of the Turner-Prize-winning British sculptor Antony Gormley, who was knighted for his efforts in 2014. There's a free car park at the base of the statue, or you can take Bus 21 from Eldon Square in Newcastle-upon-Tyne. With typical northern humour, the statue has earned its own affectionate nickname – the 'Gateshead Flasher' – a sure sign that the town it's located in has taken it to heart.

From left: Antony Gormley's *Angel of the North*; Whitby Abbey; Whitby harbour

of ammonites, trilobites and other geological treasures which have been buried for countless millennia in the fragile, fast-eroding cliffs. A hike or drive south takes you to Robin Hood's Bay, or north to the picturesque fishing town of Staithes; both figure in Yorkshire's top 10 list of postcard-worthy views, and the fractured cliffs and windy bluffs are great for seabird-spotting.

THE INLAND LOOP TO NEWCASTLE

After a blustery spin along the coast, turn your EV inland, skirting around the southern edge of Middlesbrough to seek out a couple of classic Yorkshire castles. The first is in Richmond, where the 12th-century keep commands a panoramic position looking across to the Yorkshire Dales: it's quite a view, and not at all hard to understand why its builders chose this spot for their strongpoint. The next is in Durham, where the city's hilltop Norman castle has been repurposed as a part of the prestigious university here – it can be visited, but only on a guided tour. Durham has another landmark, too: its monumental Anglo-Norman cathedral, resplendently Romanesque and, since 1986, a Unesco World Heritage Site.

Last stop on this drive is Newcastle-upon-Tyne, a dynamic city that combines industrial grit and artistic adventure with a rich legacy of Victorian architecture, built during the days when this was one of the great northern powerhouses of the Industrial Revolution. Explore the city's past at the Discovery Museum and the Great North Museum; delve into the darkness of the extraordinary Victoria Tunnel, which runs for 2.5 miles (4km) under the streets; and admire the collection at the Baltic, a grain factory turned modern art gallery.

And, of course, don't forget to make a pilgrimage to the *Angel of the North*, Antony Gormley's post-industrial masterpiece, which looms unforgettably over the A1, 6 miles (10km) south of the city.

© Andrew Montgomery / Lonely Planet; DavidGraham86 / Shutterstock; Neal Rylatt / Shutterstock

➜ **Distance: 87 miles
(140 km)**

➜ **Duration: 2-3 days**

Winchester to Brighton

ENGLAND

The medieval city of Winchester and the seaside party town of Brighton bookend a road trip that weaves and winds through southern England's most ancient and storied landscapes.

To drive between Winchester and Brighton is to experience England's history in microcosm, from the Neolithic age right through to the modern era. Your first port of call is the medieval period. The Romans had a settlement in Winchester, but many of the city's architectural highlights – like its magnificent cathedral, college and Great Hall – date back to the Middle Ages; some terrific, creaky old inns remain from the period, too.

HIKING & HISTORY

Hop in your EV and head 9 miles (14km) east to Beacon Hill National Nature Reserve. The stirring South Downs views from here give a good taste of what's to come; take a stroll and you can claim you've walked some of the South Downs Way – the old drover's route that rambles 100 miles (161km) between Winchester and Eastbourne passes over the chalk hill here. Narrow country lanes wind from Beacon Hill to today's lunch stop, the Harrow in Steep. Order a ploughman's and choose which period to eat it in: the beamed 16th-century bar, complete with blackened inglenook, or the Victorian saloon. It's then 15 miles (24km) on to another unique slice of history. The Weald & Downland Living Museum's collection of rural buildings spans 900 years, from medieval flint cottages

© Myles New / Lonely Planet

92

© Malcolm McHugh / Alamy Stock Photo

Tips for EV drivers

All the major car-hire companies in England offer EV options, though not as many as petrol/diesel vehicles – be sure to book ahead. Download the Zap-Map app (Android and iOS) for charging maps, route planning and live-status data across the UK. Southern England is well served by charge points. If you need a quick top-up, the car parks of large supermarkets and retail parks will often deliver.

Where to stay

Winchester Royal Hotel, Winchester (winchesterroyalhotel. com), has served as a bishop's residence and a convent over its 500-year existence. Goodwood Hotel, Goodwood (goodwood.com), has characterful bedrooms, superb dining and 12,000 acres (5658 hectares) of country estate on the doorstep. Drakes Hotel, Brighton (drakesofbrighton. com), sits right on the seafront; individually decorated rooms have sea or city views and there's a great cocktail bar.

When to go

There's never a bad time to take this trip – roads are mostly in good condition and amenities stay open throughout the year. School holidays and the height of summer see the most tourists, so visit in the shoulder seasons of spring and autumn to avoid crowds. The region's landscapes can look particularly magical under the hard frosts and lingering mists of winter.

Further info

The speed limit on most roads in Brighton is just 20mph (32kph), and there's a plan to introduce a city-wide 20mph limit in Winchester. Away from the car, there are numerous walking and cycling trails across the region. The entire South Downs Way is 100 miles (161km), but can easily be split into smaller chunks. The South Downs National Park website (southdowns.gov.uk) has route suggestions and downloadable maps, as well as info on other activities such as photography.

South Downs stargazing

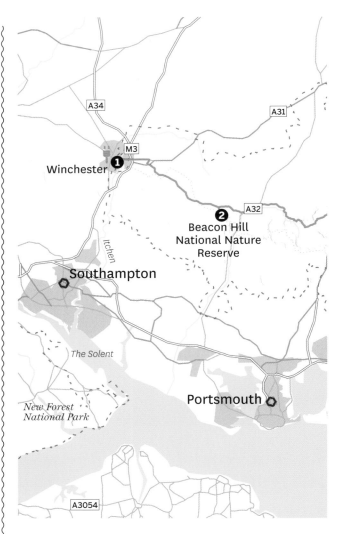

When the sun sinks below the horizon for the day, a whole host of new sightseeing opportunities are revealed. The South Downs National Park was designated an International Dark Sky Reserve in 2016, one of only six in the UK – meaning this is one of the finest places in the country in which to tilt back your head and gaze up at the stars. With little light pollution, there are good chances to see the Milky Way in all its ethereal, sweeping wonder here – no telescope required. The park's website (southdowns. gov.uk) lists a number of stargazing locations, known as 'dark sky discovery sites', a smattering of which fall on the route between Winchester and Brighton:

try Butser Hill, Iping Common and Bignor Hill for starters. If you're here in February, check for details of the park's annual two-week-long Dark Skies Festival, which includes events such as nocturnal wildlife walks, stargazing suppers and expert astronomy talks. At any time of year, it's worth calling into the Winchester Science Centre and Planetarium (winchestersciencecentre. org) to quickly swoop through the solar system before setting off on your slightly more run-of-the-mill trip on terra firma.

Above: dark skies in the South Downs National Park
Right: the hammerbeamed Barons' Hall, Arundel Castle

to a 19th-century blacksmith's. Some might recognise its thatched barn from BBC TV programme *The Repair Shop*. Demos of weaving, wattle-and-daubing and milling bring England's traditional crafts and industry to life.

Bed for the night (and a charge-up) are just 3 miles (4km) away. With stylish rooms and a choice of three restaurants for dinner, the Goodwood Hotel sits in the massive Goodwood estate, which hosts events throughout the year – including the Goodwood Revival, a stomping good-time celebration of vintage motorsports and fashion.

ARUNDEL TO BRIGHTON
After breakfast, drive back in time once again, to the 11th century and Arundel. Much of the town's imposing stone castle has been destroyed, rebuilt and added to over the centuries, but there are enough turrets and ramparts to satisfy the most committed medieval fantasist. The Barons' Hall, with an extraordinary hammerbeam roof,

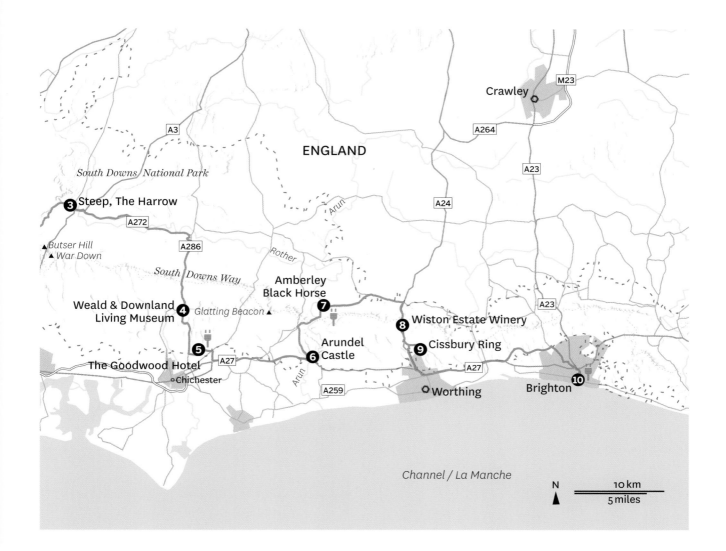

certainly looks the part, but was only completed in 1903.

There's no pretence at your country-pub lunch stop, the delightful Amberley Black Horse – just honest good food made with seasonal local produce. It'd be easy to while away the afternoon here, but head 8 miles (13km) east to sample more local produce. The Wiston Estate Winery's sparkling wine, rosé, Pinot Noir and Blanc de Blancs can be sampled on tours, tastings and dinners (or buy a bottle to enjoy when the designated driver is off duty).

There's one last stop before Brighton. Cissbury Ring has seen six millennia of human activity, with Neolithic flint-mining, Bronze Age agriculture and Roman defences just some of its varied uses. The age-old human activity of drinking is again in order once parked up in Brighton. But before exploring its many bars and pubs, shoot into the air on the seafront's futuristic British Airways i360 viewing tower. Toast your trip 450ft (137m) up at its Sky Bar, looking back over the route you've just completed.

→ **Distance: 104 miles (167km)**

→ **Duration: 3-5 days**

Salisbury to Cirencester

ENGLAND

Wiggle around ancient Wessex and into the dreamy Cotswolds, taking roads slightly less travelled to discover some of England's most delightful countryside, stately homes and chocolate-box towns and villages.

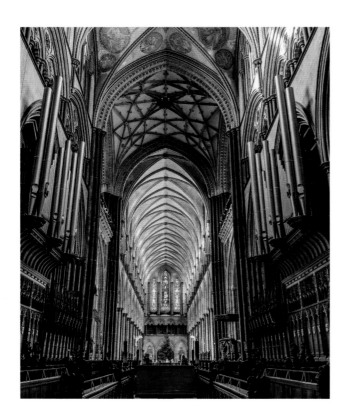

I s it sacrilege to be so close and not visit Stonehenge? Well, no – not when there's so much else to see in this wonderful wedge of the West Country and the southern Cotswolds. Flitting between Wiltshire, Dorset, Somerset and Gloucestershire, this EV excursion is an unfurling of idyllic Englishness, from rolling, verdant hills to ancient history, elegant manors and inviting country pubs.

IN-SPIRING

It's hard to imagine what medieval wayfarers must have thought when they arrived in Salisbury. The piercing spire of the 13th-century cathedral – Britain's tallest, at 404ft (123m) – is mind-blowing enough nowadays. One of the four remaining copies of the Magna Carta (the groundbreaking charter of rights, signed in 1215) is kept inside, too.

Tiny Salisbury itself is a pleasant jumble of shops, cafes and architectural eras. Explore the centre, or walk (or drive) 2 miles (3.2km) north to Old Sarum. This mighty mound has been the site of an Iron Age hill fort, a Roman settlement, a Saxon stronghold, a Norman castle and Salisbury's original cathedral. Wander the ramparts for views of the 'new' cathedral soaring below.

© Vivvi Smak / Getty Images

Plan & prepare

Tips for EV drivers

The undulating terrain on this drive, including the chalk downlands of Cranborne Chase and the rolling hills of the southern and central Cotswolds, will affect battery range. There are a fair number of public charging points on the first half of this route, including in Shaftesbury, Frome and Bath; there are far fewer chargers available between Bath and Cirencester. Plan accordingly.

Where to stay

Woolley Grange Hotel (woolleygrangehotel.co.uk), just outside Bradford-on-Avon, is a Jacobean manor turned elegant family-friendly hotel; there are chargers on site as well as pools (both indoors and out) and extensive grounds. The Hare & Hounds Hotel (cotswold-inns-hotels. co.uk), on the Bath Rd near Westonbirt Arboretum, has a Cotswold country house atmosphere, a welcoming bar and charging facilities for guests' use.

When to go

Spring is a super time to visit these green and pleasant lands: the hills and woodlands will be alive with wildflowers and birds. Warm summer days are delightful, but roads and accommodation will be busier. Autumn sees the honeystone buildings glow in the low light and fiery displays of fall colours, especially at Stourhead and Westonbirt. Crisp winter days can be atmospheric and peaceful. Bath hosts a magical Christmas market (late November to early December).

Further info

The most convenient airports for Salisbury are London Heathrow (80 miles/129km), Bristol (60 miles/97km) and Southampton (25 miles/40km). Try to avoid travelling during rush-hour periods (roughly 7am to 9.30am and 4pm to 6pm), when roads can get congested, especially in and around hotspots like Bath. Country roads can be narrow and winding, so drive slowly and considerately.

Trusted sites

Before embarking on this drive, consider joining the National Trust (NT; nationaltrust.org.uk), the charity that cares for many historic and natural sites across England, Wales and Northern Ireland; members can visit NT properties for free (though note that many sites close over winter). In addition to Stourhead and Dyrham, there are lots of NT properties on or near this route. Start with Mompesson House in Salisbury's Cathedral Close, where the interior has been restored to look as it might have done in its Georgian prime. Or detour en route to Shaftesbury to roam Dinton Park – on a clear day, Salisbury Cathedral's spire can be seen from here. There's a cluster of NT sites around Bradford-on-Avon:

Westwood, a 15th-century stone-built manor, with intricate plasterwork and topiary gardens, is walkable from the town. In nearby Holt you'll find medieval Great Chalfield Manor, which sits within moated Arts and Crafts grounds; and Courts Garden, which is like an assembly of 'outdoor rooms', with lily ponds, a stone temple and an arboretum. In Bath the NT runs the elegant Assembly Rooms (where Jane Austen once danced) and Prior Park, a hill-set estate with a rare Palladian bridge.

Above: the gardens at Great Chalfield Manor
Right: Sunday market on Catherine Hill, Frome

It's tempting to detour from here to Stonehenge, 10 miles (16km) north. No one would blame you: the Neolithic stone circle and surrounding ancient landscape are world class. But for tracts less trodden, steer west instead, into the rolling chalk downs of Cranborne Chase. The billowing hills and woody thickets of this Area of Outstanding Natural Beauty (AONB) line the 20-mile (32km) drive to Shaftesbury, in Dorset's scenic Blackmore Vale. Shaftesbury has famously featured in Thomas Hardy's novels and in a classic 1970s advert for British bread-brand Hovis – don't miss your own climb up cobbled, cottage-lined Gold Hill, where it was filmed. Afterwards, browse the artisan shops of Swans Yard, then visit ruins of the town's Abbey, founded in 888 CE, and its associated museum.

TIMELESS TOWNS

Next, head 11 miles (18km) north, back into Wiltshire, to reach the National Trust's Stourhead, a Palladian manor and landscaped garden that's been likened to a 'living work of art'. Follow the trails around the estate, via the Greek-style temples, arches, grottoes, exotic trees and mirror-like lake before refuelling in the cosy pub.

Then continue through the northwestern corner of Cranborne Chase, emerging 10 miles (16km) on near Frome. This creative Somerset town is worth a detour, especially on Independent Market Day (first Sunday of the month, March-December), when artisan craft and food stalls tumble down hip Catherine Hill. Otherwise, drive a further 11 miles (18km) on to Bradford-on-Avon, a handsome market town built on six centuries of wool and weaving wealth amid the Cotswolds' southern fringes. After checking in to the Woolley Grange Hotel, just outside the centre in Woolley Green, stroll through Bradford-on-Avon via the Norman-era Town Bridge, the narrow Shambles, the independent shops and delis, the Saxon church and the Georgian townhouses, then walk along the river to the huge 14th-century Tithe Barn and leafy Kennet & Avon Canal.

It's a 10-mile (16km) walk along the Kennet & Avon towpath to Bath, via magnificent Dundas Aqueduct. By road, it's around 8 miles (13km); you can view the aqueduct en route, if you stop at Brassknocker Basin car park. Bath – designed for carriages and sedan chairs rather than cars – isn't a lovely place in which to drive, but it's a lovely place to be. No city in England has such a homogenous centre – a feast of honeystone Georgian gorgeousness. It's also spectacularly set, amid bulbous green hills, and liberally strewn with good bars and cafes. Get a memorable view on a tower tour at the city's ancient Abbey, or via the breathtaking Bath Skyline walk.

N

20 km
10 miles

Brown Hill

WALES

A449

M5

A433

Cirencester 🔟

Tetbury 9️⃣

8️⃣ Westonbirt,
The Hare
& Hounds Hotel

A417

Thames (Isis)

A420

Thames

M4

M48

A4

M4

⬡ Swindon

*Severn
Estuary*

7️⃣ Dyrham Park

A46

Bristol ⬡

ENGLAND

A350

A346

M5

A4

Avon

Bath 6️⃣

5️⃣ Bradford-on-Avon,
Woolley Grange Hotel

A34

Weston-super-Mare ⬡

▲ *Black Down*

A36

A338

A38

A37

Frome

Stonehenge
★

Bourne

A303

Glastonbury Tor
▲

4️⃣ Stourhead

2️⃣ Old Sarum
1️⃣ Salisbury

M3

Winchester

*South Downs
National Park*

A303

A36

Ham Hill
▲

3️⃣

Win Green
▲

Shaftesbury

Stour

Avon

*New Forest
National Park*

Southampton ⬡

© Nigel Jarvis / Shutterstock

Water world

Bath is home to a natural thermal spring, extremely rare in Britain. It's why the Romans built a town here in around 60 CE, which they named Aquae Sulis. You can tour the ancient remains and taste the (disgusting) mineral water at the town's excellent Roman Baths (romanbaths.co.uk); you can also sip it from a fountain in the fancy Georgian Pump Room restaurant next door (thepumproombath. co.uk). To soak in the hot water, you'll need to visit the modern Thermae Bath Spa (thermaebathspa.com). Detox in its steam rooms and saunas, and enjoy the fine city views from the roof-top pool. Alternatively, take a dip in Britain's oldest lido. Dating back to 1815 but closed since the 1980s, Grade-II* listed Cleveland Pools (clevelandpools. org.uk) reopened in 2022 following a huge restoration project. Although not fed by the thermal spring, the pools are warmed with a water-source heat pump.

Clockwise from top: Pulteney Bridge over the Avon, Bath; Dyrham Park; Hare & Hounds, near Westonbirt

COTSWOLDS CRUISING

From Bath, head 9 miles (15km) up the A46, above the splendid Woolley Valley, to Dyrham Park. Another National Trust stunner, the baroque 17th-century manor sits in sloping parkland. Admire the collection of Dutch art and walk trails that offer views across the Bristol Channel.

Continue northeast, plunging deeper into the Cotswolds, to the Hare & Hounds. Around 13 miles (21km) from Dyrham, this traditional rural hotel is handy for Westonbirt, the country's National Arboretum, where 2500 species of trees rustle together; explore via marked trails and the wonderful Tree Top Walkway. The hotel is also only 3 miles (5km) south of the pretty wool town of Tetbury, a home of the King and Queen Consort (well, Charles III's private Highgrove Estate is close by, visitable on pre-booked garden tours). Tetbury itself is heaven for antiques shopping and cafe hopping.

If your EV has plenty of charge remaining, you could steer left down any country lane to fall deeper into the Cotswolds' folds. But stick to the main road and, in 14 miles (23km), you'll reach Cirencester – aka Corinium Dobunnorum. That was the name of the Roman city that once stood here, encased in walls over 2 miles (3km) long. The fascinating Corinium Museum tells the story of the area, from Stone Age hunter-gatherers to Roman times. For a wider scope, seek out the town's 50-plus plaques, which mark moments of Cirencester's history – from the Brunel-designed train station to the site on which a fleeing King Charles II stayed in 1651. Finish in beautifully landscaped Cirencester Park, for a final Cotswolds stroll.

→ **Distance: 83 miles (133km)**

→ **Duration: 3-5 days**

King's Lynn to Norwich

ENGLAND

Ease your foot off the accelerator and slow down to Norfolk pace: this rural East Anglian county of big beaches, bigger skies and easy charm is the perfect place for an unhurried EV drive.

Norfolk seeps in. There's just something about it. The way late-afternoon light hits the reedbeds; the ales and accents in flinty, fire-warmed pubs; the prolific birds; the golden beaches and that sky – that enormous, forever sky. There's interest all over the county, but combining the genteel north coast and the greatly likeable regional capital is a good start.

AVIAN ENCOUNTERS & A-LIST SHORES

King's Lynn, on the River Great Ouse, did a roaring trade from the 13th century as a Hanseatic League port. Those days are long gone, but you can delve into this history on the town's self-guided Hanseatic Trail (pick up leaflets locally). Then it's time to hit the countryside. It's 12 miles (19km) north to Snettisham (unless you detour to the Royal Family's Sandringham Estate en route). The village's Rose & Crown pub-with-rooms is a cosy base for lovely Snettisham Beach and RSPB Snettisham, a wild-bird reserve on the shores of the Wash, renowned for its winter influx of pink-footed geese. Indeed, birds are constant companions on this drive. Once you meet the north coast at Hunstanton and follow the A149 east, reserves come thick and fast: 10 miles (16km) beyond Snettisham, bitterns boom and avocets and marsh harriers nest in the

© Frances Browne / Alamy Stock Photo

Plan & prepare

Tips for EV drivers

The charger network is not extensive in Norfolk; look out for accommodation with charging facilities. Fortunately, the county is very flat, so gradients won't deplete your battery life here. Also, Norfolk has no motorways – there's little chance of exceeding 60mph (100kph) on its slower A- and B-roads, which should help eke out your range.

Where to stay

Snettisham's Rose & Crown (roseandcrownsnettisham. co.uk) is a proper village pub that also serves award-winning food; it has 16 bedrooms and EV chargers for those staying overnight. The stylish Blakeney Hotel (blakeney-hotel.co.uk) sits right on Blakeney Quay, with views over the moored boats, creeks and salt marshes. It has an AA-rosette-awarded fine-dining restaurant, a swimming pool and EV chargers for guests' use.

When to go

North Norfolk is often glorious year-round, although the long, sunny days of peak summer can mean chock-a-block roads – expect jams. Spring and autumn offer pleasant weather (good for walks) without the crowds. Winter can be an absolute knockout: colder weather, but fewer people, thousands of migratory birds, pupping seals, empty beaches and brilliantly dark, starry skies.

Further info

Norwich International Airport is 4 miles (6.5km) north of the city centre. Its route network isn't extensive but daily, year-round flights to Amsterdam Schiphol, taking under an hour, make it quick and easy to connect to most corners of the globe. The handy Coasthopper bus links many seaside villages between Wells-next-the-Sea and Cromer – useful for getting back to your EV after linear walks along the Norfolk Coast Path.

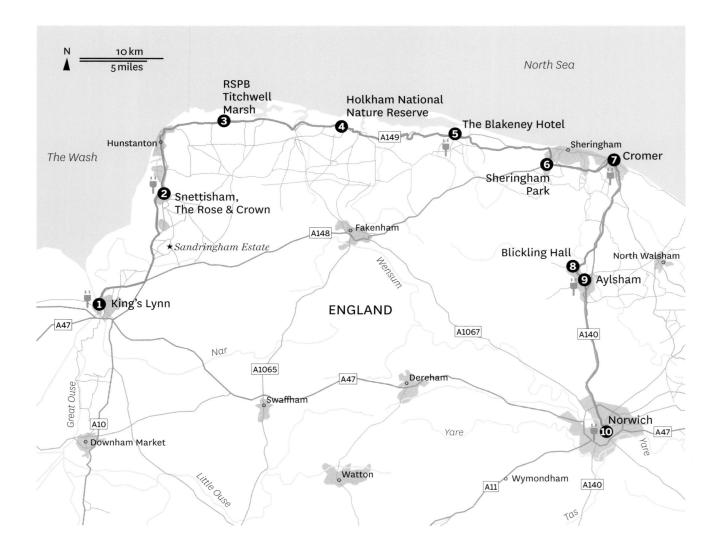

reedbeds, lagoons and salt marshes of RSPB Titchwell Marsh. Nearby Thornham has a lovely pub and deli.

The same marshes keep the sea at a distance as you continue on the A149 to Holkham, 10 miles (16km) on. The eponymous National Nature Reserve is north Norfolk at its most showstopping, especially so at Holkham's immense, golden beach, backed by dunes and pine trees. The loop-walk from here to the fishing harbour of Wells-next-the-Sea, via grand Holkham Hall, is a cracker. Another 10 miles (16km) brings you to the comely flint cottages and super-smart restaurants and hotels of Blakeney (including the estuary-side Blakeney Hotel). The biggest draw, though, is Blakeney Point, home to the country's largest seal colony; boat trips offer the chance to get close.

TO THE CITY
The mood changes over the following 5 miles (8km). At Sheringham, the coast starts to rise to cliffs. Head

to Sheringham Park, laid out by landscape designer Humphry Repton in the early 19th century: from Repton's Gazebo, you get one of the best views in the county.

The Victorian seaside town of Cromer is only 15 minutes further on: walk along its classic pier and gorge on local crab. Then veer inland for 10 miles (16km) to Blickling Hall, the Jacobean mansion (with glorious estate) where Anne Boleyn was born, before heading to nearby Aylsham. This handsome market town is full of little shops and tea rooms; its central square, lined with fine 18th-century houses, hosts markets every Monday and Friday. Norwich lies about 13 miles (21km) south. Once England's second hub, and its first Unesco City of Literature, Norwich has a striking cathedral, a Norman castle, a well-preserved medieval centre, a covered market that's been there for 900 years – and a very appealing vibe. Finish in the Lanes, the warren of alleys near the old Guildhall, where you can celebrate journey's end in the independent bars and cafes.

Norfolk nibbles

As you'd expect from a rural, sea-lapped county, local produce is good here. Look for big, juicy Brancaster mussels (in season from September to April); grey-blue Stiffkey cockles; and samphire, also known as 'sea asparagus', which flourishes on the salt marshes. Cromer crab is legendary, renowned for its sweet, delicate flavour and high proportion of white meat. Cromer holds a Crab Festival every May. Or give gillying (crabbing) a try yourself, a traditional Norfolk pastime that's especially popular in Wells-next-the-sea; reusable metal buckets and eco-friendly tackle can be hired from the Gilly Hut on Wells Quay. In Norwich it's all about Colman's Mustard. In 1814, Norwich miller Jeremiah Colman devised a method of powdering mustard seeds that didn't destroy their heat-giving properties, creating the punchy, bright-yellow British condiment. There are plenty of good beers, too. Award-winning Woodforde's Brewery produces a range of ales, including best-selling Wherry (named for the sailboats that once plied the Broads) and dark, citrusy Nog. Or try a dram of Nelson's Blood – Admiral Horatio was born in Burnham Thorpe, near Holkham, and in the 1970s the landlord of the Lord Nelson pub here created a rum-and-spice concoction in his honour.

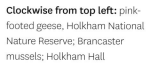

Clockwise from top left: pink-footed geese, Holkham National Nature Reserve; Brancaster mussels; Holkham Hall

→ **Distance: 236 miles (380km)**   → **Duration: 4-5 days**

Bordeaux to Biarritz

FRANCE

This Atlantic adventure explores France's most hallowed wine region and takes a spin down the breezy southwest coast. Taste wines, climb Europe's largest dune and experience Basque culture in Bayonne and Biarritz.

This trip begins in the Unesco-listed city of Bordeaux, France's viticultural capital. You can get an excellent grounding in the art of the vine at the Cité du Vin, then head off around the city to explore its shady backstreets, *hotels particuliers* and grand squares. Next, with designated driver nominated, drive out for a loop around the vineyards of the Médoc: you'll lose count of the signs for local *caves* (cellars) offering tours and tastings.

After a night (or two) in Bordeaux, spin down the Atlantic coast to Arcachon, an elegant seaside town overlooking its eponymous bay. Across France, Arcachon is renowned for its *huîtres* (oysters), which are farmed in the bay's shallow waters, and prized by connoisseurs for their taste and texture. Swing by quayside shacks to taste them straight off the boats, and settle in for the night at Hôtel d'Hiver. Southwest of Arcachon looms one of the Atlantic Coast's strangest sights: the mighty Dune du Pilat, the largest pile of sand this side of the Sahara: 1.7 miles (2.7km) long, 1640ft (500m) wide and up to 360ft (110m) high. You might see local daredevils paragliding off it or sandboarding down its slopes. South of the dunes sprawls the flat, scrubby, marshy expanse known as Les Landes de Gascogne, much of which is protected by a *parc naturel regional* (it's very good for birdwatching). To most

© Justin Foulkes / Lonely Planet

Plan & prepare

Tips for EV drivers

EVs can be hired in Bordeaux and Biarritz. Both have reasonable charger concentrations, but coverage is much sparser in between. Parking can be a challenge, so it's best to choose hotels with car parks and EV charging. Many public car parks and supermarkets have charging stations, but it's worth registering in advance with the big operators: Freshmile (freshmile.com), Allego (allego.eu) and others have large presences. When planning your trip, factor in costs for autoroute tolls.

Where to stay

Bordeaux, Bayonne and Biarritz are awash with hotels; all our choices offer private parking and EV charging. The InterContinental Le Grand Hotel (bordeaux. intercontinental.com) is a Bordeaux landmark overlooking Place de la Comédie, with a swimming pool and spa. In Arcachon, the Hôtel d'Hiver (hotelvilledhiver. com) is a Belle Époque beauty. Hôtel du Palais (hyatt.com) is the former home of Napoleon III and Empress Eugenie, its luxurious rooms offering Biarritz's finest sea views.

When to go

Late summer marks the peak of the grape harvest in the vineyards of Bordeaux and the Médoc, but it's a busy time of year: July and especially August are the main months for French holidaymakers. Autumn is a good alternative: temperatures remain warm in September and October, the coastal towns and beaches are less crowded and, with a bit of luck, you may get to taste some of the season's early wine blends.

Further info

The main French road rule to remember is *priorité à droite*: you should mostly give way to merging traffic approaching from the right, eg on autoroute slip roads. You'll earn some hoots and fruity language if you forget. By law you need to carry emergency items including reflective jackets for each passenger and a warning triangle in case of a breakdown. If you're hiring an EV these should be included, but check before you drive off.

Clockwise from top left: Cité du Vin, Bordeaux; oysters and *bigorneaux* (winkles), Arcachon; ascending the mighty Dune du Pilat

Arcachon's oysters

Oysters may not be to everyone's taste, but for aficionados, the best *huîtres* in all of France are raised in the gleaming blue waters of the Baie d'Arcachon. Though it only takes a second or two to shuck one and gobble it down, each oyster is in fact the product of four hard years of loving graft. Arcachon's *ostréiculteurs* (oyster farmers) tend their beds day-in, day-out, all year round, with the oysters kept on man-made frames suspended in the water. Connoisseurs assert that it's possible to taste the difference between oysters raised in different areas of the bay, thanks to the varying *terroir* of each of the spots. You might detect hints of mushrooms and crème fraîche in oysters from Banc d'Arguin, a sandbank in the channels connecting the bay to the ocean, at the foot of the Dune du Pilat; those from Île aux Oiseaux, the largest and oldest of the beds, are distiguished by mineral and metallic notes. The sheltered Cap Ferret beds produce tangy oysters with hints of citrus and green fruit, while (so they say!) the velvety bivalves from Grand Banc are redolent of roasted hazelnuts and even breadcrumbs. The best way to eat them is freshly shucked from the shell, adding a twist of lemon (or not, depending on your preference), and ideally washed down with a glass of crisp local white or rosé wine.

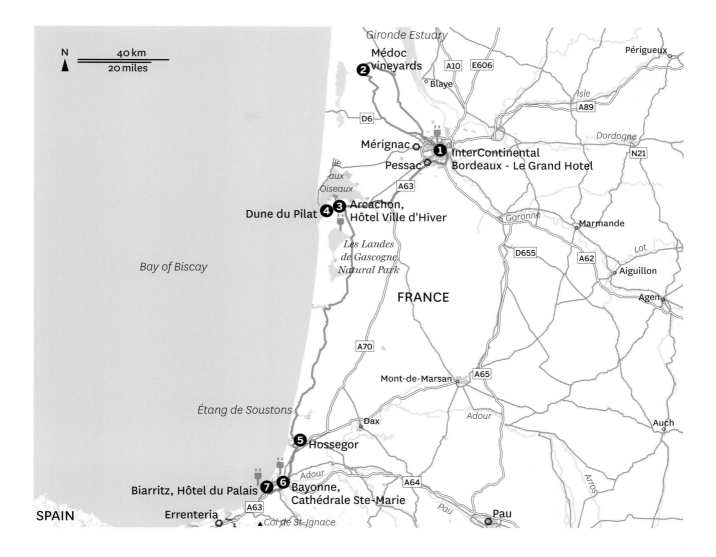

French people, however, it's known for its beaches: there are scores of them, from little coves to big white-sand affairs, perfect for sunbathing and sunset walks – albeit a little blustery. This windy coast is also legendary for its surf: Atlantic swells roll in reliably for much of the year, attracting surfers who congregate en masse around the beachy town of Hossegor. If you feel like learning how to catch a wave, this is as good a place as any to do it.

THE FRENCH BASQUE TO BIARRITZ

Driving your EV South of Les Landes takes you into the French Basque country, a distinct cultural corner of France that has much in common with its cousin across the Spanish border – not least a taste for spicy *piment*-peppered food, tapas and Basque ball game pelota. Be aware, there's also a heritage of bullfighting. With its own festivals, dress, customs and, perhaps most significantly, language, the French Basque feels like a little country within a country. The riverside town of Bayonne makes a great introduction: it hosts France's biggest Basque-themed party, Fêtes de Bayonne, every July, and has an interesting Basque-themed museum as well as plenty of restaurants where you can sample plates of *pintxos*, the Basque take on tapas. And don't miss a visit to the Cathédrale Ste-Marie, a Gothic marvel whose towers dominate the town's skyline.

Biarritz marks your drive's end. Since the 19th century, this elegant seaside city has been one of France's most popular beach resorts, its seafront lined with magnificent hotels and townhouses, many of which were built during the Belle Époque era (there are a few concrete carbuncles dotted around, too). These days, it's half glitzy summer getaway, half surfer's hangout. Stroll along the Grande Plage, cross the footbridge to the Rocher de la Vierge and climb the 248 steps of the town's 240ft-high (73m) lighthouse for widescreen Atlantic views.

Below: *quenelle Lyonnaise* in a city *bouchon*
Right: peering down across Lyon

➡ **Distance: 410 miles (660km)**

➡ **Duration: 4-5 days**

Lyon to the Alps

FRANCE

France's historic second city is the place to indulge before departing on an Alpine drive that will push your road trip experience to giddy new heights.

Strolls under the plane trees along riverside quays; bistros tucked down the lanes of the 5th *arrondissement*; the funicular trundling up the hill crowned with its iconic white basilica; that fin-de-siècle fluted tower of crisscrossed girders punctuating the skyline – it can only be Lyon. The Romans intended this to be the main city of Gaul, and though it's had to play second fiddle to Paris for most of the subsequent two millennia, Lyon knows how to console itself. Above all, by eating.

The tubthumping about being the 'gastronomic capital of France' is justified not so much by the 16-odd Michelin-starred restaurants here, but by the many *bouchons* – the Lyonnais take on the bistro. Pork features prominently, even in a *salade Lyonnaise*. Restaurant Le Musée, in the Presqu'île district between the Rhône and Saône rivers, is an exhibition-worthy example of what a *bouchon* should be, beginning with the red-checked tablecloths and ending with a lava-pink slice of *tarte aux pralines*.

ROAD-TRIPPING THE ALPS
A bon viveur's continuation to this trip would lead north or south to the winelands of Burgundy or the

© lauadibi / Shutterstock

Plan & prepare

Tips for EV drivers

Planning ahead for where to find the next charger is especially important in the French Alps, not just because of faster power consumption on steep roads, but because away from the main motorway routes – which usually have a good network of fast chargers – options become sparser. The longest dry patch on this route (at the time of writing) was the mountainous 45 miles (72km) between Modane and Val d'Isère; you'll need to make a recharge stop in one or both.

Where to stay

Book ahead for hotels in the mountain stages. In Briançon, the Hotel de la Chaussée (hotel-de-la-chaussee. com) is a centrally located three-star option with chunky Alpine furnishings. For a unique stay in Val d'Isère, try Le Refuge de Solaise (lerefuge-valdisere. com) – a smartly converted ski-lift station up at 8369ft (2551m), with road access in summer. The best rooms at La Sapinière in Chamonix (chalethotelsapiniere chamonix.com) have Mont Blanc views, and there are charger points on site, too.

When to go

If you're taking the full route over the high mountain passes, the drive will only be possible when these are snow-free and open to traffic, which might be just July, August and September. June and October may still be doable, though mountain resorts aren't always fully open in shoulder seasons. If you're determined to try this as a winter trip, the direct route from Grenoble to Chamonix via Albertville and Megève is driveable year-round, barring exceptional snowfalls.

Further info

Although this route doesn't use any motorways or expressways in its small Swiss portion, remember that you'll need to buy and display a Vignette sticker if you do drive on those roads. In France and Italy, the payment is at toll booths. In French summer holiday periods, check the Bison Futé website (bison-fute.gouv.fr) for information on congested routes.

Passing grade

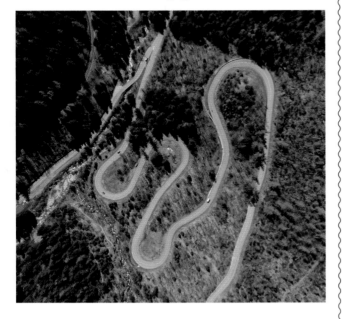

A mountain pass – that liminal space that's both high point and low – is the star of many a driving challenge, and the Alps are prime territory for pass-bagging. One planning challenge (aside from plotting routes that cover as many passes as possible without doubling back on yourself) is what actually counts for scoring purposes. The highest paved road in Europe is not in Alpine lands at all, but at 10,827ft (3300m) near the summit of Veleta, in the Sierra Nevada of southern Spain. But as it no longer descends the other side, and its upper reaches are limited-access only, it's of more interest to cyclists than drivers. A similar dead-end is the Ötztal Glacier Road

in Austria, up to 9285ft (2830m), though this time you can take your car all the way. Europe's highest continuous road is the 9193ft (2802m) Cime de la Bonnette, in a particularly desolate stretch of the southern French Alps, but it's not a true pass, rather a loop embellishing the actual V-point down at 8908ft (2715m). All of which makes the Col de l'Iseran, near Val d'Isère, the winner – at 9088ft (2770m) – of the distinction of highest paved mountain pass in Europe.

Above: Col des Montets, en route to Chamonix
Right: the gondola up to Fort de la Bastille, Grenoble

Rhône valley, but loftier ideals might draw you east, via Grenoble, into the Alps. As to where a French Alpine drive should end, the obvious answer – looming 15,774ft (4808m) high – is Mont Blanc, or rather the resort of Chamonix at its foot.

The most direct route, though, is rather dull given the possibilities of the surrounding landscape. Between Grenoble and Chamonix, the Isère and Arly valleys line up almost ruler-straight, and the highest pass is barely above 3600ft (1097m), occupied by the posh ski village of Megève. Alternatively, you could throw directness to the mountain winds and take this celebratory route around two national parks, over the highest road pass in the Alps (plus two others in the top 15) and briefly through neighbouring Italy and Switzerland to loop back on Chamonix, almost catching it by surprise.

GRENOBLE TO THE COL DE L'ISERAN

The first inkling of the mountains comes shortly before Grenoble, as you follow the Isère upstream between the ranges of the Vercors and Chartreuse, the latter home to the secretive monks who first made that signature green liqueur. At the range's southernmost point, a gondola shuttles up from the historic centre of Grenoble to the panoramic terrace of the Fort de la Bastille – acclimatisation for greater heights to come.

Military history looms large on the hill-bound road south: a horseback statue of Napoleon in the village of Laffrey recalls his abortive attempt at a comeback in 1815, between his exiles on Elba and St Helena. Until you turn off just before Gap, you'll be following (in reverse) the commemorative Route Napoléon that starts in Cannes. Among the huddled houses of Corps, where the emperor spent a night, the Distillerie Salettina concentrates the herbal flavours of the mountains into liquid form.

Skirting round the massif of the Écrins National Park, you come at last to Briançon, a worthy place for an overnight stop, and one of the most obsessively fortified places in the world. Its Unesco-listed bastions were begun by the engineering genius Vauban 300 years ago, to protect one of the lowest Alpine crossing-points from Italy into France. You, however, are aiming high, snaking in your EV up first to the 8668ft (2642m) Col du Galibier, with the sharp summit of La Meije to your back. Then, after an advisable recharge in the valley at Modane, it's a heady ascent through the majesty of Vanoise National Park to the Col de l'Iseran at 9088ft (2770m). Pity the Tour de France riders in the years that include this as a climb.

N
40 km
20 miles

Bourg-en-Bresse

Geneva
Lake Geneva

SWITZERLAND

A9 Rhône

Matterhorn

A40

Annecy

Chamonix ❾

Mont
Blanc

❽ Great St Bernard
Hospice

Megève

La Thuile ❼

Aosta

Lyon,
Restaurant
La Musée ❶

Villeurbanne

A41

E25

Mt Glacier

Bourgoin

Albertville

Val d'Isère,
Le Refuge de Solaise

Gran
Paradiso

Gran Paradiso
National Park

A47

Chambéry

FRANCE

❻

Col de l'Iseran

Orco

A48

Vanoise
National Park

Isère

Arc

N6

Romans-sur-Isère

Isère

A49

Grenoble, ❷
Fort de la Bastille

Modane

Briançon, Hôtel
de la Chaussée

❺

ITALY

A32 Riparia

Turin

A7

Valence

Laffrey

Col du Galibier

Mont Aiguille

Barre des Ecrins

Corps, ❸
Distillerie Salettina

Ecrins
National Park

❹

A6

PO

N85

Montélimar

Gap

N94

Savigliano

A7

A51

On firmer footing

In French-speaking parts of the Alps, you might see 'dahu' incorporated into the names of local businesses. It's a tribute to a legendary creature with Nike-tick horns that resembles a chamois, but has a peculiar adaptation to steep slopes. Like the fabled 'wild haggis' of Scotland, its legs are shorter on one side, giving it an upright stance on the gradients, but condemning it always to circle the mountain clockwise or anticlockwise, depending on the subspecies. You stand a more realistic (though still slim) chance of spotting an Alpine ibex. In the mid-19th century, these splendid wild goats – known for the males' large, semicircular horns – had been hunted to extinction everywhere except Italy's Gran Paradiso region (a private reserve of the kings of Sardinia) and the remote Vanoise mountains, now in France. Today the population, though fragmented, has rebounded to over 50,000.

From left: Alpine ibex, Mont Blanc; hairpin bends on the Great St Bernard Pass; St Bernards on their eponymous Pass

© imageBROKER / Alamy Stock Photo; jakubtravelphoto / Shutterstock; Porojnicu Stelian / Shutterstock

IN THE SHADOW OF MONT BLANC

For the last stage beyond Val d'Isère – shorn of its ski clothes but no longer a dead-end town in summer (bed down at its year-round Refuge de Solaise) – you twice touch the sacred. The Little St Bernard Pass, strangely broad and open after some determined zigzagging to reach it, leads you into a French-tinged corner of Italy. Through La Thuile (the tunnel leaving town is the one of Lamborghini Miura notoriety from the opening scenes of *The Italian Job*) and the regional capital of Aosta, you climb again to the Great St Bernard Pass on the Italian-Swiss border, forgoing the road tunnel to stop at the lakeside Great St Bernard Hospice where the monks once bred that shaggy symbol of Alpine rescues. The official kennels are now down in Martigny, though in summer you can meet a few of the dogs up on the pass.

Europe's tallest mountain (outside the Caucasus), Mont Blanc teases first in glimpses along the horizon on the descent to La Thuile, but takes centre stage soon after you cross a small bridge over a forest stream back into France. Framed in the valley that leads from Vallorcine to Argentière is a rampart of jagged spires, and behind them, the deceptively benign snow-white dome of Mont Blanc itself. By the time you still your EV's motor among the chalets and mountaineering monuments of Chamonix, its glacier-draped slopes convey nothing but awe.

Below: Cannes
Right: EV bling – BMW
i8 plug-in hybrid in
Monte Carlo, Monaco

**Distance: 44 miles
(70km)**

Duration: 2 days

The Côte d'Azur

FRANCE/MONACO

The Côte d'Azur is named for the Mediterranean horizons that are a constant along its coast roads, but its hilltop villages, exotic foliage and art collections add more colour to the palette.

What you need to remember – as you stand at the steps in Cannes where film stars pose on the red carpet each May, or when you read delight and disappointment in the faces of punters leaving Monaco's ornate casino – is that it hasn't always been this way on the Riviera. Cannes was once just a fishing village on the overlooked fringe of France, Monaco a near-bankrupt principality you'd need a magnifying glass to find on the map.

And what changed all that was, put simply, the sun. Moneyed travellers from further north started to come here for the mild winters, then – once fashion decided that the tan was in – the radiant summers, too. Add a new enclave of legalised gambling, plus invasions of artists entranced by the light, and the groundwork was laid for those palm-lined boulevards where you can cruise between seafront hotels and the blue beyond (perhaps using a bit of solar power in the mix).

ON THE ART TRAIL FROM CANNES

Running for over a mile along the bay at Cannes, the Croisette passes monuments to glamour both vintage – such as the 1911 Carlton InterContinental Hotel – and more recent, like the angular convention centre

Plan & prepare

Tips for EV drivers

Though most EVs could easily get from Cannes to Monaco (and back) on one charge, be aware that fast chargers are mainly found along the A8 'La Provençale' *autoroute*, which runs parallel to the drive detailed here, but inland. Monaco appears to be a blank on some online maps of charger availability, though it does actually have an extensive network. Remember to keep an eye on how much power the aircon is using if driving in high summer.

Where to stay

Of the three cities covered, you'll pay a premium to stay in Monaco, while Nice can be excellent value for money. In Cannes, the three-star Villa Claudia (villa-claudia-cannes.com) is a pastel-pink mansion from 1872, with chargers located just across the road. Hotels in Nice with their own charging points seem to be biased towards Tesla users; Hôtel La Pérouse (hotel-la-perouse.com) doesn't have on-site parking, but its view of the coast is perhaps the best in town.

When to go

Why not do as the first tourists to the region did and visit outside the peak summer months, when roads are quieter? Even in its coldest month, Nice is around twice as warm as Paris (with days averaging 10°C/50°F), and half as rainy. While some hotels and restaurants along the coast might close from around October to April, urban hubs like Nice with year-round attractions mean it's a viable route even then.

Further info

To schedule some beach time – whether at a paid-for beach club or on the public shore – peruse the explorenicecotedazur.com clickable map of attractions in and around Nice. If you do a slightly longer version of this route, and in reverse, you'll find one of the best views down to Monaco from the chargers at the Beausoleil services on the eastbound A8, before the exit to Menton.

Podium finish

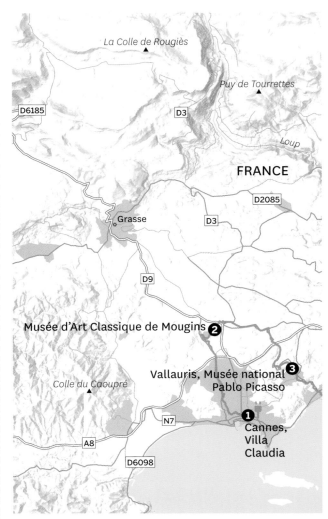

You're in Monaco with your own wheels – are you really going to miss the chance to try out a rare Grand Prix circuit that's open freely to drivers most of the year? As essential a date on the Formula One calendar as it is generally disliked by those who have to race it (since overtaking on the narrow streets is nigh-on impossible), the Monaco Grand Prix has been running since 1929; since 2015, the principality has also hosted the semi-regular Monaco ePrix for electric cars. To emulate them, begin on Boulevard Albert 1er, where you'll see race-starting positions painted on the tarmac year-round. A right curve and a long uphill lead to the Place du Casino, in front of the 1860s Casino de Monte-Carlo. Take Avenue des Spélugues, first to an ultra-tight hairpin and then right again through a seaside tunnel under the Fairmont Hotel. After emerging, follow the road around the main harbour to complete your 2.1-mile (3.4km) lap with two right turns in quick succession. But just remember that on non-race days, Monaco's usual speed limit is 31mph (50kph) – and you do need to stop at zebra crossings.

Above: the Fairmont Hairpin, aka Loews Curve, on Monaco's hallowed Grand Prix circuit
Right: Musée Picasso in Antibes

where the film festival is held. It would be easy to follow this lead, keeping the beach clubs and parasols immediately to your right for most of the drive to Nice. But there's also an artistic hinterland to discover if you strike out perpendicular to the seaside.

It's a short drive in your EV through Cannes' suburbs to Mougins, a genuine old Provençal hilltop village amid the sprawl of swimming-pool-land. In its curled *escargot* of streets, you'll find both a photography centre and the Musée d'Art Classique de Mougins, which pairs artefacts from ancient Greece, Rome and Egypt with similarly inspired works by the likes of Chagall and Cocteau.

The name that rings loudest here, though, is that of Picasso, honoured in two different castle-museums just four miles apart. In Vallauris, the walls of an old chapel – now the Musée national Pablo Picasso – are given over to his own 1951 epic *War and Peace*. And back on

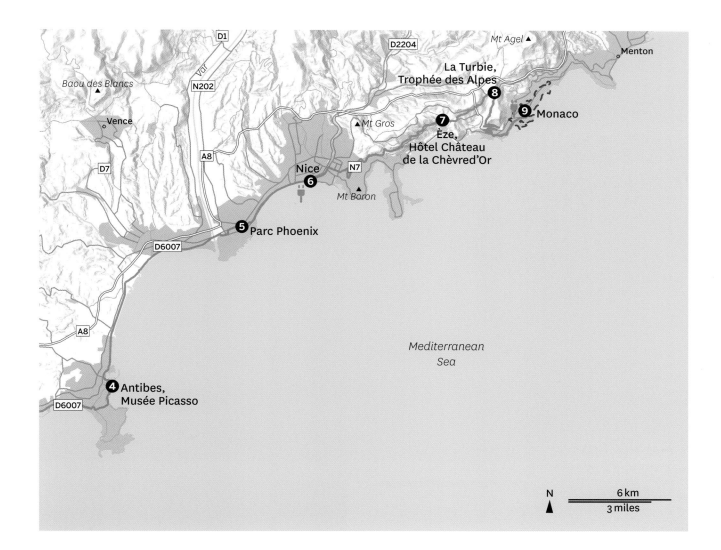

the coast in Antibes, waves break on the rocks right under the medieval battlements where Picasso set up a studio in 1946, now the Musée Picasso.

The ongoing risk is that if you diverted to every art museum near the route – the Musée Renoir in Cagnes-sur-Mer, the Fondation Maeght in St-Paul de Vence – you'd be stopping every five minutes. Along these shores, it can sometimes feel simpler to list the great names of late 19th to mid-20th century art who did not come here.

EN ROUTE TO NICE

For some different sightseeing on the way into Nice, and a possible charge top-up for your car nearby while you do, consider Parc Phoenix, whose tropical plants make great use of the microclimate, with assorted parrots, flamingos, lemurs and wallabies completing the picture.

Say it with flowers

While Cannes has its Film Festival and Monaco its Grand Prix, the biggest event of the year in Nice is its two-week Carnival (en.nicecarnaval.com). Held in February or early March, it's the largest such celebration in France – indeed, it claims to rank behind only Rio de Janeiro and Venice in the globe's pre-Lenten revelry stakes. The earliest mention of a carnival in Nice was in 1294, but it was only in the decades after the city passed definitively to France, in 1860, that the signature elements of the festivities took shape. The twin strands are the Corso, a parade of giant sculptural floats including a King of Carnival, made to a different theme each year and ritually burnt on the last night; and the Battle of the Flowers – despite the name, expect further floats and scatterings of mimosa and lilies rather than petal-strewn carnage.

Clockwise from top: Promenade des Anglais, Nice; dining at Château de la Chèvre d'Or, Èze; Carnival in Nice

Running right past is Nice's riposte to the Croisette: the Promenade des Anglais, which continues most of the way along the city's 3-mile (5km) curve of beach, the name a reminder of those winter exiles two centuries ago. It's as fine a way as ever to arrive in town. Just before the Old Town and the hilltop remains of the Château de Nice, you're diverted inland, as the promenade's continuation – the Quai des États-Unis – is westbound only.

Nice deserves more than just a pit stop, and with a day here (and a night at Hôtel La Pérouse) you're bound to be sucked back into the art vortex, whether at the Musée Matisse, sitting stately between olive groves and Roman ruins; or the contemporary collections of MAMAC, fronted by a giant, enigmatic statue with a cube for a head. But the last stage of the drive is the most cinematic, along the steeply flanked Corniches towards Monaco.

THE CORNICHES TO MONACO
With three parallel Corniches to choose from (Grande giving lofty views from the top, Petite down by the seaside, and Moyenne in between at the heart of the landscape), you must either choose two for outbound and return, or – as here – pick and mix, using connecting roads. Start on the Corniche Moyenne and aim for the village of Èze, clustered on a hump of rock that stands out from the mountainside.

A recharge for yourself – if not your car – could involve lunch at one of three panoramically sited restaurants (one with a double Michelin star) at the Château de la Chèvre d'Or. Shortly after Èze, shimmy up to the Grande Corniche to reach La Turbie, where the terrace at the Trophée des Alpes (a monument built to celebrate the conquests of the Roman emperor Augustus) reveals your first view of Monaco.

Using the D37 to zigzag back to the coast at Cap-d'Ail, you enter the 2-mile-long (3.2km) realm of Prince Albert II discreetly, by way of a roundabout planted with tropical foliage. Here, of all journey's-ends – beside Monaco's yacht-filled harbour and palace-crowned rock – is the place to do a victory lap.

Below: Château de Saint Paterne, Alençon
Right: Haras national du Pin, France's 'Versailles for horses'

→ **Distance: 178 miles (286km)**

→ **Duration: 3-4 days**

Caen to Tours

FRANCE

History is writ large across this route, with medieval castles and cathedrals, half-timbered houses, Renaissance chateaux and the vestiges of the Normandy battlefields to discover along the way.

Over the years, this corner of northern France has been the setting for a rich – but often brutal – unfolding of events. Caen was badly hit during the Battle of Normandy in 1944, and its hugely impressive Mémorial de Caen is justifiably regarded as one of Europe's best World War II museums. After a visit, reach further back in history with a trip to 11th-century Château de Caen, stronghold of William the Conqueror. Walk the castle's ramparts, visit its medicinal garden and Musée des Beaux-Arts, then head to the Romanesque Église St-Étienne to see William's tomb.

CASTLES, CATHEDRALS & COTTAGES

Heading south of Caen to Falaise, you can visit William the Conqueror's birthplace, blocky Château de Falaise, which lords over the town from atop a rugged outcrop. Take in the views, then head down into the medieval streets to visit the powerful Falaise Memorial, a museum telling the story of civilian life during World War II.

Next, wind your way southwest to Haras national du Pin, the French national stud, where you can tour the grand stables, tack rooms and courtyards. Built by Louis XIV, its stately architecture earned it the nickname 'Versailles for horses'.

© Château de Saint Paterne

Plan & prepare

Tips for EV drivers

Caen's small airport only serves domestic flights; the nearest international airports are in Paris, where you can rent electric vehicles – but be aware that the availability of EVs with local car rental businesses is steadily increasing across France. The infrastructure here is now generally well set up for EV drivers, with regular charging points along most major highways.

Where to stay

In Caen, Clos Saint-Martin (clossaintmartin.com) offers handsome rooms in an old mansion, while just outside Alençon, stunning Château de Saint Paterne (chateau-saintpaterne.com) has chic guestrooms, an outdoor pool and oodles of character. La Demeure de Laclais (lademeuredelaclais.fr) is a characterful guesthouse in Le Mans' historic quarter, with free parking nearby; in Tours, La Maison Jules (lamaisonjules.com) is a 19th-century mansion in the cathedral district, with a leafy terrace and garden.

When to go

May to September is a great time to visit. In May, Tours' VitiLoire festival showcases wines from local vineyards, while in early June the anniversary of the D-Day landings is marked with commemorations and historical reenactments. In mid-June, car fanatics flock to Le Mans for its 24-hour race; Bastille Day on July 14th sees celebrations in most large towns, with outdoor music and theatre performances continuing throughout July and August in Le Mans.

Further info

Read up carefully on how local driving regulations apply to you and your EV. When driving in France, you're legally required to carry a warning triangle to use in the event of a breakdown or accident, and a reflective jacket for each occupant. If you're taking your own car from the UK or Ireland, you'll also need to adjust the beam of your headlights or apply headlamp-beam deflectors.

The D-Day beaches

In the early morning of June 6 1944, 135,000 Allied soldiers stormed onto the beaches north of Caen as part of Operation Overlord, the largest seaborne invasion in history. In the 76-day Battle of Normandy that followed, over 435,000 soldiers were killed or wounded. Driving through the pastoral countryside today, it's hard to comprehend how brutal the fighting was, but several excellent museums put events into historical and human context. At Arromanches-les-Bains, you can still see the remnants of the prefabricated Mulberry Harbours that were hastily installed here, while the Musée du Débarquement explains the logistics of the landings, and the 360-degree cinema shows archive footage. German gun emplacements remain intact at Longues-sur-Mer to the west, while nearby Omaha Beach, site of some of the most ferocious fighting, is overlooked by the deeply moving Normandy American Cemetery and Memorial, with its seemingly endless rows of white-marble crosses. The visitor centre tells the poignant stories of some of the 9387 soldiers buried here. Further west, at Pointe du Hoc, is perhaps the most visceral of experiences: the ground here is still pitted with huge bomb craters.

Clockwise from top left:
Mulberry Harbours at Arromanches-les-Bains; Château du Lude; 24 Heures du Mans victory parade

Back on the road in your EV, it's worth a stop in Sées to visit its ornate Gothic cathedral and episcopal palace before bedding down for the night at the glorious Château de Saint Paterne, on the outskirts of Alençon. With its perfect combination of Renaissance architecture and chic, contemporary styling, it's possible you might never want to leave.

Tear yourself away in the morning to weave along the rolling backcountry roads of the Mancelles Alps to Saint-Céneri-le-Gérei on the River Sarthe. The village's jumble of narrow, cottage-lined streets, charismatically set between forested hills, were once a favourite of Impressionist painters. Downstream is scenic Fresnay-sur-Sarthe, a larger town with a traditional market hall, quaint streets and willows reaching down from the castle ramparts to the river.

LE MANS TO TOURS
From Fresnay-sur-Sarthe, it's only 40 minutes' drive to Le Mans, home to the famous 24-hour car race and a handsome medieval core. The cobbled lanes, wonky half-timbered houses and imposing cathedral have provided a backdrop for period dramas such as *Cyrano de Bergerac*, *Man in the Iron Mask* and *The Three Musketeers*. And for those with petrolhead proclivities (even EV drivers!), Le Mans' Musée des 24 Heures awaits.

© Herve Lenain / Alamy Stock Photo, TWilliam Perry / Getty Images

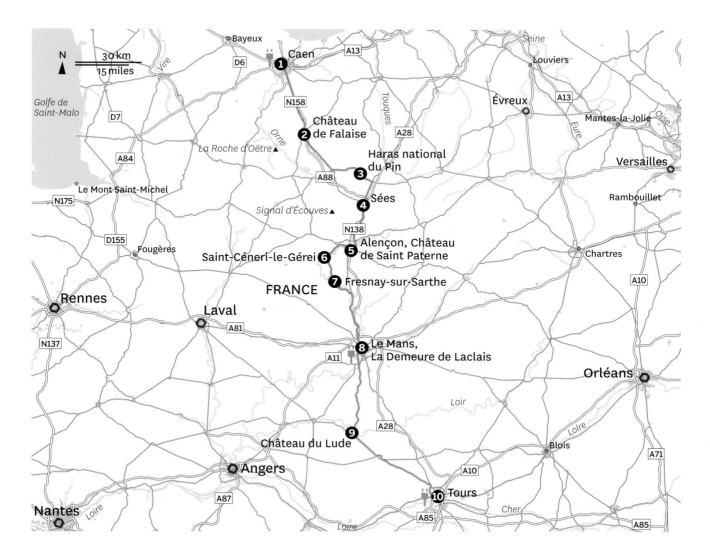

From Le Mans, head south on the D307 for 50 minutes to reach Château du Lude, the most northerly of the Loire Valley chateaux. An Italian Renaissance masterpiece with six towers, a dry moat and lavish private apartments, it's well worth a tour and a stroll through the formal gardens. Stop for a traditional lunch at the Auberge des Isles on the riverfront, then continue on to Tours, about an hour's drive away.

From Place Plumereau at the heart of Tours' medieval quarter, narrow cobbled streets flanked by half-timbered houses fan out to the Gothic Cathédrale St-Gatien, with its exquisitely detailed facade and soaring nave. Nearby, the Musée des Beaux-Arts shows work by Degas, Monet, Rembrandt and Rubens. Pick up some local nougat, dried pears or *rillettes*, watch the world go by at a riverfront bar and finish your day at Bistrot des Belles Caves, where you can dine on French classics accompanied by the pick of Touraine wines.

Below: vineyards around Würzburg
Right: Schmiedgasse, Rothenburg ob der Tauber

→ **Distance: 239 miles (385km)**

→ **Duration: 3-4 days**

The Romantic Road

GERMANY

Running from the vineyards of Würzburg to the foot of the Alps, through a cultural and historical cross-section of southern Germany, the Romantic Road is the most popular and renowned of Germany's tourist routes.

Würzburg is the northern starting point for the Romantic Road (Romantische Strasse), and beguiles even before you reach its city centre. With a designated driver alongside, you can sample delicate locally-produced white wines in amongst rococo wonders such as the immense Residenz, a Unesco World Heritage-listed 18th-century palace. Also sizeable is the city's student population, the presence of which means its cobbled streets thrum throughout the day and night.

Heading 31 miles (50km) southwest, the hills above the small village of Bad Mergentheim – a particularly restful place for an overnight stop – are lined with vineyards. A further 25 miles (40km) on is medieval Rothenburg ob der Tauber, its twisting cobbled lanes and pretty architecture enclosed by stone walls punctuated with towers. Fudge vendors and year-round Christmas shops proliferate here.

Pointing your EV due south again, you'll cross bridge after bridge traversing the waterways that lace this verdant region. After around 45 minutes on the road, you'll come to immaculately preserved Dinkelsbühl, which proudly traces its roots to a royal residence founded by Carolingian kings in the 8th century. This is arguably the Romantic Road's quaintest and most authentically medieval destination, right down to its moat and watchtowers.

Plan & prepare

Tips for EV drivers

The number of EV charging stations in Germany is growing rapidly; the government has pledged to have at least a million established across the country by 2030. Most towns and cities – especially on the Romantic Road – have large parking areas at the edges of their centres, to allow for pedestrianised precincts and a less frenetic atmosphere. Increasing numbers of these public car parks have charging stations, so you can top up while heading in for a stroll.

Where to stay

Amidst the green space that rings Bad Mergentheim, the luxe Ringhotel Bundschu (hotel-bundschu.de) is within sight of some of the vineyards that supply the region's highly drinkable white wines, and is a good base from which to get out in nature after a day experiencing the over-the-top glories of Würzburg. The Augsburger Hof (stadthotel-landsberg.de), in tiny Landsberg am Lech, is a traditional inn which fits right into the old-timey vibe of the Romantic Road.

When to go

The Romantic Road welcomes visitors year-round, although it can be swamped in July and August. In towns like Rothenburg ob der Tauber, it's always Christmas: huge trinket emporiums line the main streets, some posing as 'museums' of the holiday. Consider enjoying the drive and the towns during the spring and autumn, when crowds are fewer and there are either the vivid greens of spring or the golden shades of fall to take in along the way.

Further info

The Romantic Road runs through western Bavaria, covering 239 miles (385km) between Würzburg at its north end and Füssen near the Austrian border. Given its many transport options and ease of car rental (EVs included), Frankfurt is the most popular gateway for driving the route north to south – but if you prefer to tackle it the other way round, Munich is a sound jumping-off point for starting at nearby Füssen and heading north.

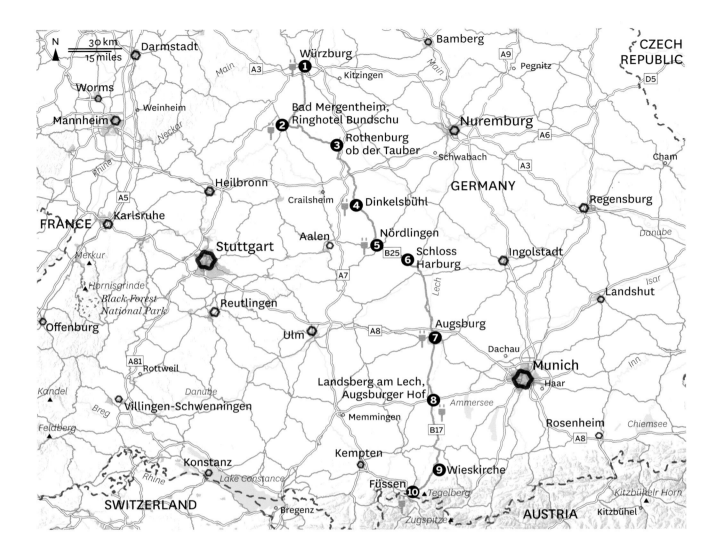

One of the charms of this drive is catching your first sight of old towns set amid rolling hills and fields. A case in point lies 30 minutes further on, where delightfully medieval Nördlingen retains an air of authenticity that comes as a relief after some of the Romantic Road's kitschy extremes. The intact 14th-century walls form an almost perfectly circular surround to the town.

To the southeast, rising dramatically above the Wörnitz River, Harburg is famous for one thing – its 12th-century castle. Get lost in its parapets, towers, turrets and red-tiled roofs, so perfectly preserved they seem like a film set.

SOUTH TOWARD FÜSSEN

Next up is Augsburg, established by the Romans and later a centre of Luther's Reformation. Today it's a lively provincial city, with streams crisscrossing streets lined with period buildings, and an assortment of beer gardens and beer halls that rival those of Munich.

Lovely Landsberg am Lech is often overlooked by Romantic Road-trippers on their town-hopping way between Augsburg and Wieskirche to the south. But it's this very absence of crowds that make this walled town, prettily set on the Lech River, a peaceful option for a sleep.

Towering over Wies, 45 minutes' drive south, the Unesco-listed Wieskirche is a truly wondrous work of 18th-century rococo excess; it's built where, in 1730, a farmer is said to have witnessed the miracle of his statue of Christ shedding tears. Some 16 miles (25km) southwest, you reach the southern tip of our route at 'Mad' King Ludwig's two castles in Füssen. Hohenschwangau was his childhood home; adjacent Neuschwanstein was his creation (with the help of a theatrical designer). With plenty of evidence of his twin obsessions (swans and Wagnerian operas), it's a fantastical architectural pastiche, both overwhelmingly beautiful and over the top, and is said to have inspired Disneyland's fairy-tale castle.

The spark of romance

A tourism official once said that if each of Germany's cities, towns and villages had their way, they'd all be on the Romantic Road – so popular (and such a driver of tourist income) has it become: two million visitors head along here each year. Ignoring for the moment the bewildering prospect of a route linking every settled spot in the country, the Romantic Road has a history that goes back to 1950, when Germany was still digging out from the destruction of WWII. Tourism officials in southern Germany – whose names are now lost, otherwise they'd be worthy of statues on the main squares of towns from Würzburg to Füssen – saw the fascination American soldiers had with relatively untouched towns that embodied every half-timbered German cliche. In response, the original route linking some 20 villages was carved out and branded the Romantic Road. At the time, the use of 'romantic' was more motivated by Germanic conventions linking the word *'romantische'* to ideas of quaint cosiness rather than to the idea that you're likely to find or rekindle romance along the way – although that confusion certainly hasn't hurt the Romantic Road's popularity.

Clockwise from top left:
Landsberg am Lech;
the perfect romantic
backdrop at Disneyesque
Neuschwanstein Castle; rococo
wonders and fabulous frescoes
at the Wieskirche, Wies

➡️ **Distance: 180 miles (291km)**

➡️ **Duration: 5-7 days**

The Black Forest

GERMANY

Legendary land of chocolate cake and cuckoo clocks, the Black Forest is awash with cliches – but it also makes an extraordinary place for a road trip.

Even if you've never set foot in this improbably picturesque corner of Germany before, you'll almost certainly have tasted a slice of it. Schwarzwälder Kirschtorte, that classic cherry-topped chocolate gateau, is undoubtedly the region's most famous export, but the Black Forest isn't just about indulgent teatime treats. Forest trails, spa towns, sparkling lakes, cosy beer halls, cuckoo clocks and even the odd lederhosen-wearing local: the Schwarzwald is as near as you'll get to the Grimm Brothers' Germany of your childhood imagination.

Kick off in Baden-Baden – the spa town that's so good, they named it twice. Its mineral-rich waters are said to have healing properties (everyone from Queen Victoria to Barack Obama has come here for a restorative dip), and the town has an air of fin-de-siècle grandeur, with turreted villas and Art Nouveau buildings galore. For a luxurious bath option, book a session at fabulous, Roman-style Friedrichsbad, where you can get scrubbed, scarified and purified to your heart's content. Leave inhibitions at the door: nudity is the norm here, and bathing mostly mixed.

ON TO THE BLACK FOREST HIGHWAY

From Baden-Baden, take the Schwarzwaldhochstrasse (Black Forest Highway), also known as the B500, a

Tips for EV drivers

With over 50,000 chargers (and counting), Germany has one of Europe's most extensive EV charging networks. Maingau (maingau-energie.de) and Ladenetz (ladenetz.de) are two of the biggest charger operators. This is a rural route, however, and you will find chargers a bit scarce outside the towns: plan charge stops at Baden-Baden, Freudenstadt, Trossingen and Konstanz. Due to the hilly mountain roads, err on the side of caution when it comes to range predictions.

Where to stay

There's no shortage of places to stay in the Black Forest, from timbered mountain inns to traditional small-town guesthouses, but it's worth noting that on-site EV charging is, for now, a rarity. Hotel Merkur (hotel-merkur.com) in Baden-Baden is a modern, eco-friendly choice: guests get free e-scooters to explore the town, plus access to EV charging stations. Hotel Bad Horn (badhorn.ch) has views of Lake Constance and a very contemporary spa; there are chargers in its underground car park.

When to go

Autumn is the most attractive time of year in the Black Forest, for obvious reasons: if Europe has a great leaf-peeping drive to rival the USA's Blue Ridge Parkway, then the Black Forest Highway is surely it. The autumnal palette is stunning: October is the peak month. Alternatively, come in spring for leafy foliage – but avoid summer, which can be crowded around the lakes and mountain towns.

Further info

Check into almost any hotel in the Baden-Württemberg region, pay the nominal Kurtaxe (resort tax) and you'll receive the money-saving Gästekarte (Guest Card), entitling you to free entry to local swimming pools and attractions, plus hefty discounts on everything from bike hire and spas to ski lifts and boat trips. Versions with the KONUS symbol offer free use of public transport.

131

Clockwise from top left: Black
Forest glade; cuckoo clocks, Triberg;
traditional nightwatchman sounding
a bull's horn, Wolfach

Like clockwork

Baden-Württemberg has given the world some important inventions and discoveries: the spark plug (Robert Bosch), the astronomical telescope (Johannes Kepler), DNA (Friedrich Miescher) and the Zeppelin (Ferdinand von Zeppelin), to name but a few (you may also have heard of a bright spark by the name of Albert Einstein, born in Ulm, who came up with a little idea called general relativity). But if there's one innovation this corner of Germany is known for, it's the Kuckucksuhr (cuckoo clock). This peculiar timepiece was said to have been invented in the 1730s by one Franz Anton Ketterer, a clockmaker from the Black Forest village of Schönwald, who was inspired by the bellows of a church organ. Recent research, however, suggests cuckoo clocks were being made in the area as early as the mid-1600s, pre-dating Ketterer's claim by nearly a century. Using an intricate system of bellows, pendulums and gears to keep time, the clocks' trademark 'coo coo' is generated by air being pushed through two wooden whistles to create the familiar two-note call. Kuckucksuhr range from simple designs to highly ornamented pieces: and antique clocks by the top Black Forest artisans can fetch thousands of euros at auction.

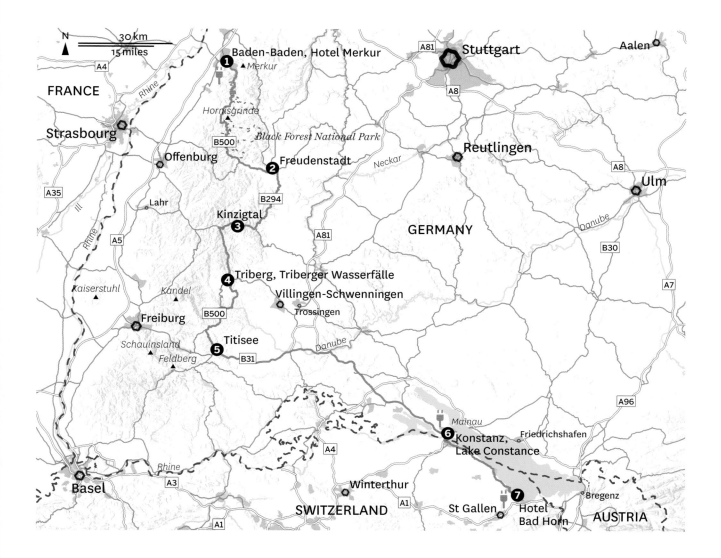

brilliant mountain road which takes in big views of woods, peaks and waterfalls as it meanders south into the Black Forest proper (officially known as the Nationalpark Schwarzwald). It's one of Germany's oldest scenic roads, winding along a mountain ridge that tops out at the high point of the Bühlerhöhe, and zips past the impressive 3819ft (1164m) peak of the Hornisgrinde, the highest point in the northern Black Forest. It's only a journey of 37 miles (60km) or so from Baden-Baden to Freudenstadt, but you'll want a whole day to make the most of it. Freudenstadt itself was almost entirely flattened during WWII, but it makes a handy overnight stop.

THE KINZIGTAL

After Freudenstadt, venture south along the B294 as it travels into the Kinzigtal, a dramatic valley that follows the babbling course of the Kinzig River. The valley's inhabitants survived for centuries on mining and logging,

and it's peppered with pretty half-timbered towns and villages: Gengenbach, Haslach, Schiltach and Wolfach are well worth a stop. Gutach is a renowned area for hikers, and you can also drop in to the Vogtsbauernhof for a glimpse into the area's rural past: it's a kind of living museum where you can watch traditional crafts being carried out, pet farmyard creatures and learn about everything from sheep-shearing to butter-making. Traditional inns along the valley make ideal pit stops for an extremely filling lunch.

CLOCKS & CAKES

Triberg is perhaps the quintessential Black Forest town. It's the heir to the original 1915 Black Forest gateau recipe, and there are plenty of cafes around town where you can treat yourself to an absurdly generous slice. The town is also an historic centre of cuckoo-clock making. The Weltgrösste Kuckucksuhr claims to be the world's

The Zeppelin Museum

The lakeside town of Friedrichshafen on Lake Constance is home to one of the region's most interesting museums. Near the eastern end of the waterfront promenade is the Zeppelin Museum, with an aviation theme that commemorates the town's claim to fame as birthplace of the Zeppelin airship. The centrepiece is a full-scale mock-up of a 108ft (33m) section of the *Hindenburg* (LZ 129), the largest rigid airship ever built, measuring 804ft (245m) long and outfitted as luxuriously as an ocean liner. Infamously, the hydrogen-filled craft burst into flames, killing 36, while landing in New Jersey in 1937. Various other aviation exhibits are on show, including a motor gondola from the *Graf Zeppelin*, which circumnavigated the globe in 21 days in 1929. Friedrichshafen is also one of the only places on the planet where you can take a Zeppelin trip: contact Zeppelin NT (zeppelinflug.de).

From left: Zeppelin Museum, Friedrichshafen; Mainau Island, Lake Constance; Triberger Wasserfälle

largest of these, and took local clockmaker Joseph Dold three years to build entirely by hand. Just watching the mechanism in action is enough to boggle your brain as to how it's all put together. While you're here, follow the trail up to the Triberger Wasserfälle. Dropping 535ft (163m) over a series of seven cascades, the waterfalls are the highest in Germany, and remain lit up until 10pm. Keep your eyes peeled for red squirrels here.

TITISEE TO LAKE CONSTANCE

When you simply can't find any more room for another slice of gateau, it's time to head on to Titisee (no giggling!). Named after its glittering lake, this is a pleasant summer resort and a popular place for sailing and watersports. If you feel up for a bracing dip, head to the lakeside lido here.

From Titisee, take the B31 east, exiting the Black Forest as you travel on towards Germany's southern border with Switzerland and Austria. Final destination on this route is

Lake Constance, the vast body of water that's really closer to an inland sea. Fed by the mighty Rhine, at 39 miles (63km) long by 9 miles (14km) wide, it's the third-biggest lake in Europe and spans three nations: locals often joke that you can have breakfast in Germany, nip to Switzerland for lunch and make it to Austria in time for afternoon tea. It's a massive area that offers several weeks' worth of sights, from Benedictine abbeys to Roman forts, medieval castles to baroque churches – not to mention plenty of opportunity to indulge in watersports.

One expedition definitely worth your time is the boat ride to Mainau: this 111-acre (45-hectare) Mediterranean garden in the middle of Lake Constance was the brainchild of the Bernadottes, relations of the Swedish royal family. Two million visitors flock here every year to admire lake views from the castle, wander tree-lined avenues and visit glass hothouses bristling with exotic palms and orchids.

→ **Distance: 367 miles
(590km)**

→ **Duration: 3-5 days**

The Fairy Tale Road

GERMANY

Take an EV road trip through a beautiful swathe of Germany and learn the real stories behind Grimms' fairy tales along the way. You might just live happily ever after!

Bremen is well known for its fairy-tale characters. On the western side of the ornate 1410 Rathaus you'll find the city's unmissable and famous symbol, direct from a Grimms' tale: *Bremen Town Musicians* (1951), by the sculptor Gerhard Marcks, depicts a dog, cat and rooster, one on top of the other, on the shoulders of a donkey (the latter's nose and front legs incredibly shiny after being touched by countless visitors for good luck).

An hour and a half's drive southeast of Bremen, Hanover is known for its huge trade shows, but it also has many elegant parks – stroll them while you and your car recharge. This is a great place to spend your first night.

TALL TALES

Half-timbered Hamelin is only 30 miles (48km) southwest of Hanover. According to the Brothers Grimm in their 19th-century version of *The Pied Piper of Hamelin* (a story which dates to the Middle Ages), the Pied Piper (Der Rattenfänger) was employed by Hamelin's townsfolk in the 13th century to lure its rodents into the river. When the people refused to pay him, he picked up his flute and led their kids away. Today the rats rule once again: fluffy and cute stuffed rats, wooden rats, and tiny brass rats adorning the sights around town.

Plan & prepare

Tips for EV drivers

At the time of writing, around one in five new cars sold in Germany were EVs, a proportion increasing with the German government's offers of incentives for buyers, and with the efforts of Germany's major car companies to catch up with Tesla, which has a huge factory near Berlin. Chargers have also proliferated, with many petrol stations converting to accommodate fast EV chargers.

Where to stay

Marburg's swankiest digs, the Vila Vita Rosenpark Hotel (rosenpark.com), are a short stroll from the centre of town in an attractive spot by the river, close to chargers. With a lovely terrace bar-restaurant overlooking Hanover's leafy Ernst-August-Platz, the small Central-Hotel Kaiserhof (centralhotel.de) makes for a fine stop; it's directly opposite Hanover's main train station, the Hauptbahnhof, where many EV chargers can be found.

When to go

The Fairy Tale Road is not so thronged with road-trippers as certain other themed routes in Germany, such as the Romantic Road. In some regards it's best enjoyed from May to October, when the days are long and the weather is mild. However, in December nearly every town and city will have one of Germany's famed and fun Christmas markets.

Further info

The start point for this trip, Bremen (where you get whiffs of the North Sea in the air) is less than an hour's drive southwest of busy, rollicking Hamburg – a hub for international sea, rail and air travel, and with EV rental options. Frankfurt, 16 miles (26km) west of Hanau at the end of this route, is well connected for international flights, and also has EV rental and potential drop-off options.

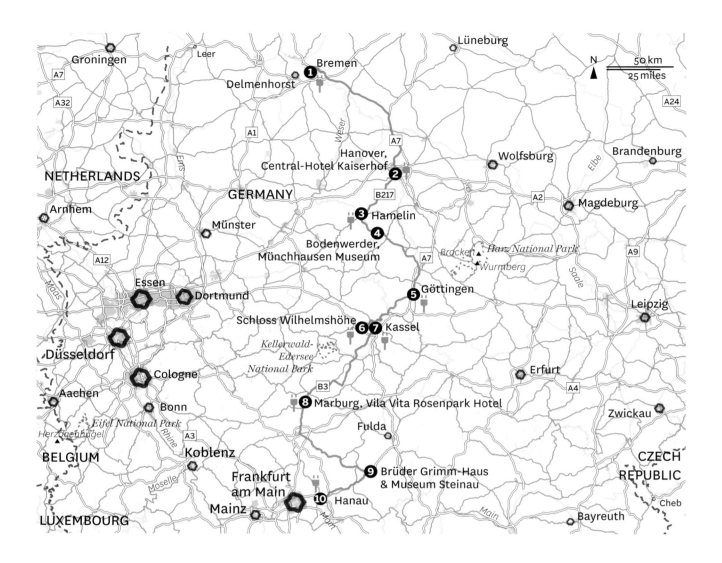

It's a mere 20 minutes' drive to Bodenwerder. This was the home of the notorious Baron Hieronymus von Münchhausen (1720–97), one of history's most shameless liars (his whoppers were no mere fairy tales) and the inspiration for Terry Gilliam's cult film, *The Adventures of Baron Munchausen*. Learn more at the Münchhausen Museum, which tackles the difficult task of conveying the chaos and fun associated with the 'liar baron'.

ON THE GRIMM TRAIL TO HANAU

Drive southeast via deeply forested valleys replete with bedtime-story atmosphere. After a little over an hour, you'll reach Göttingen. With over 30,000 students, this quaint yet lively town in a corner of Lower Saxony offers a good taste of college life in Germany's north. Georg-August Universität once hosted the fairy-tale-writing Brothers Grimm as teachers; they were dismissed in 1837 for their liberal views.

Less than an hour southwest, in the leafy Kassel suburb of Wilhelmshöhe, is the baroque Bergpark. You could easily spend a day exploring the formal gardens but prioritise the Schloss Wilhelmshöhe, a late-18th-century palace. Kassel proper is a short hop east, and is home to an unmissable attraction: Grimmwelt (Grimmworld), which houses the planet's most significant collection of Brothers Grimm memorabilia. Barely 60 miles (96km) southwest, hilly, historic Marburg has an Old Town laced with narrow lanes, and is a splendid place to halt for the night.

To delve deeper into Grimm lore, drive southeast through the hilly Vogelsberg to riverside Steinau, where the Brüder Grimm-Haus and Museum Steinau occupy the building where the Grimm family lived from 1791 to 1796. A further 31 miles (50km) on, in Hanau, the 18th-century Schloss Philippsruhe sits on the banks of the mighty Main River. As the birthplace of the Grimms (Jacob in 1785, Wilhelm in 1786), Hanau makes a fitting journey's end.

Following storylines

The Grimm brothers travelled extensively through central Germany in the early 19th century, documenting folklore. Their collection of tales, *Kinder- und Hausmärchen*, was first published in 1812 and quickly gained international recognition – and the original stories within were much earthier and more violent than the Disneyfied versions popular today. The book's 209 yarns include such fairy-tale staples as *Hansel and Gretel*, in which (spoiler alert) a mother tries to ditch her son and daughter, a witch tries to eat them, and Gretel outsmarts her; the kids and father are reunited (the evil mum had died). *Cinderella* is the story which gave stepsisters a bad name – when the prince fits the shoe on our heroine, all is good with the world (although in the Grimms' version, the stepsisters are blinded by vengeful doves). *Rapunzel* is a morality play starring an adopted girl with very long hair, a prince who goes blind, and some evil older women; it ends on a love note when the prince stumbles upon an outcast Rapunzel and his sight is restored. In the first edition of the Grimms' book, Rapunzel bore children out of wedlock.

Clockwise from top left:
Münchhausen Fountain, Bodenwerder; *Hansel and Gretel* illustration from the 1812 *Kinder- und Hausmärchen*; Weidenhäuser Bridge, Marburg

Below: linger in
Berlin to sample the
city's bars and beers
Right: the Spree River,
overlooked by Berlin's
Fernsehturm TV tower

➡ **Distance: 190 miles (306km)**   ➡ **Duration: 6-9 days**

Berlin to Dresden

GERMANY

There's a world of surprises on this trip between two great German cities, from a canal-lined rural idyll where the gherkin is king to a town famous for its porcelain.

I f ever two cities were to embody the phrase 'like a phoenix from the ashes', it's the ones flanking this trip. There's Berlin, which continues to fizz with creative energy decades after the fall of its Wall; and Dresden, rebuilt after its near-total destruction in WWII.

You could spend weeks in Berlin and barely scratch the surface, meandering between art galleries, drinking in some of Europe's best bars, and trying to understand the city's remarkable history. When you're ready to leave, head west. In good weather, stop for a swim at Strandbad Wannsee before continuing to Potsdam, where Hotel Brandenburger Tor Potsdam is home for the night. There's an embarrassment of riches in this Unesco-listed city, so don't be in any hurry to check out. If you like a stately home, you're well served here, with numerous palaces to ogle, from elegant Sanssouci to Tudor-style Cecilienhof. The Dutch Quarter, built for Dutch immigrants in the 18th century, is good for a ramble. You'll not forget dinner at another historic property, Villa Kellermann, with a menu devised by Michelin-starred chef Tim Raue.

TAKE TO THE WATER
Once you've had your fill of Potsdam, ditch history and culture and have some good old-fashioned fun splashing

Plan & prepare

Tips for EV drivers

All the main rental companies in Germany hire out EVs, and are increasing the number of vehicles in their fleets. You'll have little trouble finding a charger here: Germany has one of the highest densities of charge points in Europe and ambitious plans to increase the numbers. The PlugShare (plugshare.com) and ChargeFinder (chargefinder. com) websites are good resources, or download the Zap-Map app.

Where to stay

SO/ Berlin Das Stue (so-berlin-das-stue.com), in the former Danish embassy, has a fine-dining restaurant and a spa; Hotel Brandenburger Tor Potsdam (hotel-brandenburger-tor.de) has crisp, neutral rooms in an historic villa. In Spreewald, try riverside Strandhaus Boutique Resort & Spa (strandhaus-spreewald.de). Hotel Wellness Goldenes Fass Meissen (goldenes-fass-meissen.de) is a cosy option in a 17th-century building. Finish your trip at smart, modern INNSiDE Dresden (melia.com) in the Old Town.

When to go

There are plenty of opportunities to get active on this trip, and late spring, summer and early autumn are the most enjoyable seasons for that. If you can, avoid the region's summer school holidays, which fall from mid-July to late August in Berlin and Brandenburg (for Spreewald) and early July to mid-August in Saxony (for Meissen and Dresden). There's a good chance of snow and subzero temperatures in winter.

Further info

Don't assume you can drive as fast as you want on the autobahn – they tend to have variable speed limits, with only about one in 10 having no limit at all, so check road signs before flooring your EV. In the event of snow, roads are cleared very quickly, but you must have winter tyres fitted when driving between November and March. Check germany.travel for more inspiration and info.

Clockwise from top left: Besucherbergwerk Abraumförderbrücke F60; cucumber harvest, destined for transformation into Spreewald gherkins; Schloss Moritzburg, a stately spot for lunch

Pickle perfection

Is there a region in the world that loves a gherkin as much as Spreewald does? Probably not. In Lübbenau, there's a gherkin museum, and the Gurkenmeile, a permanent row of market stalls devoted exclusively to gherkin products. There's the Gurkenradweg, a 160-mile-long (257km) gherkin cycle path. There's an annual gherkin festival in Golssen, in which a gherkin king and queen are crowned. There are gherkin statues and gherkin murals. And in the shops you can buy gherkin hats, fridge magnets, key rings and Christmas decorations. And gherkins, of course. The region harvests some 40,000 tonnes of cucumbers a year, which go into the million-plus jars of pickles produced each day. The vegetable has been grown here since the 14th century, when it was introduced by the Dutch, who recognised that the damp, mineral-rich soil and mild climate provided the perfect growing conditions. The 'Spreewälder Gurken' has now been recognised for its quality by the European Union and is protected by law. To get on top of your gherkin game, take a tour and tasting at a pickling factory in Lübbenau (spreewaldrabe.de). You can even stay the night in an old pickling barrel at Restaurant & Café Hanschick (spreewald-hanschick.de).

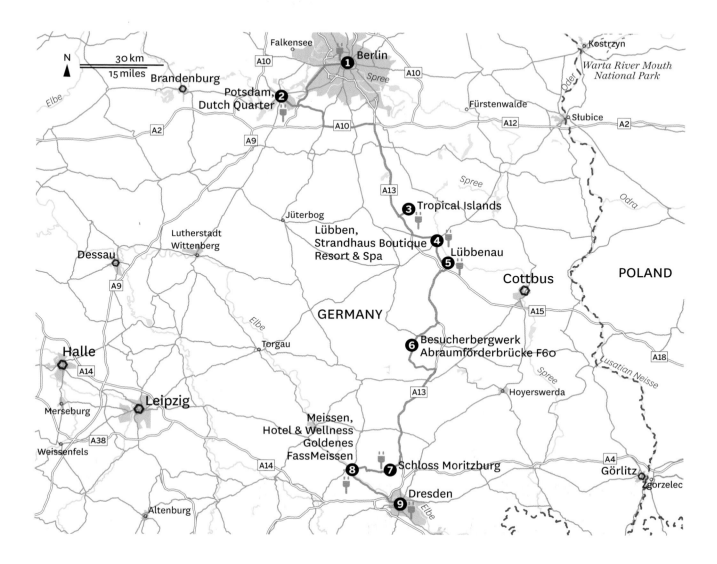

around at Tropical Islands, an hour's drive southeast; you'll spot the water park's enormous domed roof long before you arrive. There's further water-based distraction at the next destination. Spreewald is a bucolic region crisscrossed with canals, many flanked by pretty cottages; hop on a sightseeing boat, or rent a canoe and explore the network under your own steam. Lübben's Strandhaus Boutique Resort & Spa is a fine spot to recharge yourself and the car, and don't miss a stroll around regional hub Lübbenau, where there's no escaping the local speciality, the Spreewald gherkin, on restaurant menus.

Continuing south, it's worth a detour to an unusual attraction. The Besucherbergwerk Abraumförderbrücke F60 is a conveyor bridge that happens to be the world's largest moveable piece of machinery. Pre-book a guided tour to clamber about the colossal steel structure known as the 'reclining Eiffel Tower'. A man-made wonder of a different nature is found 40 miles (64km) further on.

Schloss Moritzburg is a moated palace whose 200 rooms were magicked into life by Saxony's finest 17th-century craftsmen. Its restaurant terrace, with views over the water, is a good spot for lunch.

There's a final stop before journey's end: 16 miles northwest of Dresden is Meissen. There are many reasons to visit this castle-topped town on the banks of the Elbe, but many people come for one alone – china. In the 18th century, Meissen was the first place in Europe to discover the secret to making porcelain. You can learn its fascinating story at the museum devoted to the subject, and see it being made at the factory.

After a night at Hotel Wellness Goldenes Fass Meissen, you'll arrive bright and perky in Dresden. There are enough magnificently restored churches, palaces, galleries and museums to fill a good few days here – and make sure you plonk yourself in the beer garden of SchillerGarten and toast your trip with a local Pilsner. Prost!

➡ **Distance: 195 miles (312km)**   ➡ **Duration: 2-3 days**

Dublin to Galway

IRELAND

Weave your way across the country on a route peppered with stately homes and early Christian ruins, visiting Ireland's oldest licensed whiskey distillery and sampling some of the country's finest oysters.

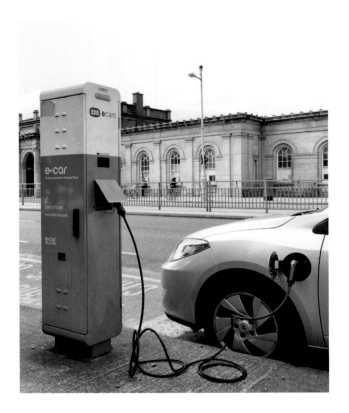

A small city with a whopper of a heart, Dublin is a place of castles, cathedrals and sophisticated Georgian terraces, and with a reputation as a cultural hothouse that has produced more than its fair share of great writers and musicians. Start by exploring Trinity College's Old Library to see the Book of Kells illuminated manuscript in the Long Room, then nip into the National Gallery and head for Kilmainham Gaol to learn about the country's journey to independence.

Along the way you'll come to realise that more than anything, it's Dubliners' humour and attitude that make the city sing, and an evening spent over 'a few scoops' in a local pub will put you at the heart of the action. Follow in the footsteps of Joyce, Beckett and Behan and head for McDaids, Toners, Davy Byrnes or the glorious Long Hall.

WEST TO CASTLETOWN

Just 40 minutes' drive west of Dublin on the M4 is the Palladian mansion Castletown House, Ireland's largest and most imposing Georgian estate. A testament to the vast wealth of the Anglo-Irish gentry in the 18th century, it was built for William Conolly, Speaker of the Irish House of Commons, in the style of an Italian palazzo. Take a tour of the house, then stroll through the landscaped gardens.

© Gabriel Casson / Alamy Stock Photo

Plan & prepare

Tips for EV drivers

Dublin airport is just north of the city and has several companies offering electric vehicle hire. You'll find rapid chargers in larger cities and standard fast chargers in many towns along this route; most are part of the ESB public charging network. Download the ESB app ahead of your trip (esb.ie/what-we-do/ecars).

Where to stay

In Dublin, the Wilder Townhouse (thewilder.ie) offers boutique charm within walking distance of St Stephen's Green. For a waterfront retreat complete with spa, award-winning restaurant and electric-boat hire, try the Wineport Lodge in Glasson (wineport.ie); the Prince of Wales Hotel in Athlone (theprinceofwales. ie) is a cheaper alternative. Galway offers lots of options; our pick is the Hardiman (thehardiman.ie), set in a landmark Victorian building on the city's main square.

When to go

May to October is the best time to travel, with long days and warmer weather, but a road trip in mid-March means you'll catch St Patrick's Day festivities across the country. In mid-June, Joycean fans come out in style for Bloomsday in Dublin. The Galway Arts Festival in July features a wealth of performances, while in September oyster lovers descend on Galway and Clarenbridge.

Further info

Driving west out of Dublin on the M4, you'll have to pay a small toll between Junction 8 (Kilcock) and Junction 10 (Kinnegad East). Tolls can be paid by cash or card. A second toll is payable on the section of the M6 between Junction 15 (Ballinasloe West) and Junction 16 (Loughrea).

Galway's traditional music scene

Combine an abundance of buskers, bands and boozy students with a location on the edge of a Gaeltacht (Irish-speaking area) and you'll get some measure of why Galway is so famous for its traditional music. Trad is a big deal here, and you'll find live music pouring out of almost every pub in the evenings. Just wander around and you'll be lured in by the siren call of fiddles, tin whistles and *bodhráns* (goatskin frame drums) belting out melodies that often speak of times of great social upheaval and political oppression. Crowd-pleasers such as *The Fields of Athenry* always result in a rowdy singalong at the end of the night. Serious music lovers head for the Crane Bar on Sea Rd; if it's

rammed, try the Róisín Dubh or Monroe's nearby. Back on the main drag, you can't miss the crowds pouring out into the streets from Taaffes, Tig Cóillí and Tigh Neachtain. And if you're feeling inspired to have a go at playing yourself, head to Powell's Music Shop (aka the Four Corners) on Williams St (powellsmusic. ie); it's been serving the city's musicians since 1918 and is the place to buy instruments of all kinds.

Above: busking, Galway-style
Right: high cross at the 6th-century monastic site of Clonmacnoise

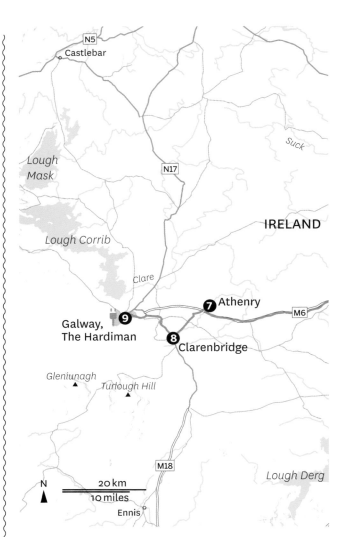

CASTLETOWN TO GALWAY

From Castletown, drive 45 minutes west to Kilbeggan. Founded in 1757, the Kilbeggan Distillery here is the oldest licensed distillery of its kind in Ireland. Take a tour with one of the distillers to hear the poignant story of its salvation from dereliction by the local community – and sample the whiskey (designated drivers can set some aside for later). Follow it up with lunch at Julimay's or whiskey truffles at the Kilbeggan Chocolate and Coffee Bar.

It's just a 30-minute drive west of Kilbeggan to Clonmacnoise, a 6th-century monastic site set on the River Shannon. Early churches, high crosses and a round tower are remnants of an ecclesiastical city that once trained monks from across Europe. Viking invaders put paid to all that learning, and by the 12th century Clonmacnoise had fallen into decline. After another half an hour shadowing the River Shannon's upstream path, the Wineport Lodge makes a good stop for the night,

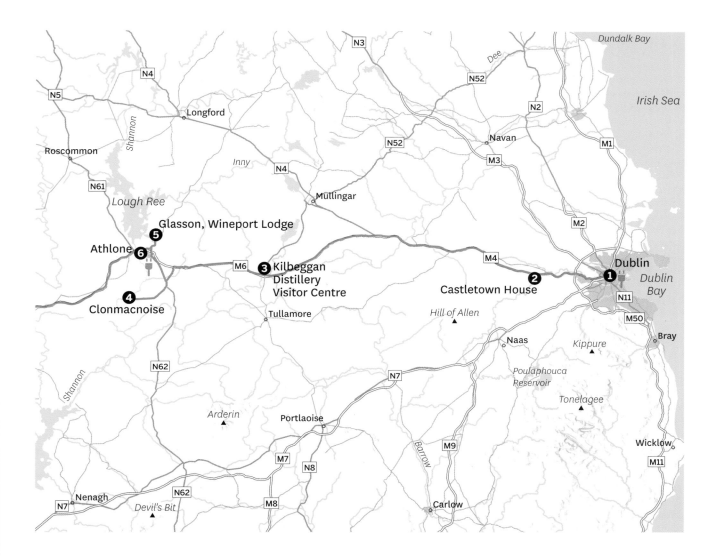

its waterfront location and excellent food both balm
for weary souls. In the morning, take a riverside stroll
before heading into Athlone to charge your EV while you
explore the former garrison town, its Norman castle and
the excellent Luan Gallery. You'll find another Norman
castle, a medieval parish church and a Dominican friary in
Athenry, 45 minutes' drive west; displays at the Heritage
Centre help give context to all. From there, it's only 20
minutes' drive to little Clarenbridge, where you can
rummage the antiques stores before settling in at Moran's
Oyster Cottage for a feast of fresh seafood.

Head round the bay into boho Galway, a city that seems
to teem with life, even in the pouring rain. There's a castle
and cathedral here, and a windswept promenade, but
Galway is all about its *ceol, caint agus spraoi* (music, chat
and fun). The colourful pedestrianised streets at the heart
of town, with their little galleries, cosy pubs and glut of
buskers, give it a celebratory vibe at any time of year.

➔ **Distance: 130 miles (208km)**   ➔ **Duration: 4-6 days**

Killarney & the Ring of Kerry

IRELAND

Cut a swathe through moss-draped forests, inky lakes and rugged peaks along a road that clings to the edge of Europe and takes you through a glut of gorgeous landscapes.

Circling the wild and rugged Iveragh Peninsula, the Ring of Kerry is undoubtedly Ireland's most famous drive – and rightly so, for its patchwork of ancient woodlands, gushing waterfalls, steely lakes, deep-purple mountains and golden beaches are unmatched in their beauty. You could breeze around the loop in a single day, but to do so would mean missing everything that makes this place so special.

INTO KILLARNEY NATIONAL PARK

Most travellers start their trip in Killarney, a lively base that offers easy access to the sublime beauty of its namesake national park. Make the most of the scenery by hiring a bike for the short cycle ride to restored 15th-century Ross Castle, at the edge of Lough Leane and within the national park. Tour the castle before loading your bike onto an open rowing boat and making the hour-and-a-half trip across the park's three lakes to Lord Brandon's Cottage. Little survives of the original hunting lodge here except a crumbling tower which, according to local legend, is where the lord imprisoned his young wife after hearing of her affair with Lord Melbourne (William Lamb), who later became Britain's prime minister. There's a cafe here; have some lunch before cycling the Gap

Plan & prepare

Tips for EV drivers

Kerry airport is about 20 miles (35km) north of Killarney, but the transition to offering electric vehicles for hire – both here and in Killarney – hadn't yet happened at the time of writing. EV chargers are dotted along this route, some at high-end hotels, others part of the ESB public charging network. Download their app ahead of your trip (esb.ie/what-we-do/ecars).

Where to stay

Muckross Park Hotel (muckrosspark.com) is the grande dame of Killarney hotels, hosting royalty, celebrities and the well-heeled since 1795; the lovely Cahernane House Hotel (cahernane.com) is more intimate. If you're after decadence, the Park Hotel Kenmare (parkkenmare.com) delivers with excellent dining, tranquil grounds and a spa, gym, pool and EV charger on site. The Kells Bay House near Cahersiveen (kellsbay.ie) is an old hunting lodge set in magnificent subtropical gardens.

When to go

Late spring and early autumn are the best times to visit as there is far less traffic on the roads, and far fewer visitors in Killarney National Park. These shoulder seasons are also the time to catch either the vibrant bloom of rhododendrons (between April and June), or the dramatic deer rut (October and November).

Further info

Although the direction of travel makes little difference in terms of what you can see, the route gets understandably busy between June and August. If you must travel then, consider that you'll need to make a choice between driving anticlockwise behind the tour buses, or meeting them head-on around narrow bends.

The wonder of the Skelligs

Two uninhabited islands flung out into the Atlantic 7 miles (12km) off the tip of Kerry, the Skelligs are places of legend. These jagged pyramids of rock were once what must have been the most inhospitable religious site in Europe, settled in the 6th century by the monks of St Fionán who built beehive cells, water cisterns, vegetable gardens and two oratories here, the structures set impressively atop foundation platforms built on the steep slope using nothing more than earth and drystone walls. Now a Unesco World Heritage Site, Skellig Michael is still difficult to reach, with sea swells meaning boats are only able to land in fair weather. Once here, a hike up 618 roughly hewn steps

awaits – but the rewards are spectacular, with the incredible views dwarfed only by a sense of awe at the tenacity and determination of the monks who lived here. The island is the final point on the St Michael Axis that links sacred sites all the way across Europe to the Middle East, though it may be more familiar as the location of Luke Skywalker's Jedi temple in two of the *Star Wars* prequels. The smaller of the two islands, Little Skelllig is a protected gannet colony with up to 35,000 breeding pairs nesting here between May and September.

Above: beehive cells on Skellig Michael
Right: Henry St, Kenmare

of Dunloe, a 7-mile (12km) stunner of a mountain pass wedged between the MacGillycuddy's Reeks – Ireland's highest mountains – and Purple Mountain.

Making your way up and over the pass, you'll encounter a steady flow of jaunting cars (horse-drawn traps), tiny streams, inland lakes and countless photo opportunities before descending the twisting road and meeting the cycle path back into Killarney. There's no shortage of places to eat or drink in this buzzing town, but for a taste of traditional Irish food try Bricín, where the *boxty* (potato pancake) is the house speciality.

SOUTH TO KENMARE
In the morning, head south on the N71, stopping off on the outskirts of Killarney at Muckross Abbey, a ruined 15th-century friary with a magnificently twisted yew tree growing in its midst. Just beyond is the commercial – but nonetheless impressive – Elizabethan revival

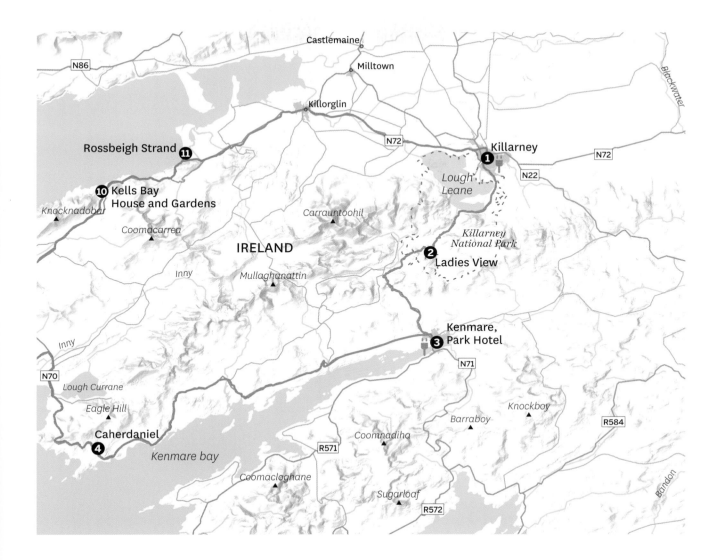

Muckross House; its vast estate forms the core of Killarney National Park. From here it's just two minutes' drive to Torc Waterfall, where peaty water gushes down the mountainside in a torrent, its spray draping the surrounding forest in a heavy blanket of moss.

Following the twisting N71 towards Kenmare, you'll pass a procession of heathered hillsides and brooding lakes. The most picturesque stops are at Ladies View, where Queen Victoria's ladies-in-waiting were said to have been much impressed; and Moll's Gap, where the eponymous Moll ran a shebeen (unlicensed pub) for the road workers in the 1820s.

Continue on for another 10 minutes and you'll arrive in Kenmare, home to some of the best pubs and restaurants in the county. Before hitting the nightlife, however, take a stroll to the town's Bronze Age stone circle or look into the little galleries along the main street. Check in to the elegant Park Hotel and, if you can tear yourself away from

Hiking Iveragh Peninsula

With ancient woodlands, the country's highest peaks and dramatic coastal cliffs, the Iveragh Peninsula offers some of Ireland's most rewarding hiking. Start off on the flat with the 9-mile (15km) Muckross Lake Loop, a scenic trail through the gnarly Reenadinna Woods and along waterside paths. For sweeping views over the Killarney lakes and the MacGillycuddy's Reeks, you could take on mountains Torc (1755ft/535m) or Mangerton (2749ft/838m), but if you're up for a challenge, the real prize is an ascent of Carrauntoohil, Ireland's highest peak (3407ft/1038m). For coastal scenery, Bolus Head offers blustery ocean views, and Portmagee sheer cliffs that plunge into the Atlantic; on Valentia Island, Geokaun Mountain delivers views of the Reeks, the Blaskets and the Skelligs. Alternatively, you could tick them all off on the 135-mile (215km) Kerry Way long-distance hiking trail.

From left: hiking the Iveragh Peninsula from Kenmare; Muckross Abbey's magnificent yew tree; cemetery on Abbey Island, Derrynane

its luxury, nip out later to catch some live music at PF McCarthy's on Main St.

COMPLETING THE LOOP

After breakfast, take the N70 through Sneem to tiny Caherdaniel, just under an hour's drive away. This former smugglers' haven was home to local hero Daniel O'Connell, who campaigned for Catholic emancipation in the 19th century. His family home, Derrynane House, is set in lush gardens with a pathway down to the turquoise waters and golden sands of Derrynane Beach.

Continue on through Waterville, turning west onto the R567 to join the far more tranquil Skelligs Loop through the Kerry Gaeltacht (Irish-speaking area). In tiny Ballinskelligs you'll find the Cill Rialaig Arts Centre and café, where you can browse local work and stop for lunch.

Just north of Ballinskelligs, the 1000ft (300m) Kerry Cliffs offer the chance for a walk with dramatic Atlantic views before heading into Portmagee, a little town with a busy pier and a single street of colourful houses. Tours to the Skellig Islands depart from here; across the bridge to Valentia Island, at the turf-roofed Skellig Experience Visitor Centre, you can learn about the islands' early Christian monastic settlement.

Drive east across Valentia Island on the R565 to Knight's Town, where a five-minute car ferry takes you back to the mainland and the N70. Recharge your battery in sleepy Cahersiveen as you explore the striking Old Barracks Heritage Centre, then check in at the glorious Kells Bay House just outside town.

After breakfast the next day, take the time to explore the exotic Kells Bay gardens; the Gulf Stream supports an array of tree ferns and subtropical plants. Back on the road, it's a 20-minute drive to Rossbeigh Strand, a tendril of golden sand that juts out into Dingle Bay and makes a wonderful stop for a morning walk. From here, it's just 40 minutes' drive, via Killorglin, back to the busy streets of Killarney where you began.

Below: Château
d'Urspelt
Right: Abbaye
de Neumünster,
Luxembourg City

➜ **Distance: 111 miles (180km)**

➜ **Duration: 2-3 days**

Around Luxembourg

LUXEMBOURG

Sandwiched between the mighty nations of Western Europe, this is a compact country with a compact capital city – yet it has large-scale appeal for a short road trip.

Among the nations of the world there are republics, kingdoms, principalities and sultanates – but there is only one Grand Duchy. Luxembourg is a geopolitical anomaly: a sliver of land at the heart of Western Europe, ruled by a Grand Duke. Miniature though it may be, it is a nation ideally sized for a road trip over a long weekend. Start in the eponymous capital – an unsung treasure, with a handsome Old Town ringed by steep gorges. Promenade along the Chemin de la Corniche – a walkway following the city ramparts – for a watchman's view over the picturesque jumble of spires and turrets, weirs and terraced gardens.

CASTLE TO CASTLE
Hôtel Le Place d'Armes lies just a short stroll from Luxembourg's Gothic Notre-Dame Cathedral – rest up under its gabled roofs before striking out in your EV into the Luxembourgeois hinterland. The north of the country is dominated by its castles – some former Roman frontier forts, others bastions from the heyday of the Holy Roman Empire; some crumbling, others still upright. Driving due north from the capital, you'll eventually happen upon medieval Château de Bourscheid – it's impossible to miss, being the

Plan & prepare

Tips for EV drivers

Companies at Luxembourg International Airport offer EV hire. Luxembourg has a higher density of chargers compared to the neighbouring regions of Belgium, France and Germany – especially in Luxembourg City, where they fringe the Old Town; and also along the A7 highway. Luxembourg is a relatively flat country with mild winters, which will help your charge sustain. Chargy (chargy.lu) is the main charging-point operator – their website has an easily navigable map of charging stations throughout the country.

Where to stay

Hôtel Le Place d'Armes (hotel-leplacedarmes.com) has some 28 luxurious rooms in the capital, overlooking the leafy square of the same name. Château d'Urspelt (chateau-urspelt.lu) occupies a turreted pile in the Our Valley, with a spa and pool. In Mondorf-les-Bains, Mondorf Parc Hôtel (mondorf.lu) has smartly sparse rooms, and sits within parkland flush with the French border.

When to go

Luxembourg is a year-round destination. Spring can be an appealing time to visit the north of the country – look out for Buergbrennen celebrations on the first Sunday in Lent, when towns and villages light huge bonfires to ward off the winter (allegedly a legacy of a pagan ritual). Summer heralds festivities centred on the Grand Duke's birthday (23 June); autumn sees wine festivals in full swing on the banks of the Moselle; and Christmas markets pop up in December.

Further info

If ever you feel like parking up your EV and making a short detour, remember that public transport in Luxembourg will cost you absolutely zilch. Since early 2020, all buses, trains and trams have been funded by general taxation and are free for anyone to use. The exception is first-class train tickets, which are very reasonably priced (albeit necessarily so, given the short journey times here).

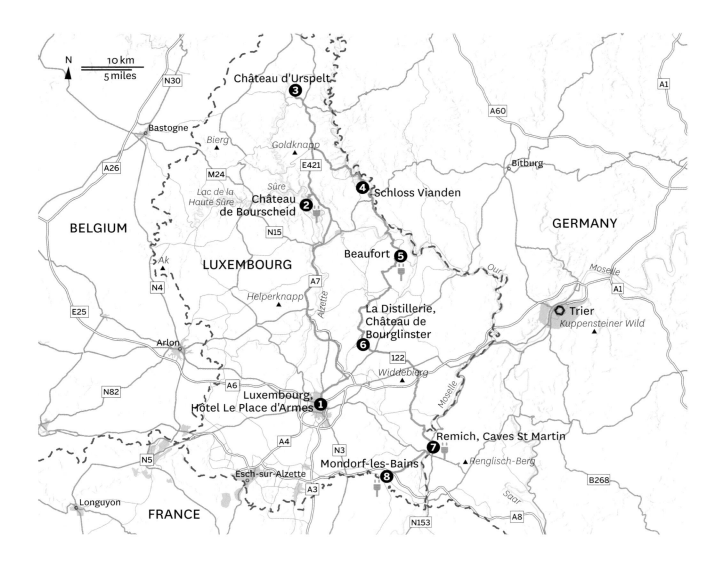

biggest castle in the country. Leave your car charging at the bottom of the hill before storming its draughty battlements – which have pointed turrets like witches' hats, and arrow slits looking down to the Sûre River that makes its march south.

You're sure to see more river valleys as you press north toward the tri-border with Belgium and Germany. Stop short to spend the night at Château d'Urspelt – an 18th-century country-house hotel, aristocratically poised amidst rolling lawns and neatly trimmed box hedges.

SOUTHBOUND TO THE SPA

The next day rise early to return south, skirting the German border to tick off (yes, you guessed it) yet more castles – the hulking Romanesque pile of Schloss Vianden is a prelude to the smaller, greenery-swathed castle at Beaufort (which has charging points nearby). Last comes the 11th-century Château de Bourglinster,

where you'll find Michelin-starred La Distillerie – one of the Grand Duchy's most distinguished restaurants, its menu focused around fresh vegetables.

As you enter the southeastern nook of Luxembourg, the landscape subtly changes, with rows of vines chequering the hills beside the banks of the Moselle, planted to supply the country's small but thriving wine industry. Sparkling and dry white wines are the Luxembourgeois signature, and many wineries open to visitors – Caves St Martin in Remich has been in business since 1919, and offers guided tours of their maze of cellars (there's also a shop, so drivers can stock up for later). Follow the Moselle downstream, and look out for the tiny village of Schengen, which gave its name to the agreement that allows breezy, passport-free travel across European frontiers.

Most motorists in these parts are heading into France, but instead swerve westwards to hit the village

of Mondorf-les-Bains, Luxembourg's preeminent spa town. Mineral-rich waters were accidentally discovered here by prospectors digging for salt in the mid-19th century – those waters still bubble up from the innards of the Earth at a balmy 24°C (75°F). Spend an afternoon stewing in alfresco pools before retiring to the adjoining Mondorf Parc Hôtel, which lays on abundant spa treatments. Exfoliated and pummelled into contentment, you'll end your foray into the Grand Duchy feeling suitably grand indeed.

What did you say?

Despite being one of Europe's smallest countries, Luxembourg is a modern-day Babel. French is near-universal, spoken particularly in the capital and within the hospitality sectors, while about 80% of the population also speak German – which, curiously, is the dominant language in newspapers here. Switch on the radio or TV, or hear a politician on a soap box, however, and you're more likely to hear Luxembourgish – a language closely related to German and one which, confusingly, can also be heard over the border in Germany proper. In recent decades Luxembourg has acquired a fourth de facto language: being a hub of business, English has emerged as the lingua franca of commerce.

And just to make things even more exciting, a wave of immigration starting in the 1960s means some 15% of Luxembourgers are of Portuguese descent – Portuguese can be heard amidst cafes selling *pastéis de nata* and Super Bock beer. Locals living at this crossroads of the continent take all this in their stride, of course. If this might sound baffling to a visitor, do not fear: the tourist board reassures that 'it is a rare occurrence not to find a common language in Luxembourg.'

Clockwise from top left: an EV pit stop at Beaufort Castle; Kirchberg's European quarter, Luxembourg City; Moselle vineyards, Schengen

 **Distance: 186 miles (300km)**

 **Duration: 4-5 days**

Rotterdam to Groningen

NETHERLANDS

Some of the easiest EV driving in the world can be found in the Netherlands. Combine a visit to innovative Rotterdam and atmospheric Amsterdam with the lesser-visited north of the country.

Container-stacked ships chug by on the Nieuwe Maas as locals lounge on the lawns of Holland Amerikaplein, the square from where, a century ago, over half a million people departed for the United States. Massive as they are, the ships are dwarfed by the skyscrapers dominating Rotterdam's Kop van Zuid neighbourhood, one of the city's buzzing, revitalised areas. Soak up the impressive architecture, then head out of the city across the Erasmus Bridge – another local icon.

Student town Delft is a mere half-hour drive along the motorway, but its medieval centre feels like it belongs in a different country. Take a stroll around town to visit one of the artisan workshops producing intricate blue-and-white Delfts blauw pottery, then it's back in the car to head northeast. Brick buildings alternate with ever-flat fields until the urban sprawl of Amsterdam fills the horizon.

AMSTERDAM TO THE AFSLUITDIJK
Don't attempt to take on the centre in your EV – it's not worth the hassle. Instead, drive to Volkshotel in hip Oost, then rent a bike to explore Amsterdam on two wheels. Pedal past the Amstel River, full of houseboats and pretty bridges, to De Pijp, where you'll find merchants flogging their wares at the country's largest outdoor market, Albert

© Sjoerd van der Wal / Getty Images

Plan & prepare

Tips for EV drivers

The Netherlands has the highest total number of chargers of any European country, so range anxiety is a non-issue. Shell Recharge (shell.nl) offers the best EV charge card: order it well ahead and use it to charge at all the stops with AC chargers on this route. For a quick top-up, use the Shell Recharge app to find rapid DC chargers. Alternatively, download the Fastned app (fastnedcharging.com), add your bank-card info, and charge at their numerous (and excellent) rapid stations.

Where to stay

In Rotterdam, Room Mate Bruno Hotel (room-matehotels.com) offers funky design at a fantastic location in Kop van Zuid. Occupying former newspaper offices in Amsterdam-Oost, Volkshotel (volkshotel.nl) has a great rooftop bar. Boutique Hotel de Eilanden (hoteldeeilanden. nl) in Harlingen has comfy rooms and canal views. The Social Hub (thesocialhub. co) located in Groningen's Ebbingekwartier is a fab base for exploring. All hotels have paid public parking, and AC chargers under five minutes' walk away.

When to go

The summer months of June to August are when the Netherlands truly comes alive, with the Dutch heading out to parks, terraces and the water in droves. The shoulder seasons are quieter, but fickle weather is almost guaranteed. Winter brings its own charm, with outdoor ice-skating rinks and, if you're very lucky, a few days of ideal conditions for skating on frozen canals and lakes.

Further info

If you're not bringing your own car, you can rent an EV in Rotterdam (via sixt.nl) and drive it back from Groningen in just three hours. Rotterdam is easily reached by train and ferry, while Amsterdam Schiphol airport is also close. Roads in the Netherlands are of excellent quality, but, especially along the first part of the route, they can get very busy: try to avoid driving during rush hour. Check holland.com and visitwadden.nl for more.

Clockwise from top left: Amsterdam *stroopwafel* stall; juvenile seal, Wadden Sea; Zaan River windmills, Zaanse Schans

Wadden Sea wonders

The Netherlands is one of the world's most densely populated countries, and yet there's a place here where you won't hear any traffic and can still see the night's starriest skies. A Unesco World Heritage Site (waddensea-worldheritage. org), the Wadden Sea forms the northernmost part of the country and stretches northeast across Germany to Denmark. It's the largest inter-tidal system in the world, and its waters mostly retreat at low tide, leaving behind a watery world of mudflats and sand that offers sanctuary to seals, porpoises and over 300 bird species. Some of the best experiences in the area include heading out on a mudflat walk with a guide, or boarding a sailing ferry for a unique experience called *droogvallen*: the flat-bottomed vessels are allowed to come to rest on the sea floor at low tide, enabling passengers to hop out and explore. If you have longer to linger, jump on a ferry to one of the five Dutch Wadden Islands – Texel, Vlieland, Terschelling, Ameland and Schiermonnikoog – all popular with locals in summer. Expect tiny villages, dune landscapes crisscrossed with bike paths, and miles and miles of uninterrupted beach – however crowded the islands may get, you can always find a deserted stretch of sand for a shoreline walk. Check visitwadden.nl for inspiration and more information.

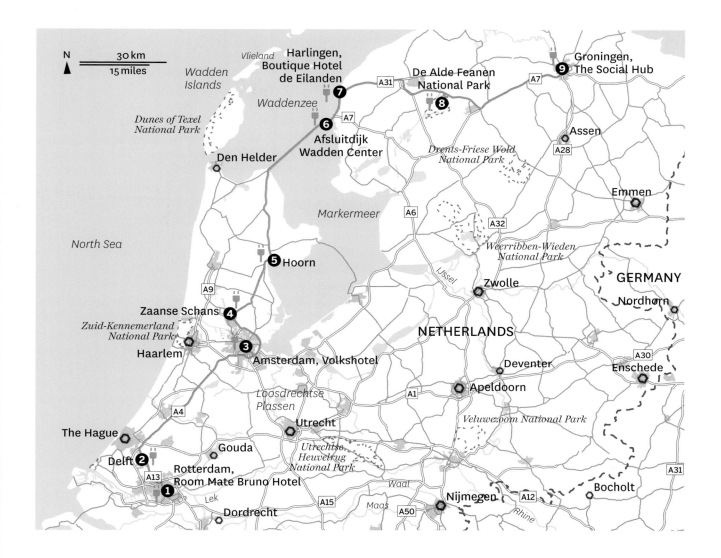

Cuypmarkt. Taste local treats like warm *stroopwafels*, then seek out one of many excellent restaurants in the area. Bike north after dinner for a relaxed ride through the centre. When twilight hits and the street lanterns cast their golden glow, the canals are magical.

Driving north the next morning, you'll be hard-pressed to find a place more archetypically Dutch than Zaanse Schans. Windmills from the 17th century line the Zaan River, while traditional shops include a cheesemaker and a clog factory. The village is a popular day-trip destination from the capital – come early to sidestep the rush and you might catch the mills framed by fog clinging to the river. Leave the crowds behind during a pit stop in Hoorn, a tiny port town on the banks of the Markermeer that's easily explored on foot. Then continue north, driving on reclaimed land, to the Afsluitdijk. An incredible feat of engineering, this causeway dammed off the Zuiderzee (South Sea) upon its completion in 1932. It's one of the best examples of the country's epic water management – learn more in the brand-new Afsluitdijk Wadden Center.

EAST TO GRONINGEN

From here, it's a short drive north to Frisian Harlingen. Take in the picturesque centre on foot or park at the harbour for a day trip by ferry to Vlieland or Terschelling, two of the serene Dutch Wadden Islands, just 3 miles (5km) off the coast.

Time to head east towards De Alde Feanen National Park. This excavated peat bog forms an interconnected area of lakes and rivers that you can explore at a leisurely pace in a rented electric boat. Back behind the wheel, enjoy big, blazing skies as you drive the final stretch towards Groningen, a student city famed for its nightlife. Start with a walk around the centre, then toast reaching the finish line with a Dutch beer and a plate of piping hot *bitterballen* (meatballs) on one of the terraces.

Below: Cathedral
Quarter, Belfast
Right: green and serene
on the Causeway Coast

➜ **Distance: 98 miles
(157km)**   ➜ **Duration: 3-4 days**

Belfast to the Causeway Coast

NORTHERN IRELAND

Along an underrated stretch of the Irish coastline, this journey features brilliant beaches embraced by rocky cliffs, gushing waterfalls, geological wonders and crumbling castles teetering on the edge of history.

Belfast's past casts a long shadow, but today the narrative is far more about the city's triumphs than its troubles. The glittering bulk of Titanic Belfast lords it over the former docks and tells the story of the ill-fated liner from conception to launch. It's a great place to begin a tour of the city, and its Titanic Experience delivers as much background on the history of Belfast and its people as on the construction of the ship itself.

From here, make your way back to the city centre to admire the grandiose architecture of Donegall Sq and the leafy mansions of South Belfast's Queens Quarter before nipping into the wonderful Crown Liquor Saloon, a flamboyant Victorian pub complete with stained-glass windows, polished brass taps and an elaborately sculpted ceiling – all illuminated by gas lights.

Next, hop in a black taxi for a tour of West Belfast to see the political murals and hear about the sectarian divide that has riven the city for much of its history. Finish your day with a stroll through the restored warehouses of the Cathedral Quarter, where bars, brasseries and bottegas showcase the city's vibrant arts and nightlife scenes.

CLIFFS & A CASTLE
From Belfast, it's just 40 minutes' drive north on the A2 to

© Anthony Livingstone / 500px

Plan & prepare

Tips for EV drivers

Belfast has two airports, and you can rent hybrid vehicles from operators at both of them; however, at the time of writing, there were only a small number of EVs on offer. You'll find EV chargers dotted along this route; most are part of the ESB charging network. Download their app for locations (esb.ie/what-we-do/ecars).

Where to stay

Belfast's central Merchant Hotel (themerchanthotel.com) offers 19th-century Italianate opulence; in south Belfast, the Harrison Chambers of Distinction (chambersofdistinction.com) is all about eclectic style. Elegant Kilmore Country House in Glenariff (kilmorecountryhouse.com) is a rural bolthole with sweeping valley views. The Bushmills Inn (bushmillsinn.com) offers tasteful, traditional lodgings; Elephant Rock in Portrush (elephantrockhotel.co.uk) has contemporary style and sea views.

When to go

The long days and milder weather make May to September the best time for this trip. Visit in May and you'll catch Belfast's Cathedral Quarter Arts Festival. The Bushmills Salmon and Whiskey Festival in mid-October is a great opportunity to feast on the province's finest produce, while at the same time Belfast celebrates its International Arts Festival.

Further info

It's worth booking the Causeway Experience online before you visit (nationaltrust-tickets.org.uk): along with timed entry to the Giant's Causeway Visitor Centre, you'll get reserved parking. On July 12th each year, the Orange Order celebrates William of Orange's 1690 win at the Battle of the Boyne with parades across the province. Sectarian tensions heighten at this time and security can be tight.

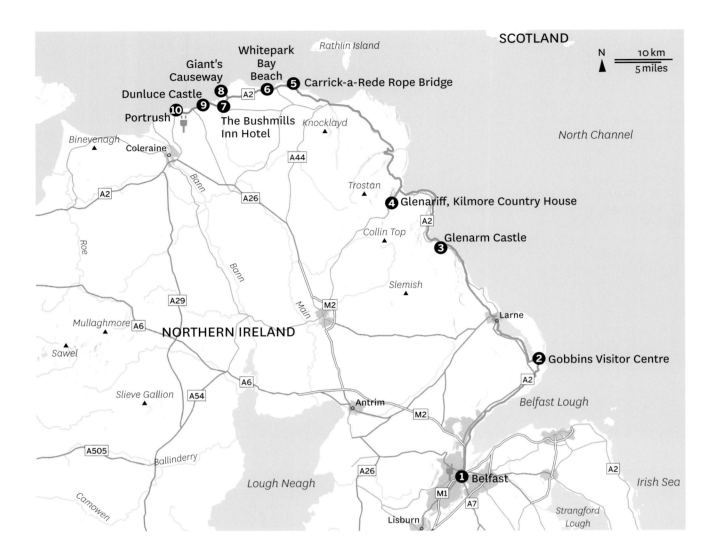

the magnificent Gobbins Cliff Path, a marvel of Edwardian engineering. Guided walking tours depart from the Visitor Centre, along the cliff-face and over a series of dramatic suspension bridges linking narrow coves and sea caves.

Suitably buffeted by the elements, continue your drive north to Glenarm Castle, family seat of the MacDonnell family, Earls of Antrim, since 1750. The impressive castle remains the family home and is only open for tours on selected dates, but you can still plan to visit the walled garden, Heritage Centre and Coach House Museum, take a wander through the woodlands or hire an e-bike to explore the estate.

UP THE COAST TO THE CAUSEWAY
From Glenarm, continue north to your bed for the night at Kilmore Country House in Glenariff, where you can soak up views of a sweeping valley from the expansive lawn. After breakfast, stop at the nearby Glenariff Forest Park for

a walk along a rocky gorge where tumbling waterfalls are surrounded by woodlands blanketed in moss.

Make your way back to the coast road and meander on through the handsome towns of Cushendall and Cushendun. It's a scenic 45-minute drive to the white-knuckle rope bridge at Carrick-a-Rede. Swinging gently over the churning sea below, the bridge allows local fishermen to check nets laid from the tiny island here. Make it across and you'll get bragging rights as well as views of Rathlin Island and Fair Head.

Nearby Ballycastle is a good spot for lunch; just 10 minutes on you'll come to Whitepark Bay, a gorgeous stretch of golden sand framed by steep cliffs. You'll often see a herd of cows wandering the waterfront, grazing here as part of local conservation efforts.

Continue on to Bushmills for a stay at 17th-century Bushmills Inn, a former coaching inn with beamed ceilings and traditional styling. In the morning, make an

Causeway Coast food finds

The Irish may well be renowned for their love of potatoes, but this tired stereotype is being blasted apart by a new generation of artisan food producers across the country. Ballycastle on the north coast has become something of a gourmet hotspot, with locals breathing new life into classic products. At the North Coast Smokehouse (northcoastsmokehouse. com) you'll find award-winning smoke-roasted organic salmon, trout and dulse (seaweed), and if you call ahead you can drop in to see the team at work. Just down the road, the Ursa Minor Bakehouse (ursaminorbakehouse.com) is a great stop for lunch, and if you're impressed with their bakes you can join a class or workshop and learn how to make them yourself. Just outside Ballycastle, Broughgammon Farm (broughgammon. com) is an award-winning sustainable farm specialising in kid goat, free-range rose veal and seasonal wild game. Drop into their shop or slow-food cafe, or join a tour to hear their story. Another great foodie experience is the Catch and Sea food tour in Portstewart (causewaycoastfoodietours. com), an early morning fishing trip that gives you insight into local food heritage before returning to shore to cook your catch for breakfast.

Clockwise from top left:
Carrick-a-Rede rope bridge; sourdough at Ursa Minor Bakehouse; Whitepark Bay

Rathlin Island

Six miles (10km) off the shore of Ballycastle but seemingly half a world away, Rathlin Island is home to only around 100 people – and about 250,000 nesting seabirds. Wild, rugged and wonderfully welcoming, it makes for an easy day trip but a magical overnight stay. In summer, friendly staff at the harbourside Boathouse Visitor Centre can provide historical and cultural context for your visit as well as tips on walking, cycling and wreck-diving. Make your way to the 'upside down' lighthouse at West Light Seabird Centre for sweeping views of sea stacks teeming with guillemots, kittiwakes, razorbills and puffins. To the north, the Ballyconaghan Trail offers views of dramatic sea cliffs and the Scottish islands of Islay and Jura, while the Kinramer Trail weaves along steep clifftops providing memorable views of the angular basalt columns of the mainland.

From left: razorbill, Rathlin Island; Giant's Causeway; Dunluce Castle

early start to beat the crowds to the Giant's Causeway, the region's headline attraction. Although legend has it that the columns of hexagonal basalt here are the remains of an ancient causeway to Scotland built by the giant Finn McCool, geologists tell a story of 60-million-year-old lava cooled and contracted into angular shapes. The Visitor Centre throws light on it all, and provides audioguides and maps of the various walking trails. Leave at least a couple of hours to walk here, as there's far more to see than the frequently photographed basalt steps slipping into the sea.

WEST TO PORTRUSH

Whipped by the wind, awed by nature and ready for some warmth, make your way back to Bushmills from the Causeway to visit the handsome Old Bushmills Distillery. It was granted a licence by King James I in 1608, and the whiskey produced here is triple-distilled in copper-pot stills with 100% malted barley. Take a tour to learn about its production and the crippling taxes, devastating fires and prohibition eras that the business has survived.

Afterwards, press on west for a stop at the arresting Dunluce Castle, just outside Bushmills. Perched on a basalt crag surrounded by the sea, this ruined bastion was the seat of the McQuillan and MacDonnell families in the 16th and 17th centuries. You'll have to pass over a narrow bridge to reach the ruins, some of which have collapsed dramatically into the sea.

From here, it's a short spin in your EV into buzzy Portrush, an old-fashioned seaside resort and Northern Ireland's premier surf spot. A short way further west, genteel Portstewart has a more dignified air, a sandy beach and a popular golf course. Take your pick for the last night, perhaps starting with some fine local seafood – beachside Harry's Shack in Portstewart is one of the best places to indulge – before hitting the bright lights and bars of Portrush.

Below: *moliceiros*,
traditional transport
in Aveiro
Right: Porto from the
Douro River

➡ **Distance: 293 miles
(472km)**

➡ **Duration: 6-7 days**

Porto to Lisbon

PORTUGAL

Portugal's breezy Atlantic coast forms the backbone for this drive – but there are also inland detours to see monasteries, castles and fairy-tale villages, as well as the two dynamic cities that bookend the route.

Ranged attractively along the banks of the Rio Douro, Porto is one of Portugal's most handsome cities, and makes a princely place to begin this road trip down the Atlantic coast. Shaded alleyways, chapels and courtyards define the ravishing Old Town, but this is a city that's also very young at heart, with striking modern museums like the Museu de Arte Contemporânea and the Casa da Música, and a bevy of rooftop bars where you can sip cocktails and nibble *petiscos* (Portuguese tapas) late into the night. Don't miss a stroll around Gaia's Jardim do Morro, a peaceful hilltop garden with excellent cross-city views.

BOATS, BEACHES & BASTIONS

After Porto, it's time for a breezy drive down the coast to the 'Venice of Portugal', Aveiro, set on a crisscross of canals. The traditional way of getting around is the city's *moliceiros* (the Portuguese version of a gondola), which float serenely along the waterways. Aveiro is also a good place for some beach time and, a little to the north, to indulge in the excellent walking and birdwatching of the São Jacinto nature reserve: this is a quiet, pleasant corner of the coast, characterised by dunes, fragrant shrubs and the salty blue expanse of Aveiro Lagoon.

Plan & prepare

Tips for EV drivers

Portugal's EV network is developing fast (around 3200 public chargers at the time of writing), but it's not as extensive as in many other European nations – and the hilly roads and hot weather (meaning enthusiastic use of aircon) can drain charge fast. Portugal has a centralised charging system, mobi.e (mobie.pt), which allows you to use pretty much any charger from any provider – but you will need to sign up to an app such as Miio (miio. pt) in order to access them.

Where to stay

Unusually for Portuguese hotels, many in the Vila Galé chain (vilagale.com) offer EV charging facilities for guests. Choices include the riverside Vila Galé Porto Ribeira, a stylish small hotel that overlooks the Douro River, with artist-themed rooms. Vila Galé Coimbra feels a little institutional, but its superior rooms have views over the Mondego River. Lisbon's Vila Galé Opera, in the lively Belem neighbourhood, is handy for drivers – it's right next to the city's Golden-Gate-style Ponte 25 de Abril.

When to go

The vast majority of visitors pitch up to Portugal in summer to maximise beach time, but be prepared for scorching temperatures and high hotel prices in July and August. Prices drop markedly between November and March, even at many top luxury hotels; April, May, September and October offer an attractive combination of sunny days and way fewer crowds. February is carnival month in Portugal, with colourful pageants in Lisbon, Ovar, Sesimbra, Torres Vedras and several other locations.

Further info

To make the most out of a Portuguese road trip, it's nearly always worth getting off toll-paying auto-estradas (motorways) and exploring the backroads. From quiet villages to country chapels, tiny beaches and village restaurants, you'll have a more rewarding experience. If you go onto the motorways, note that main toll roads now have automated toll booths, meaning you won't be able to simply drive through and pay an attendant. Most car-rental agencies hire out the small electronic devices needed for automated tolls.

Clockwise from top left: Castelo do Montemor-o-Velho; partaking of port in Lisbon; live *fado* in Lisbon's Bairro Alto

Any port in a storm

Porto wouldn't be Porto without port, the rich, fruity fortified wine made here for at least 2000 years. Roman soldiers were the first to plant grapes, but port really took off in the 17th century. During one of its periodic wars with the French, Britain's wine supplies dried up, so it turned to ally Portugal for help. The dry Douro wines were too astringent for British tastes, so they chucked in some grape juice and *aguardente* (distilled grape spirits similar to brandy), and voilà – port wine was born. Grapes are harvested in autumn, crushed and fermented until alcohol levels reach 7%. At this point, one part *aguardente* is added to every five parts wine. Fermentation stops immediately, leaving the unfermented sugars that give port its distinctive sweet flavour. The main varietals are Ruby, Tawny, Aged Tawny, Vintage and LBV (late-bottled vintage). The rocky slopes of the Douro Valley, especially the Vila Nova de Gaia, are the heart of the port-making industry, with prestigious names like Taylor's (taylor. pt), Graham's (grahams-port.com), Cockburn's (cockburns.com), Ramos Pinto (ramospinto.pt) and Cálem (tour.calem.pt) offering tasting sessions and tours; several have restaurants with menus pairing port with local fare. For obvious reasons, driving and port-tasting don't go well together, so catch a tram instead and sip away.

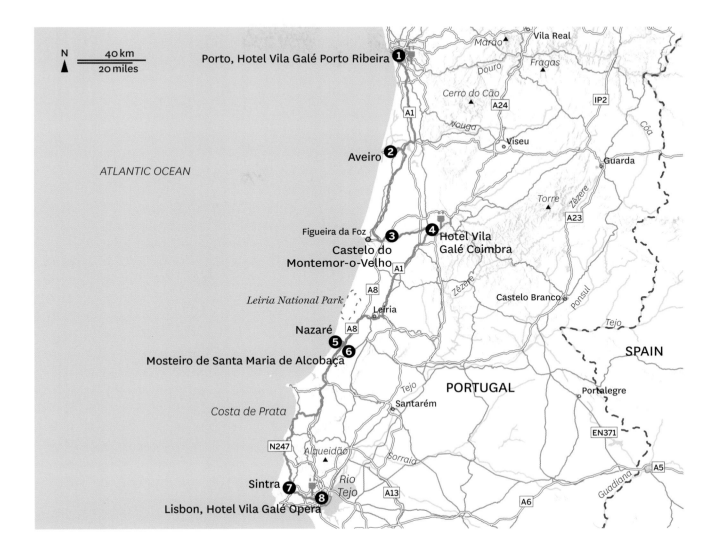

N
40 km
20 miles

Porto, Hotel Vila Galé Porto Ribeira ❶

ATLANTIC OCEAN

Aveiro ❷

Figueira da Foz
Castelo do
Montemor-o-Velho ❸ ❹ Hotel Vila
Galé Coimbra

Leiria National Park
Leiria

Nazaré ❺
❻
Mosteiro de Santa Maria de Alcobaça

Costa de Prata

N247

Alqueidão

Sintra ❼
❽
Lisbon, Hotel Vila Galé Opera

Marão Vila Real
Douro *Fragas*
Cerro do Cão A24 IP2
Vouga *Côa*
Viseu
Guarda
Torre *Zêzere*
A23
Zêzere
Castelo Branco
Ponsul
Tejo
SPAIN
PORTUGAL Portalegre
Santarém
EN371
Sorraia
A5
Rio Tejo
A13
A6 *Guadiana*

Continue along the coast to Figueira da Foz, where you'll veer inland, swapping views of sandy beaches and the Atlantic for vistas of flat, open fields and low wooded hills. One of these is home to the hilltop fortress of Castelo do Montemor-o-Velho, which was constructed during the 10th century and has witnessed many an Arab-Christian conflict over the centuries. Nowadays it's a place to walk the battlements in peace, drinking in views over the Rio Mondego rice fields below.

COIMBRA, NAZARÉ & ALCOBAÇA

The inland city of Coimbra marks a midway breakpoint. For a century during medieval times, this was Portugal's cultural capital, and it's still home to the nation's oldest and most illustrious university. The maze-like Old Town is super for late-night wanders in search of local eateries and atmospheric *fado* bars, where you can listen to haunting tunes late into the night.

From Coimbra, the main A1 cuts southwest, across rolling hills and plains and back towards the coast. It's surprising how green inland Portugal can be: the road is often lined by trees, making for a very pleasant drive. After about 42 miles (68km), you'll reach Nazaré, Portugal's surfing capital. In summer, its beaches are packed with sunseekers and board-riders, but it's winter that brings the true wave aficionados: massive, skyscraper-sized swells roll in from across the Atlantic, attracting the world's top big-wave surfers. These waves are for the pros only, but at other times of year, this is a fine place for surf lessons.

After exploring the sand-fringed coast around Nazaré, head inland to the hilltop monastery of Santa Maria de Alcobaça, one of Portugal's great religious centres. Its austerely beautiful 12th-century church exemplifies the simplicity and purity that defined the Cistercian order: wander around Alcobaça's cloisters, kitchens, refectory and the enormous dormitory where the monks slept.

Lisbon's trams

Unless you're with someone local who knows the city really well, you definitely don't want to try and drive around Lisbon's complicated, confusing and frequently cobbled street network. Far better to leave the car at the hotel and hop aboard one of the city's vintage *elétricos*. These cute little yellow-and-white electric trams have been rattling around Lisbon since 1901 (and even before that they were horse-drawn). Most iconic of all is Tram 28E between the Campo de Ourique and Martim Moniz, passing many of the city's must-see sights along the way – all for the princely price of a €3 one-way ticket. Tram 12E from Praça da Figueira through the narrow streets of Alfama is another great option – but go early in the morning or at night to avoid the likely tourist mobs.

Clockwise from top left:
Nazaré waves; Sintra's Palácio de Monserrate; Bica funicular, Lisbon

SOUTH TO SINTRA & LISBON

Alcobaça's austere restraint makes quite a contrast to the showy extravagance of Sintra, 78 miles (125km) to the south. The landscape changes notably as you head further this way, with green woods and hills gradually giving way to rocky plateaus and plains. The quickest route is to take the main A8, but following the winding coast road through quiet villages and coves is much more rewarding if you can spare the time.

Whichever route into here you choose, Sintra itself is incredible: a vivid confection of turrets, battlements, pastel-tinted manor houses and hilltop palaces looming above its namesake town. Surrounded by gardens, terraces and groves, this hilltop model village looks like something out of a fairy tale, with several fabulous palaces built as lavish getaways for well-heeled nobles and aristocrats, who spared no expense and demanded the finest views. The centrepieces are the magnificent

Palácio Nacional de Sintra, identifiable by its twin chimneys, and the madcap, onion-domed Palácio Nacional da Pena, but you'll need an entire day to explore the others: don't miss moody Quinta da Regaleira and over-the-top Palácio de Monserrate, a 19th-century fantasy built for the English merchant Sir Francis Cook. Byron adored Sintra – so will you.

After Sintra, you'll leave the wooded hills and rocky coast far behind as you enter the built-up suburbs of Lisbon, Portugal's princely capital. Surrounded by seven hills, this fascinating city surely ranks in the top tier of European capitals. Park up your EV to explore its cobbled alleyways on foot; ride a bike around the Parque Florestal de Monsanto; bar-hop around the Bairro Alto; or climb aboard one of Lisbon's trams to a myriad of *miradouros* (viewpoints) overlooking the rooftops. Finally, settle in with a pitcher of icy-cold sangria as the sun goes down over the cityscape.

➡ **Distance: 94 miles
(152km)**

➡ **Duration: 2–4 days**

The Algarve Coast

PORTUGAL

This ocean-peeping drive takes in classic Algarve beaches, Roman ruins and the nature-rich wetlands of Parque Natural da Ria Formosa, as well as leisurely lunches that showcase the best of the region's seafood.

Our jumping-off point is Lagos, a resort town with plenty of activities, restaurants and bars. Enclosed by 16th-century walls, its Old Town has cobbled streets and squares to explore, while the well-curated Museu Municipal provides insights into Lagos' pre-tourism history. Leave your EV charging in town and take a 15-minute taxi ride to have lunch at Casa Vale da Lama, a stylish eco-hotel and restaurant that prides itself on protecting and restoring local biodiversity; the plant-based meals feature ingredients from an on-site farm.

BEACH-HOPPING TO FARO

Suitably refreshed, pick up the car and head east for a quick stop in pretty Ferragudo, a former fishing village on the Rio Arade that's a gentle contrast to hectic Lagos. From here it's a short drive through resort towns built above sandy coves, before dropping down to the dramatically beautiful beach of Praia da Marinha, where limestone cliffs have been eroded into arches and stacks.

Continuing east, the coastline becomes more built up, culminating in Albufeira, where there's a chance to charge overnight and to try some of the region's high-quality eateries – including Portugal's first two-Michelin-starred restaurant at the luxurious Vila Joya, a 5-mile (8km) taxi

© M Swiet / Getty Images

Tips for EV drivers

EVs can be hired from wattsonwheels.pt with pickup in Portimão, near Lagos. Europcar (europcar. co.uk) rents from various locations, including Faro airport. This route bypasses the A22, which requires a toll. If you plan to use the A22, you'll need a transponder device, available at a charge from car rental companies – EV drivers receive a toll discount. The Miio website and app (miio.pt) advises you of charger locations, their availability and cost.

Where to stay

Just outside Lagos, Casa Vale da Lama (casavaledalama.pt) hotel and restaurant is a relaxing retreat with simple rooms. Luxurious Vila Joya (vilajoya.com) in Albufeira gives guests priority booking at its two-Michelin-starred restaurant. In the Posadas de Portugal chain (pousadas. pt), sumptuous Pousada Palácio de Estoi houses guests in a modern wing integrated into a hillside; butter-yellow Pousada Convento da Tavira is a tranquil hotel converted from a 16th-century convent.

When to go

The Algarve's summer season runs from June to August, when its towns and beaches heave with visitors. In August the Portimão Street Food Festival celebrates modern Algarve cuisine, with visits by celebrated chefs (including a few holders of Michelin stars). The lovely shoulder seasons of spring and autumn have pleasant temperatures and fewer crowds. Winter is the Algarve's secret, when its wide beaches return to their wild, empty state.

Further info

Generally excellent road conditions and clear signage make driving in the Algarve an easy experience, and distances are relatively short between destinations. However, finding parking can present a significant challenge, especially over the summer months when resort areas fill up to capacity. The historic town centres tend to have extremely narrow streets, so it's advisable to park your EV outside and stroll in.

Fruits of the sea

Before there was tourism, the Algarve was almost exclusively devoted to fishing. Tuna in particular was big business here, and in summer Portugal's fishermen would decamp to the coast to catch them as they migrated through. Migratory routes changed and tuna numbers dwindled, while holidaymakers caught wind of the beautiful beaches and fishing villages evolved into resort towns. Today the fishing industry here faces additional challenges, from depleted stocks of fish such as cod and mackerel to an ageing fleet. Seafood, however, still reigns supreme in the restaurants and markets. Look out for regional specialities like *conquilhas à Algarvia*, tiny local clams simmered with onions, garlic and Portuguese

sausage; and *cataplana de marisco*, seafood stew cooked in a large copper dish. Along the route you'll find delicious seafood everywhere, from cafes and bars to destination restaurants: in Lagos, the glass-walled Camilo sits above pretty Praia do Camilo and serves seasonal specialities like razor clams and crab; Rei das Praias near Ferragudo is a beautiful seafront restaurant specialising in grilled and baked fish. For a taste of the former Algarve, witness the crowds in Olhão's waterfront market, there for the freshest, best-value seafood in all of Portugal.

Above: Algarve speciality *cataplana de marisco*
Right: Capela dos Ossos, Faro

ride west. Albufeira itself has all but been taken over by mass tourism, its historic centre hidden behind a sea of English pubs and bars. Instead, indulge in some beach time. Starting some 5 miles (8km) east of Albufeira, Falésia is one of the Algarve's most impressive beaches, a 4-mile (6km) strip of golden sand backed by deep red cliffs.

From here, it's 30 minutes' drive to Faro, capital of the Algarve. Top up your car's charge and head into the walled Old Town, where the imposing Igreja de Nossa Senhora do Carmo, completed in 1719, is one of Portugal's finest baroque churches. Just behind, the macabre Capela dos Ossos comprises the skeletons of more than a thousand Carmelite monks, exhumed in 1816 and repurposed for the walls as a reminder of Earthly mortality.

ON TOWARD TAVIRA

From Faro, it's a brief drive inland through parched fields to Milreu, where you can see the ruins of a Roman villa,

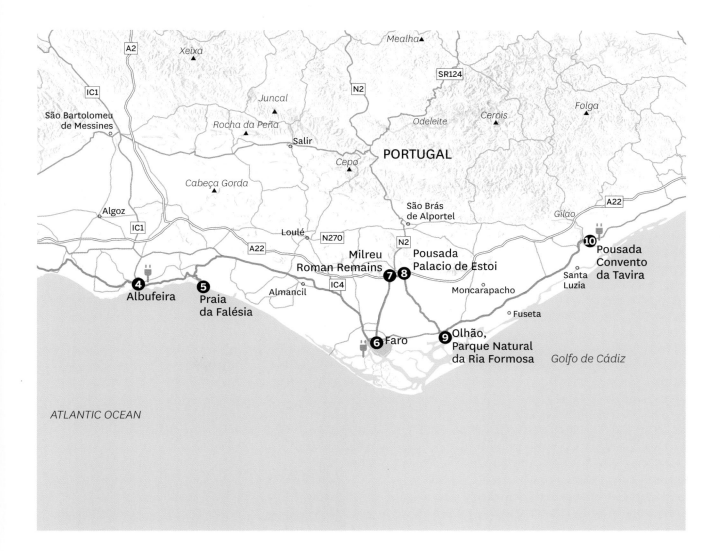

so grand that archaeologists initially thought they'd uncovered a town. A small museum provides background on the Algarve's most important Roman site. There's further opulence up the road at the rococo Pousada Palácio de Estoi – non-guests can visit the Versailles-inspired grounds and the frescoed drawing rooms.

Heading back south, plan for at least one meal in Olhão, home to the Algarve's largest active fishing port and most impressive fish market. It's also the starting point for boat trips through the Parque Natural da Ria Formosa, a vast wetland reserve separated from the sea by peninsulas and islands, and a major stopover for migrating birds: here you can hike, cycle, or snorkel among seahorses.

Back on dry land, drive along the estuary to appealing Tavira. Take time to learn about life here under Islamic rule at the Núcleo Islâmico, an impressive museum housing artefacts discovered in city excavations. Finally, put your feet up at chic Pousada Convento da Tavira.

Below: red deer stag,
symbol of the Highlands
Right: heather-covered
hills in Cairngorms
National Park

➡ **Distance: 201 miles
(322km)**

➡ **Duration: 5 days**

Aberdeen to Inverness

SCOTLAND

Mountains, castles, coastline and, at suitable moments, whisky by the barrel-load: this Highlands road-trip combines quintessential Scotland with a Cairngorms adventure and a peek at the royal retreat at Balmoral.

The North Coast 500 might get a lot of press, but our Highland jaunt challenges it for scenic showmanship. This route begins in coastal Aberdeen, known as the Granite City: many of the buildings here were built from the same distinctive, silvery-grey granite rock extracted from nearby Rubislaw Quarry, once site of the biggest hole in Europe. Aberdeen is a prosperous town, made wealthy on the proceeds of North Sea oil and gas, and has some fine cultural institutions. Foremost among them are the Maritime Museum, which explores the city's seafaring past; and Aberdeen Art Gallery, which has a stellar collection ranging from Impressionism to contemporary.

INTO THE HIGHLANDS

As you drive west from Aberdeen, it doesn't take long before you start to feel the unmistakable pull of the Highlands. In half an hour, you'll reach Drum Castle, the seat of Clan Irvine, whose 700-year history can be traced back to the days of Robert the Bruce. This is one of Scotland's oldest tower houses, and its impressive hall, chapel and library are worth seeing. Another 45 minutes or so carries you into the eastern reaches of the Cairngorms National Park, where the woodlands and

Plan & prepare

Tips for EV drivers

Scotland still has a way to go in terms of building charger infrastructure, especially beyond the cities, so plan your route carefully. Chargeplace Scotland (chargeplacescotland.org) is a nationwide network. There's a reasonable supply of chargers in Aberdeen and Inverness, but fewer in the Cairngorms – if you need a top-up, you'll find fast chargers at Ballater, Braemar, Tomintoul, Aberlour, Craigellachie and Elgin.

Where to stay

Aloft Hotel in Aberdeen (marriott.com) is a modern hotel on the northwest edge of the city, handy for the airport and with on-site charging. The Fife Arms (thefifearms.com) is a classic Highland hotel in Braemar, with tons of history and fantastic food; fast chargers are available at nearby Balnellan Rd car park. Last stop is Bunchrew House (bunchrewhousehotel.com), a chateau-like pile west of Inverness, which has on-site charging.

When to go

Winter in the Highlands is beautiful, but not ideal for a road trip. Spring comes late, and snow can linger on the ground until March – you'll usually have to wait until June or July to get proper summer sunshine. Unfortunately this is also peak midge (small biting insects) season, especially in the glens. In September and October, the hills and moors blaze with colour, and summertime crowds (and midges) have mostly left.

Further info

Visit Scotland (visitscotland. com) has a selection of road trips on its website, which you could easily weave into this route for a longer journey. The Cairngorms National Park (cairngorms. co.uk) is another handy resource, especially for hikers and wildlife-spotters, while whisky aficionados will appreciate the comprehensive info provided by the Malt Whisky Trail (maltwhiskytrail.com).

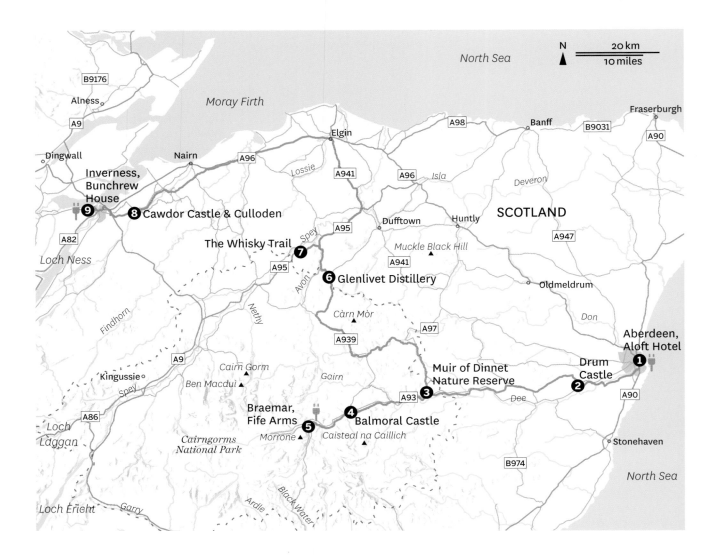

N | 20 km | 10 miles

North Sea

wetlands of the Muir of Dinnet Nature Reserve offer excellent hiking and wildlife spotting opportunities. Be sure to keep your eyes peeled for red squirrels: the Cairngorms are a key habitat for Britain's bushy-tailed native squirrel, squeezed out in most other parts of the islands by its imported grey cousin.

Further west, hills, lakes and forest spike the Highland landscape as you pass through Ballater and climb onwards to Balmoral, the royal family's Scottish residence. Built by Queen Victoria in 1855, it was said to be the favourite of the late Queen Elizabeth II's houses, and the place she finally bid the nation farewell from in September 2022. Most of the house is off-limits to visitors, but you can have a look inside the ballroom and explore the expansive grounds; an informative audio-tour is included with admission. It's worth carrying on to Braemar, which in September stages one of the largest Highland Games in Scotland, the Braemar Gathering.

You can visit the showground year-round and, with luck, you might spot someone practising.

WHISKY COUNTRY

Break overnight at the wonderful Fife Arms, a classic Highland hotel, then gear up for the drive onwards into the heights of the Cairngorms. It's a stark expanse of low hills, moors, valleys and scrub: look out for birds of prey circling overhead. The area around the River Spey also happens to be the heartland of Highland whisky making, and you'll pass a roll-call of world-famous distilleries as you spin through the hills and glens. The Spey's clean, clear waters and the rich, peaty soil are said to be key ingredients in what makes Speyside whiskies so special. Obviously it would be rude not to taste a few, so pick a designated driver.

At Tomintoul, turn off onto the B9008 and follow it to Glenlivet Distillery, the oldest and perhaps most hallowed

The fine art of whisky tasting

Speyside has been a world-famous centre for whisky for more than two centuries. Locals have been distilling spirits (often illegally) here since at least the 1500s, but the first big-name distilleries date from the early 1800s: Glenlivet was the first to be granted a licence in 1824. Whisky from each distillery has its own characteristics – connoisseurs look for smoke, peat, floral and citrus notes, burnt sugar, even Highland heather, but it takes a refined palate and a lot of practice to appreciate the subtleties. Most distilleries offer guided tours and tutored tastings where you can learn how to get the most out of your dram. The top whiskies are the single malts, which are distilled only from malted barley and are the product of a sole distillery (blended whiskies are a mix of grain and malt, while pure or vatted malts can come from several distilleries). The best way to taste them is 'cut' (diluted) with one-third to two-thirds spring water; adding water enhances the flavours and aromas. Obviously, mixers are out of the question. And remember, in Scotland, it's always spelled whisky, not whiskey as in Ireland and the USA.

Clockwise from top left: red squirrel, Cairngorms National Park; Scottish whiskies at the Cardhu Distillery shop; the lobby at Braemar's historic Fife Arms

Highland Games

Caber tossing, stone putting, hammer throwing, weight chucking, sheaf hurling: these are just a few of the 'heavy events' you'll see during a traditional Highland Games. Generally, they revolve around feats of strength to show off your brawn rather than your brains, and while it's often claimed they've been a feature of life in the Highlands for centuries, in truth, the modern-day games are largely a Victorian invention. Still, they're a highlight of the Highland calendar, and attract big crowds, many of whom turn up dressed in their traditional kilts and clan finery (including the late Queen Elizabeth II and the new King Charles III, both regular guests at the Braemar Gathering in September). It's not just sports, either – there's usually a display of traditional Highland dancing and a mass march of bagpipe bands to open and close proceedings.

Clockwise from top left: Balmoral Castle, the royal family's Scottish residence; fishing in Loch Ness; the caber toss at Gordon Castle Highland Games, near Elgin

182

name in the world of Scotch whisky. You can take three different tours, and taste whiskies ranging from a classic single malt to the Glenlivet XXV. From here, you'll join up with the official Malt Whisky Trail, which takes in many of the other big names around Speyside: Cardhu, Glenfiddich, Speyside Cooperage, Glen Grant and Glen Moray can all be factored in as you drive northwards through Aberlour, following the A95 and then the A941 towards the coast.

BEACHES, BLOODSHED & BEASTIES

When you reach Elgin, turn left onto the A96, and follow it west as it tracks the coastline. This is an especially pleasant stretch, and it's worth detouring off the main road in order to admire the beaches and sea views, perhaps at Findhorn or Nairn. The route takes you past Cawdor Castle, a moody late medieval fortress which was the seat of the Thane of Cawdor – a title Shakespeare bestowed on his Macbeth (although the real King

Macbeth died 400 years before the castle was built). Nearby is another historical landmark: the Battlefield of Culloden, where in 1746 the last pitched battle on British soil was waged, and the Jacobite Rising came to a vicious end. More than 1300 men were slain here, around 1250 of them Jacobites, loyal to the exiled Stuart family. Little evidence remains of the battle itself, but there is an informative visitor centre where you can learn of Culloden's blood-soaked history.

Last stop on this Highland tour is Inverness, at the northern end of the Great Glen. It's an excellent place in which to wander by the river, try some modern Scottish cuisine and visit imposing Inverness Castle, but nearly everyone passing through the city is actually en route to another Scottish attraction: Loch Ness. The vast, deep expanse of water sprawls for 23 miles (37km) to the southwest of the city. According to believers, it's the home of a mysterious beastie by the name of Nessie, but no-one's ever managed to snap a clear pic of the monster.

➡️ **Distance: 190 miles (305km)**   ➡️ **Duration: 3-4 days**

Ullapool to John O'Groats

SCOTLAND

Single-track roads wind past jagged peaks, ancient moorland and crofting villages on this tour of Scotland's north coast. Highlights include sandy beaches, sea caves, scallops and arguably the best scenery in Britain.

The whitewashed village of Ullapool is the biggest settlement in the northwest Highlands, and an enjoyable base for trips into the hills, out to the islands or along the coast. From here, point your EV north into Assynt, a glorious, otherworldly region of moors and lonely peaks. After half an hour, you'll pass one of Scotland's most striking mountains, the sandstone ridge of Stac Pollaidh, which rises like a great broken spine into the sky. Park up to tackle the exhilarating two- to three-hour scramble to its 2008ft (612m) summit and back – a wonderful experience for those with a head for heights.

This drive takes in quite possibly the finest scenery in Scotland, with sea lochs, islands, mountains and vast heather-strewn moors, and you can soak up some of the highlights along the coast road to Kylesku, a loch-side hamlet offering more great walking and the chance to dine on hand-dived scallops and locally sourced steaks at the Kylesku Hotel. A short hop further north, the crofting village of Scourie has more good seafood and one of the region's many luminous beaches – despite the white sand and turquoise water, the sea temperature here is bracing at best. In summer, ferries run from nearby Tarbet to Handa Island, a breeding ground for skuas, guillemots and puffins.

© Stefano_Valeri / Shutterstock

Plan & prepare

Tips for EV drivers

There currently aren't many spots to hire EVs in this region, but Enterprise (enterprisecarclub.co.uk) has a small Highland fleet, and Edinburgh-based Ecosse EV (ecosse-ev.com/north-coast-500) offers Teslas. Overall, the charging network is impressive given its remoteness, making this drive perfectly feasible: Ullapool, Scourie, Durness, Tongue, Bettyhill, Thurso and John O'Groats all have fast chargers. Many sections (especially on the west coast) are hilly: keep an eye on your charge level.

Where to stay

Accommodation fills quickly, so book in advance. Good places to stay include Mackay's Rooms (facebook.com/visitdurness) in Durness and Cloisters B&B (cloistersbandb.co.uk), outside Tongue, which has views over the Kyle of Tongue and breakfast in a converted church. Other options are the loch-side Kylesku Hotel (kyleskuhotel.co.uk) and, at journey's end, the lodges and apartments at John O'Groats (togethertravel.co.uk).

When to go

July and August bring the best weather but (especially since the launch of the North Coast 500) the route can get very busy during this period. Spring and autumn deliver relative peace and a decent chance of sunshine, with May and September the most appealing months. Winter is starkly beautiful in this part of the Highlands, but temperatures are low, days short and roads icy.

Further info

The Western Highlands is the heartland of the tiny but malevolent midge, a biting insect that's particularly active at dawn and dusk during the summer. Some claim that Avon Skin So Soft moisturiser is the best way to repel them – wearing long sleeves will at least limit your biting surface. The weather changes rapidly here – if you head into the hills, make sure you bring an effective waterproof, and stay on marked trails.

Clockwise from top left: Cloisters B&B, Kyle of Tongue; the Kylesku Bridge over Loch a' Chàirn Bhàin; Sango Bay, Durness

The North Coast 500

This great stretch of northern Scotland coast is remote – but it's also increasingly popular. The North Coast 500 (northcoast500.com) is a driving loop that starts in Inverness and heads right around the northern Highlands, connecting the EV road trip covered here with Easter Ross and the Black Isle. The NC500's success has helped many local businesses and led to improved signposting, but it's also put a strain on some sights and increased traffic congestion, especially in the peak summer months. The solution for drivers hoping to enjoy a bit of tranquillity is to go in the spring and Autumn shoulder seasons (May and September are perhaps the best times), to set out earlier in the day when the roads and sights are less busy, and to head the quieter clockwise way around the coast (most North Coast 500-ers drive the route in an anticlockwise direction). Many visitors, meanwhile, barely exit the road: spend half an hour hiking up the hills or along the beaches, and you'll leave the crowds behind – even in July and August. Thanks to its mix of experiences and stunning landscapes, the Ullapool to John O'Groats section covered in this drive is the highlight of the NC500; if you're interested in completing the whole 516-mile (830km) route, allow around six days, or more if you plan on lengthy stops along the way.

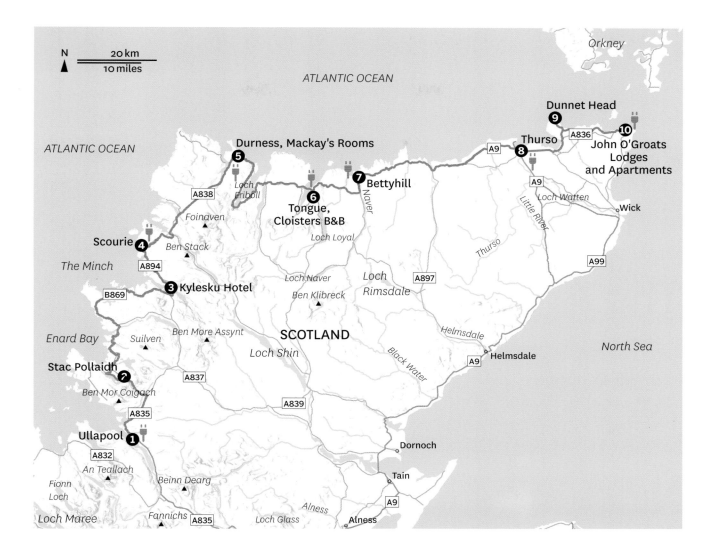

The hour or so's drive from here to Durness tracks the shore before heading inland through glens and peat bogs to the north coast, where Durness sits pretty on the sea cliffs and you can overnight at snug, hospitable Mackay's Rooms. Durness is a magical place for a walk, whether you head to the pristine beaches below the village as the North Sea shifts and the machair (coastal grass) sways in the wind, or stroll to nearby Smoo Cave, where saltwater and freshwater mingle beneath a limestone arch.

From here, you'll trace the edge of Loch Eriboll before cutting across the moors to Tongue, which has vast golden sandflats at low tide and is overlooked by ruined Castle Varrich (location for another enjoyable hike). Pause at Bettyhill, a village with a sandy beach and a museum telling the grim history of the local Clearances, which saw crofters moved off their land and many leave for foreign shores. Inland, neolithic sites and Scotland's northernmost peaks rise out of the pools and peatland of the Flow Country, the world's biggest blanket bog.

TO THE FAR NORTH

An hour or so along the coast will bring you to Thurso, the biggest town in the region, with a ferry connection to Orkney and a famously challenging surf break (Thurso East). It's a good place for lunch – try the Captain's Galley, with everything from charcuterie plates to plaice with samphire and smoked butter. From here, it's a 15-minute drive around Dunnet Bay – passing Dunnet Bay Distillery, a gin maker offering friendly tours – to the northernmost place on the British mainland, Dunnet Head. Here, rugged sea cliffs, basking seals and a great sweep of beach face the turbulent Pentland Firth. Continue to John O'Groats, Britain's northeastern corner, where you can spend a comfortable night at the imaginatively named John O'Groats, a collection of bright lodges and apartments that sit a pebble's throw from the sea.

Below: Kelvingrove
Art Gallery and
Museum, Glasgow
Right: Glen Croe,
near Arrochar

➡ **Distance: 210 miles
(338km)**

➡ **Duration: 3-4 days**

The Argyll Coast

SCOTLAND

In Argyll, Scotland's Lowlands meet the Highlands and the mainland slips
into a coast of sea lochs and islands. This route heads from the streets of
Glasgow into a watery wonderland.

N ew arrivals are often amazed at just how close the
Highlands are to Scotland's biggest city. But before
you leave Glasgow for the lochs and glens, consider
spending a night here to explore both its top-class
nightlife and its museums – including grand Kelvingrove
and the Whistler-packed Hunterian.

GOODBYE TO GLASGOW

The 'bonnie banks' of Loch Lomond are only a short drive
from Glasgow, but your trip first heads west, to hug the
coast and pass the handsome resort of Helensburgh. Cut
inland for Loch Lomond views before heading to Arrochar
village, at the head of Loch Long, where you can gaze up at
formidable peaks including the anvil-shaped Cobbler.

A 20-minute drive through the hills and you'll be at
Loch Fyne Oyster Bar, which has mountains behind and
water outside its front door. Inside, North Sea haddock
rubs up against oysters pulled from the loch. The A83
continues along Fyne's rugged northern shore for an hour,
passing the Georgian village of Inveraray, with its fairy-
tale castle. Newton Hall Guest House is a comfortable
boutique hotel here, set in a converted church.

You might spot seals and otters on the hour-long drive
to Tarbert, a fishing port that's the gateway to the Kintyre

Plan & prepare

Tips for EV drivers

Glasgow is the best place to hire an EV, with several companies at the airport. Glasgow, Helensburgh, Succoth (just past Arrochar) and Inveraray all have fast chargers. The route down to Kintyre is patchier: Tarbert only has a slow charge-point, so top up en route at Lochgilphead, or drive past Tarbert to the Kennacraig ferry terminal. On the road north, Oban, Glencoe and Fort William have good networks, with only slow chargers available elsewhere.

Where to stay

In Glasgow, try the Alamo Guesthouse (alamoguesthouse.com), a peaceful base near Kelvingrove museum. Around Inveraray are Brambles Hotel (inverarayhotel. com) and stylish Newton Hall Guest House (newtonhallguesthouse. co.uk). In Oban, besides Elderslie Guest House (obanbandb.com), Kilchrenan House (kilchrenanhouse.co.uk) has great views of the bay. Fort William's The Grange (grangefortwilliam.com) is a welcoming high-end B&B.

When to go

If you can bear the biting midges, summer is a great time to drive the route, with ferries in full swing, long days and, sometimes, even dry weather – but book accommodation well in advance, especially in Oban, Glen Coe and Fort William. Colourful leaves enliven autumn, bluebells spring up in March and rhododendrons flower around June. Winter can mean snow, bringing grandeur to the peaks and skiing to Glen Coe and the Nevis Range.

Further info

As you'd expect, the roads in Argyll are extremely winding in many places, and include sections of single-track – drive with caution. For anyone heading onwards (or home) via London, taking the Caledonian Sleeper rail service is one option for extending your adventure. Departing from Fort William and Glasgow (as well as other Scottish cities and towns), it gives a room with a moving view, and pulls into Euston Station around 8am.

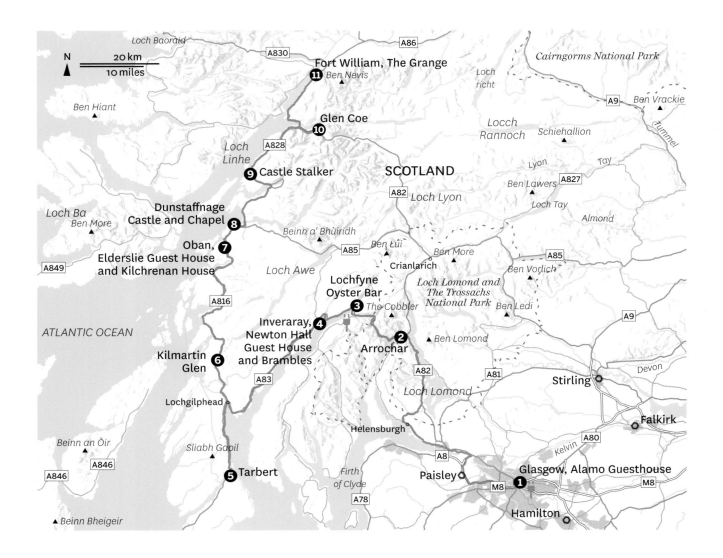

peninsula. There's great seafood here too, and it's a good base for exploring Kintyre's gentle east or wild and blustery west coasts. Next, head back north to Kilmartin Glen, where cairns, carvings, stone circles and a hill fort rise from the green hills. The Kilmartin House Museum explores the history of the monuments and the prehistoric people who built them.

Another hour or so north up the winding coast road brings you to Oban, terminus of the Glasgow railway and departure point for ferries to the islands. The advantage of overnighting here is that you have the town largely to yourself after transiting passengers have been and gone: settle in for quality seafood and views across to Mull.

TO THE TOP OF BRITAIN

North of Oban, the sea views west continue to wow while to the east the mountains rise with increasing drama. Fifteen minutes' drive takes you to squat, waterfront

Dunstaffnage Castle, which has an allegedly haunted chapel. On the hour-long drive north to Glen Coe, you'll pass Castle Stalker, the island-set fortress that featured at the end of *Monty Python and the Holy Grail*. Glen Coe itself is famous both for its brooding scenery and the grim Glencoe Massacre of 1692, in which members of the local MacDonald clan were murdered by Scottish government soldiers. A visitor centre tells the sad story. The hiking here is superb, and there's skiing in winter (though conditions can be unreliable).

You're now in the most visited part of the Highlands, and the peaceful stretches of Argyll may seem remote when you arrive in Fort William, at the base of the Nevis mountain range. You can climb the UK's highest peak, the 4413ft (1345m) Ben Nevis, ride the scenic Jacobite Steam Train, and hike, mountain bike or ski before retiring to a base such as The Grange, where log fires and Victorian baths should help your recovery from all that fresh air.

Islands in the (gulf) stream

If the weather's fine, you'll see several islands off the coast during this drive: big, small, green, rocky, topped with castles or covered with seabirds. Some of the best-known off Argyll's mainland include Islay (famous for its peaty whiskies), Jura (red deer and a whirlpool), Arran ('Scotland in miniature'), Bute (Victorian glamour) and Mull (mountains and beaches). Even the smaller isles feature sights such as puffin breeding grounds, ancient monasteries and eerily geometric rock formations. The islands add appeal to this route just by coming in and out of view on the horizon, but many are also easy to reach. A ferry between Oban and Mull takes only 45 minutes and one from

Tarbert to Arran takes an hour and 20 minutes, while the pretty former slate mining island of Seil is connected to the mainland via a bridge south of Oban. If you do plan on a diversion to the islands, check schedules in advance – services can be sporadic outside summer, and some have struggled financially in recent years. Scotland's islands contain some of the country's most fascinating corners, and the trip out to them, as seagulls gather overhead and the ferry engine throbs, is half the fun.

Clockwise from top left:
Castle Stalker, en route to Glen Coe; Isle of Jura, Inner Hebrides; Ballymeanoch standing stones, Kilmartin Glen

**Distance: 130 miles
(210km)**

Duration: 2 days

Edinburgh to Stirling

SCOTLAND

One of the world's great bridges connects Edinburgh with the historic sights
and farmland of central Scotland. This Lowland tour takes in beaches,
porridge, a royal ship, a secret bunker and some charismatic castles.

With its looming castle and atmospheric wynds (alleys), central Edinburgh is a wonderful place to visit – but it's best seen on foot. So drive north to Leith, once an independent port and now an intriguing neighbourhood of converted warehouses and excellent restaurants, where sea breezes roll down half-gentrified streets. The big sight here is Royal Yacht *Britannia*, which took Britain's royals around the world for almost 50 years. Tread the Burmese teak decks to see the well-preserved apartments and the odd royal holiday snap.

The road west shadows the Firth of Forth to Queensferry, where the Forth Bridge – built for rail traffic in 1890 and still the world's second-longest cantilever bridge – reaches across to Fife. Before crossing the parallel Forth Road Bridge, explore the bridges' history at the Queensferry Museum, which also has a display on the Burryman, the burr-covered folklore character that's long been a feature of the August Ferry Fair here.

OVER THE FORTH TO FIFE

Over the other side of the bridge, Fife was once a legendary Pictish kingdom, and you'll soon be cruising your EV along a classic coastline of beaches and fishing villages. Have a late lunch at Elie's Ship Inn, then walk if off on the

Plan & prepare

Tips for EV drivers

Car hire is available at Edinburgh's Waverly train station and airport, but EV availability is comparatively limited. This route is fairly flat, and while the roads are small and sometimes winding, there are no particularly challenging sections – for chunks of the drive you'll be following the signposted Fife Coastal Route. Good spots for fast chargers include Edinburgh, Queensferry, Kirkcaldy (on the way to Elie), St Andrews, Kinross (just past Loch Leven) and Stirling.

Where to stay

Edinburgh has a huge range of accommodation, but book well in advance – 14 Hart Street (14hartstreet. co.uk) is an elegant New Town base. En route, besides Anstruther's Spindrift (thespindrift.co.uk), you could happily base yourself in St Andrews, with 17th-century Old Fishergate House (oldfishergatehouse.co.uk) arguably the pick of the bunch. In Stirling, Victoria Square (victoriasquare.scot) and Castlecroft (castlecroft-uk.co.uk) are good options, the latter in the shadow of the city's famous fort.

When to go

Sunshine is never guaranteed in Scotland, but the days are long and the temperatures pleasant from May to September. Most sights are open year-round, and while the winter months can be damp and chilly, they're also an atmospheric time to explore the area. If you happen to be in Queensferry on 1 January, you'll catch the Loony Dook, in which brave (and often sleep-deprived) swimmers take a dip in the wintry waters of the Forth.

Further info

There are no tolls on the roads or the bridges over the Forth. If you're keen to stretch out this drive, consider stops in Dunfermline (home to a famous cathedral) and Dundee (its redeveloped dockside includes the stunning V&A Dundee). Or lace up your hiking boots and take the slow route along the coast: the Fife Coastal Path connects the seaside villages and stretches right from the Forth to the Tay.

Exploring the East Neuk

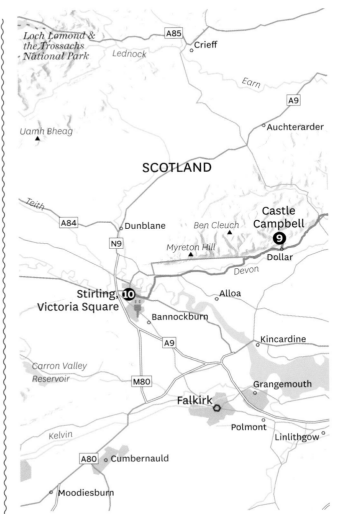

The Fife coast between Earlsferry (just west of Elie) and Crail (10 miles/16km or so past Anstruther) is known as the East Neuk. This pocket of shoreline (Neuk means 'nook', or corner) was once home to a flourishing fishing industry, with herring caught in large quantities during the 19th century. Most of the boats have gone, but the stone harbours and picturesque villages remain, and are popular with daytrippers from Edinburgh and Glasgow. The East Neuk doesn't have the look of classic Scotland: inland, the rolling scenery is reminiscent of much of the English countryside, while the coastal villages contain honey-coloured cottages and – perhaps thanks to Flemish and Baltic trading partners – houses that feature red pantile roofs and crow-step gables. But more traditional national pastimes are very evident too, with golfing links dipping down to the sea and fish and chips available just about everywhere. Looking for something a bit different? Detour to Scotland's Secret Bunker near Anstruther, a series of operation rooms, dormitories and storehouses set 100ft (30m) underground. Built in the 1950s as a regional command centre for a nuclear war, it is – thankfully – now only used as a tourist attraction.

Above: the East Neuk village of Crail
Right: fish and chips, always best by the sea

fine sandy beach here before heading on, via appealing St Monans and Pittenweem, to land in Anstruther, where the Sprindrift offers a comfortable overnight spot. Anstruther itself is a charmer, with an interesting fishing museum and the chance to take a birdwatching boat trip to the Isle of May – or just fill up on fish and chips and sea views before easing your way to bed. Kick off next morning with the Spindrift's great porridge before following the coast to St Andrews, famous as both the home of golf and the place Will met Kate. The R&A World Golf Museum is stuffed with memorabilia and has its own putting green, while the atmospheric ruins of St Andrews Cathedral – consecrated 1000 years ago by Robert the Bruce – give a sense of the city's medieval grandeur.

Turn towards the rolling farmland of central Fife to visit another great medieval relic, Falkland Palace, a vast and ornate stately home that was used as a hunting retreat by the Stewart kings. You're not far from the Highlands here,

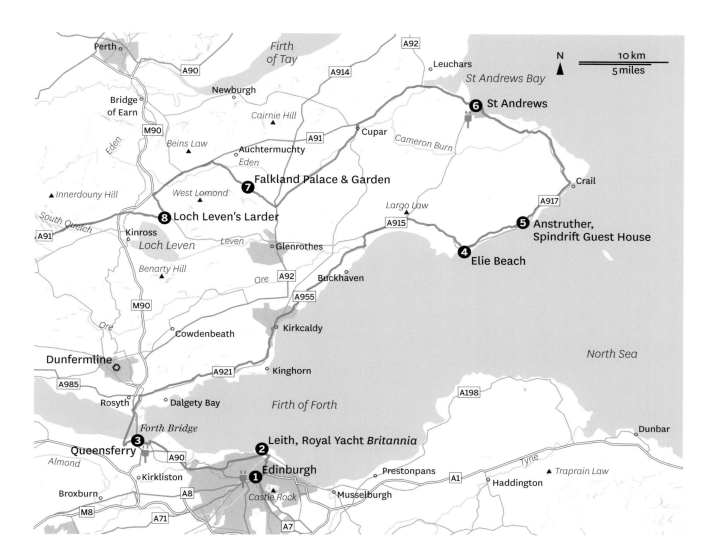

and the next leg passes the moorlands and forests of the Lomond Hills to pause for a ramble at lovely Loch Leven. Fill up at Loch Leven's Larder, a canteen-style barn with a decent deli; or classic country pub Balgedie Toll Tavern.

The mix of walking trails and grand history continues at Castle Campbell, just outside the prosperous town of Dollar. The hulking, hill-set castle may be closed for masonry renovations when you visit, but it hardly matters: take in the views and walk the lung-bursting loop that winds past the castle and through a ravine.

You should now be fully prepped for a wander round what is perhaps Scotland's greatest castle. Stirling's fortress literally towers over the city, but it isn't the only show in town: you can walk the city walls; check out what's claimed to be William Wallace's sword at the National Wallace Monument; visit Bannockburn (where Robert the Bruce won a famous victory over the English); or just rest your head at bay-windowed Victoria Square guesthouse.

Below: Lugano's lovely Old Town
Right: hairpins aplenty on the Gotthard Pass

➡ **Distance: 268 miles (431km)**

➡ **Duration: 5-7 days**

Lugano to Lausanne

SWITZERLAND

Drive your environmentally-friendly car through the most fabulous environments on a road trip from Switzerland's Mediterranean-like south to the shores of Lake Geneva, winding via the high Alps

Most drives in super-organised, scenically sensational, 60% mountainous Switzerland are enjoyable. But this one – which combines some Italian flair, looming Alpine roads, French-style lakeside living and excellent EV infrastructure – is off the scale.

INTO THE TICINO
Lugano lounges on its eponymous lake in the Italian-speaking Ticino region, a mix of piazzas, parks, Lombardy-style buildings, lip-smacking gelato and the excellent Lugano Arte e Cultura centre. Stroll the traffic-free Old Town and get an overview from Monte Brè.

The Swiss-Italian vibes continue 28 miles (45km) northwest in Locarno, on Lake Maggiore. Here, in the country's sunniest spot, palms, camellias and citrus trees bloom before a backdrop of snowcapped peaks – an appealing combination. Take in the city, lake and mountain panorama from Madonna del Sasso church.

Next stop, backtrack 14 miles (23km) to Bellinzona. This strategically located town's three medieval castles – Castelgrande, Montebello and Sasso Corbaro – were built to control traffic between the alpine passes to the north and Ticino to the south. They're now Unesco-listed and home to diverting museums.

© Buena Vista Images / Getty Images

Tips for EV drivers

Electric cars can be rented in numerous Swiss cities, including Lugano and Lausanne. There is a good network of chargers (including fast chargers) along this route, including in Piotta and Airolo (located before you hit the high passes), and in Täsch, the road-end access point for Zermatt. Note, however, that this route involves around 24,500ft (7467m) of ascent, which will take a toll on your range.

Where to stay

Switzerland Tourism's website (myswitzerland. com) has a list of eco-friendly hotels with charging stations. Options on this route include the Novotel Lausanne Bussigny (all. accor.com), which also has a natural swimming pond; the Swiss Youth Hostel in Fiesch (sport-resort.ch), near the Aletsch Glacier; the blush-pink Hotel De La Paix in Lugano (delapaix.ch); and the ibis Hotel (all.accor.com) in Locarno.

When to go

If you want to tackle the most impressive mountain passes, this is a drive for summer – the Furka Pass is usually open from the first week of June until mid-October, but heavy snowfall can cause it to open later or close earlier. Check before travel (alpen-paesse.ch). Alternative tunnels and car-train services are available if passes are closed. September is a good option – a little quieter, but still ideal for outdoor activities. The Montreux Jazz Festival is in July.

Further info

Switzerland has four official language regions – German, French, Italian and Romansh; the language used on road signs varies by canton. By law, all vehicles are required to travel with lights on during the day. Some drivers consider the best way to tackle the Furka Pass is west-to-east as it offers the most exciting climb, but it's unforgettable in both directions.

The E-Grand Tour

Our Lugano–Lausanne route follows the two southern segments of Switzerland Tourism's eight-stage E-Grand Tour, a 1021-mile (1643km) loop of the entire country designed for EV drivers. This epic circuit ticks off five Alpine passes, 13 Unesco World Heritage Sites, two Unesco Biospheres, 22 lakes, busy cities, innumerable chocolate-box villages and cow-grazed meadows – and more than 300 charging stations. Visit myswitzerland.com to download an app and GPX files for detailed maps. The E-Grand Tour can be travelled in both directions, but the recommendation is to drive clockwise, to easier navigate access roads and one-way systems; also, the route is only signposted in the clockwise direction. Driving for five hours a day, you could do the lot in around a week, though it's better to slow down and enjoy the views. From Lausanne, the full route continues to Neuchâtel, then meanders via a succession of blue-turquoise-inky lakes to capital Bern. Next are lovely Lucerne and cosmopolitan Zürich, the roaring Rhine Falls, historic St Gallen and bucolic Appenzell. From here, the route passes Swiss National Park to reach glitzy St Moritz, before plunging down the mountains to reach Bellinzona and Lugano. E-Grand Tour complete.

Above: threading through the Swiss Alps on the E-Grand Tour
Right: the mighty Matterhorn from Zermatt

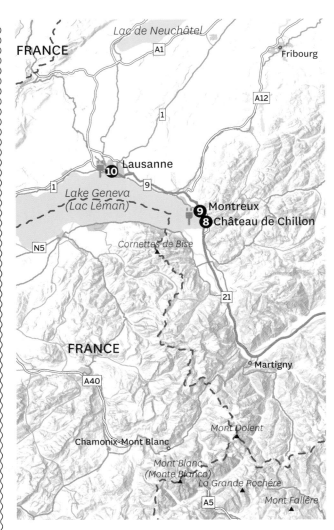

FROM MOUNTAINS TO LAKE

From Bellinzona, things get really interesting, as the road climbs towards the Gotthard Massif. Traffic tunnels burrow through the mountains these days (useful for when snow closes the passes), but driving over is far more exhilarating – especially beyond Airolo (38 miles/61km on), from where the Tremola corkscrews up to the 6910ft (2106m) Gotthard Pass; at its twistiest, this 1830s-built cobblestone road ascends about 1000ft (305m) in 24 hairpins. Negotiate the Tremola, or take the adjacent road, which affords remarkable views of the old route. At the top, 9 miles (15km) on, stop at the old customs house, now the Gotthard Pass Museum.

It's no less thrilling on the other side, where you'll soon encounter the Furka Pass. This 19th-century road switchbacks from Realp up to 7976ft (2431m) before snaking down into the Valais, past amply-photographed Hotel Bélvèdere and views of the Rhône Glacier.

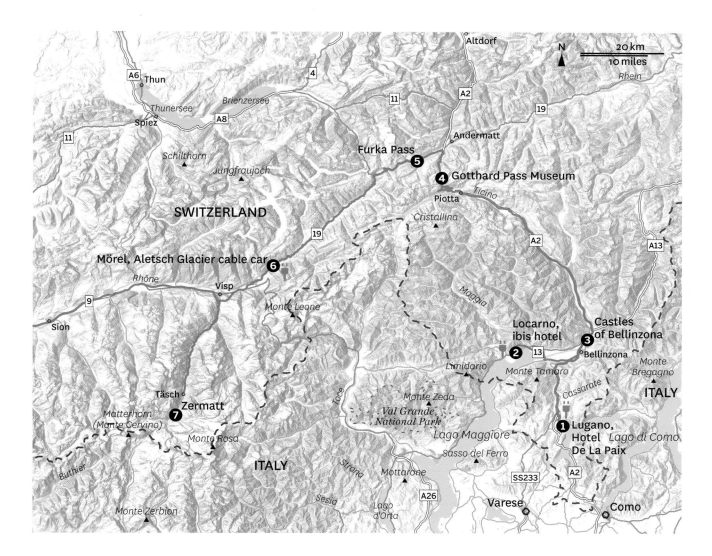

Plunging on, past geranium-bright villages, there are tempting detours at Betten and Mörel: take cable cars for close-ups of the mighty Aletsch, Europe's longest glacier.

Beyond Brig, drive 24 miles (39km) to road-end Täsch in the Mattertal valley, lined with most of the Alps' highest peaks. Take the train-shuttle to Zermatt, the characterful car-free (even for EVs) town at the foot of the jagged Matterhorn. The hiking hereabouts could distract for days.

Backtrack from Täsch, continuing west for 85 miles (137km) through the Rhône Valley via ancient Sion and the 4th-century abbey of St Maurice. At Lake Geneva, the medieval turrets of Château de Chillon rise from a rock-isle, mountains behind. It's fairy-tale stuff – take a tour to hear the centuries of stories that swill around its great halls and Gothic vaults. The lakeside Floral Path, or a 2 mile (3.2km) drive, leads to Montreux. This genteel resort has a winsome hilltop Old Town, fine villas and a creative heritage that spans from Charlie Chaplin to modern jazz.

It's an easy place to like. From here it's 17 miles (27km) around the lake, via the heady and Unesco-listed Lavaux vineyard terraces, to the lively, sporty, foodie city of Lausanne. Admire the historic centre and art galleries, and toast a great trip with a dish of Vaudois sausages and a glass of Chasselas, sipped direct from the cellar door.

➡ **Distance: 180 miles (291km)**

➡ **Duration: 2-3 days**

Geneva to Basel

SWITZERLAND

This journey through western Switzerland takes in two of the country's cultural titans, as well as the glacier-gouged lakes, handsome towns and vineyard-swathed slopes that lie in between.

A road trip from Geneva to Basel reveals a corner of Switzerland quite unlike the postcard-perfect peaks and famous passes that lie out to the east. Instead the green and gently contoured slopes of the Jura Mountains dominate here, with lowland villages and shimmering lakes forming the borderlands between French and German-speaking regions.

The starting point is Geneva – not the capital of Switzerland, but in some sense a capital of the world: it's home to the United Nations, the World Bank and other international bodies. Mingle with diplomats among its boulevards, watch the River Rhône slip away from the silvery expanse of Lake Geneva, or drive just west to CERN – the European Organisation for Nuclear Research, where exhibitions shed light on the Large Hadron Collider, the famous subterranean particle accelerator.

LAKE TO LAKE BY EV

Accelerate out of Switzerland's second city on one of the country's most scenic drives. Hwy 1 hugs the shore of Lake Geneva, the peaks of the French Alps mirrored in its waters. En route are the pretty towns of Nyon and Morges, each crowned with their own regal castle. You'll eventually arrive in Lausanne, languorously draped along Geneva's

© Erik Thom

© B&M Noskowski / Getty Images

Tips for EV drivers

Geneva has a low-emissions system by the curious name of Stick'AIR (ge.ch) – the good news is that electric vehicles are permitted in the centre at any time. EV hire is available from Geneva Airport and Basel-Mulhouse-Freiburg Airport (which is actually outside Basel in France). Parts of this Geneva–Basel road trip lie on the E-Grand Tour of Switzerland, a touring route devised with EVs in mind. Find maps for it on the Swiss tourist board website (myswitzerland.com).

Where to stay

Château d'Ouchy (chateaudouchy.ch) is a 19th-century hotel built on the site of a medieval castle in Lausanne, and presiding over the city's lakefront quays – book a room in the surviving 12th-century tower for panoramic views of the water. Built on a lakeside hill, Hôtel de l'Ours Preles (hoteldelourspreles. ch) has been run by three generations of the same family and offers suites looking out over the Jura Mountains.

When to go

Summer is the best time for this drive: July sees festivals taking place on the shores of Lake Geneva, notably the Montreux Jazz Festival – one of Europe's biggest – near Lausanne, and the Paléo rock festival in Nyon. The route from Geneva to Basel doesn't take in classic skiing destinations, but it's still attractive in winter – look out for Murten's Festival of Light in January, with illuminations along the lake shore.

Further info

Unlike some regions of neighbouring France, winter tyres or snow chains are not mandatory under Swiss law. That said, if you're detouring up into Alpine corners or travelling in the depths of winter, they are very much a good idea: your insurance might not pay out if you have an accident in wintry conditions without suitable preparation being evident.

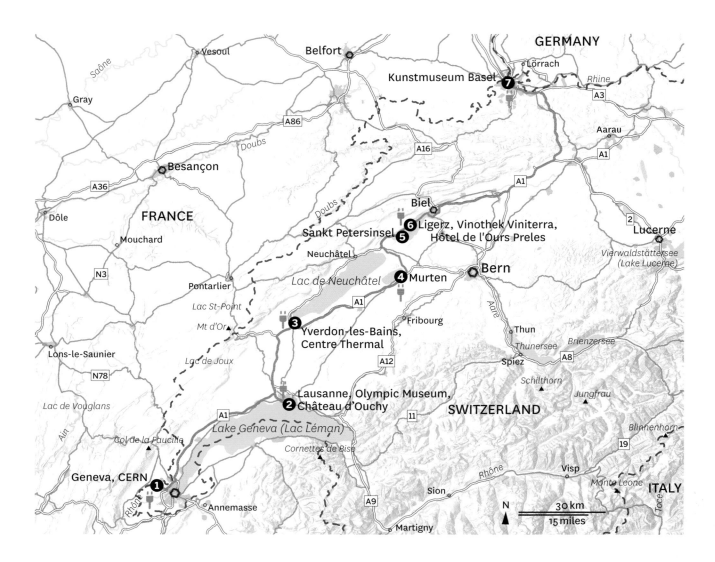

northern flank. This university town is the permanent address of the International Olympic Committee – the excellent Olympic Museum here has medals, torches, mascots and interactive exhibits where you can try out various sports. After, rest sore muscles at the Château d'Ouchy which, though it sounds like a sports-related injury, is actually a fine neo-Gothic hotel.

Lakes soon become a leitmotif – an hour north of Lausanne you arrive in the Drei-Seen-Land – the land of three lakes. The first in this trinity is Neuchâtel, where the town of Yverdon-les-Bains has a sandy beach filled with sunbathers and swimmers in high summer. You'll find balmier bathing options year-round in Yverdon's Centre Thermal – people have come to bathe in these mineral-rich springs since Roman times. Drive east until you find the smallest of the watery trio, Lake Murten, before the Drei-Seen-Land saves the best for last: blissful Biel, set under the slopes of the Jura Mountains. Park up

and wander along Sankt Petersinsel, a promontory jutting out into the lake where the Genevan philosopher Jean-Jacques Rousseau lived out 'the happiest time of [his] life.'

GREAT WINE & OLD MASTERS
Profound contentment can also be found in neighbouring Ligerz, the wine-producing hub of Lake Biel where, among rows of quivering vines, Vinothek Viniterra is an emporium stocking vintages from 60 local winegrowers. Then take your purchases to boutique Hôtel de l'Ours.

Rise early to follow Hwy 2 to Basel, a Swiss town whose suburbs spill over into France and Germany, and is best known as a centre for pan-European art. The Kunstmuseum here holds the world's oldest public art collection – amidst the Old Masters, look out for *Lake Geneva, Seen from Chexbres* by Swiss artist Ferdinand Hodler, which shows cloud formations scudding over the lake where your journey began.

Keeping watch

A drive from Geneva to Basel is a journey through 'Watch Valley' – the homeland of famous Swiss watchmaking brands like Rolex, TAG Heuer and Breitling. The industry has its origins in 16th-century Geneva when, legend has it, the advent of Protestantism under John Calvin forced jewellers to move from lavish ornamental designs to something more practical. The Watchmakers Guild of Geneva was established in 1601, with artisans aiming to produce high-quality objects in limited numbers – a philosophy that continues to the present day. Time ticked past, and as Geneva became crowded with watchmakers, the industry extended northward into the Jura, Lake Neuchâtel and Lake Biel. WWI precipitated a shift from pocket watches to modern wristwatches (soldiers used their timepieces to coordinate artillery barrages). Swiss manufacturers continued with their groundbreaking designs throughout the 20th century, producing waterproof watches in the 1920s, pioneering electric watches in the 1950s and devising the first quartz watches in the 1960s. Many watch museums can be found up and down Watch Valley – the new Omega Museum in Biel and the Patek Philippe Museum in Geneva are among the flashiest.

Clockwise from top left:
Sankt Petersinsel, Lake Biel;
Boutique Rolex, Geneva;
Olympic Museum, Lausanne

Below: pedestrianised
Augustinergasse, Zürich
Right: Zürich and its
eponymous lake from
Mt Uetliberg

➡ **Distance: 180 miles
(290km)**   ➡ **Duration: 2-3 days**

Zürich to St Moritz

SWITZERLAND

The mountain resort of St Moritz helped launch the idea of Alpine tourism, and this clean, green drive takes in lakes and valleys at the core of the Swiss apple.

The Alps are simultaneously the most and least Swiss thing about Switzerland. They offer up captivating beauty, pastures for grazing and snow-bound slopes for skiing. They encourage valley-by-valley resourcefulness and help shield the nation. But they're also a geological-scale mess. Since at least Roman times, road-builders here have furrowed their brows at the challenge of threading usable routes through zigzagging gorges and over wind-whipped mountain passes.

In Zürich, a lowland city where the trams display live connection times for upcoming stops, it's quite easy to bring good order to the transport network. More determination is called for where the land begins to rise steeply some 20 miles (32km) to the south. Since 2016, trains can take the 35.5-mile (57km) Gotthard Base Tunnel – the world's longest. The burgeoning supply of EV chargers along the high Alpine routes is a less headline-grabbing project, but what joy it is to drive towards the *grande dame* of Swiss mountain resorts without compromising the vaunted freshness of the air.

SOUTH FROM ZÜRICH

As you leave Zürich through its southern lakeside suburbs, glimpsing fleets of pleasure boats and swimming

Plan & prepare

Tips for EV drivers

Be mindful of faster battery depletion on steep mountain roads, especially in colder temperatures – though regenerative braking on the downhills can claw back some charge. There's a good run of fast-charging stations up to Silenen, but after that nothing speedy (at the time of writing) until Thusis, 75 miles (120km) later. Consider a strategic top-up part-way around Disentis, with a hotel stay or at least a lunch break to pass the hours.

Where to stay

With its spire and half-timbering picked out in red, the Hotel Vitznauerhof (vitznauerhof.ch) on the Vitznau lakeside is a classic, just calling out for a starring role in a Wes Anderson film; there's also a double Michelin-starred restaurant. To economise a bit in swanky St Moritz, consider the Hotel Sonne (sonne-stmoritz. ch) – no great shakes from the outside but near the lakeside path and (like the Vitznauerhof) with its own charging points.

When to go

The two passes on this route are kinder to drivers than many in the Alps. The Julier is usually kept open year-round (winter tyres are needed in season), while the Oberalp tends to be clear of snow by early May. Even when it's closed, you can take a car-transporter train between Andermatt and Sedrun, saving some battery charge. Shoulder seasons around May and October see many mountain hotels and other facilities closed.

Further info

While it's important to stick to speed limits in any country, be aware that Swiss speeding fines are particularly wallet-whacking. If you're taking the more direct motorway route back to Zürich via Sargans, the lakeside run by the Walensee is especially scenic.

A devilish problem

Less than a mile (1.6km) before you reach Andermatt, the road emerges from a long gallery onto the Teufelsbrücke (Devil's Bridge) – if you look in the rear-view mirror, you'll see two red-painted figures on the rock face behind. This tight gorge of the upper Reuss River has been spanned in wood and stone since at least 1300 (the current 1958 road bridge arches over its 1830 predecessor), and like many feats of medieval bridge-building, the devil got the credit. The story goes that villagers on this crucial trade route made a Faustian bargain: a safe crossing of the Schöllenen Gorge in exchange for the first soul to use it. Which turned out to be a billy goat, goaded across the bridge to attack its horned-and-hoofed rival. The cheated devil is said to have then sped down the valley and seized a giant boulder to smash his construction. But while he paused for a momentary rest, an old woman passing by made the sign of the cross, and the roadside stone became immovable – until 1972, at least, when the Teufelsstein was shifted, at great expense, to allow access to the new Gotthard Road Tunnel; it still stands sentinel over the tunnel's entrance.

Clockwise from top left: the Teufelsbrücke (Devil's Bridge); Lindt & Sprüngli chocolate factory, Zürich; lakeside Hotel Vitznauerhof

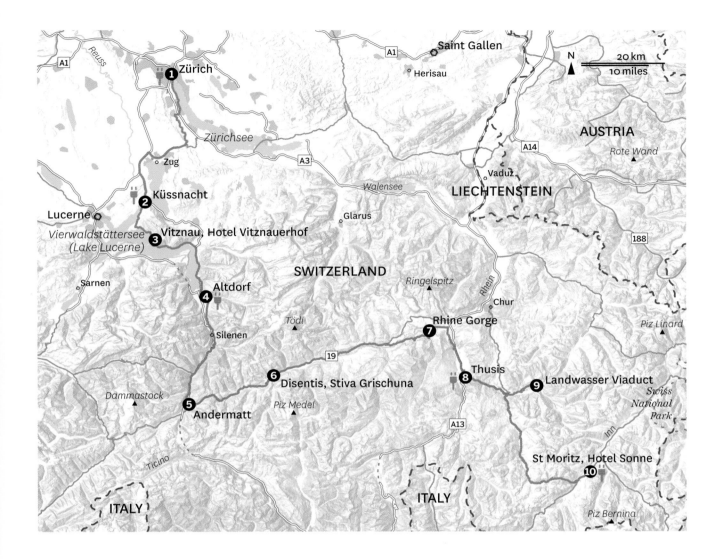

pontoons, check off one more national stock image at the Lindt & Sprüngli chocolate factory. Otherwise it's an autobahn-shunning turn away from Lake Zürich, following the gentle, wooded curves of the Sihl Valley.

Beyond the canton of Zug, with its lake and enticing corporate tax regime, lies the cradle of the Swiss Confederation – Lake Lucerne, known in German as the Vierwaldstättersee (Lake of the Four Forest Cantons). It bends and branches between mountain peaks, ensuring that the whole can never be surveyed from any one scenic viewpoint. On the road south between Ingenbohl and Sisikon, the grass-green lakeside patch to be spied beneath the cliffs and forest on the far side is the Rütli Meadow, where legend says the first three cantons swore an oath to band together around the year 1300.

But before that, at the town of Küssnacht, where this route joins the lake and within walking distance of a fast-charging station, is the first of many local sights linked

to the national origin story of William Tell. The Hohle Gasse (Hollow Alley) is a path through mossy woods where the Swiss hero is supposed to have ambushed the hated Austrian bailiff Gessler – the man who had earlier forced Tell to shoot an apple off his own son's head.

As you approach the village of Vitznau, the road hugs the lake so closely the water almost laps at your wheels, and depending on the season you may see afar the first snowcapped peaks of the drive. If not, get a panoramic boost thanks to Europe's longest-running mountain railway, which has trundled its way from Vitznau up to the 5899ft (1798m) summit of Rigi since 1871 – too late for Turner and his painting series around the peak, though it was in place when Mark Twain visited.

CROSSROADS OF THE ALPS
Travellers have been following the rushing current of the Reuss upstream from the lake for longer still. It

Fuel for mountaineers

The cuisine of Graubünden, the largest Swiss canton and location of St Moritz, seems to straddle the Alps north and south just like its German-Italian-Romansh linguistic mix. Rough, pasta-like *pizokels* and the equally hearty *capuns* (mini dumplings rolled in chard leaves, in a cheesy sauce) feature on menus in traditional restaurants such as the 200-year-old wood-lined Stiva Grischuna in Disentis. For take-home edible souvenirs, whether picked up in St Moritz or even as a cheat at Zürich Airport, the most ubiquitous are *Bündnerfleisch* (air-dried beef) and *Bündner Nusstorte*. The latter is a flat shortcrust pastry pie filled with a caramelised walnut mix. It's an odd speciality for the Engadine Valley, given that historically walnut trees struggled to grow there, but its inhabitants were once renowned as confectioners, who made their reputations as far afield as Venice and brought a few recipes home with them.

From left: Graubünden *capuns*; up high on the Julier Pass; the *Glacier Express* crossing Landwasser Viaduct

springs from a star-shaped knot of valleys centred on the small town of Andermatt, surely the crossroads of the Alps. South takes you over the Gotthard Pass, with Italy beckoning. Just west and east, separated by only 15 miles (24km), are the sources of the Rhône and the Rhine. It's the latter course you'll follow next, as a half-dozen hairpin bends take you above the tree line, over the 6706ft (2044m) Oberalp Pass, perhaps accompanied a few feet away by the red-and-white carriages of the *Glacier Express*. If you don't spot it there, you'll have other chances in villages such as Disentis, where Switzerland's fourth language, Romansh, is spoken; and from the scenic side-road overlooking the white cliffs and milky blue waters of the Rhine Gorge. The money shot of this train – also headed to St Moritz – comes as it curves round atop the tall stone arches of the Landwasser Viaduct. This is a slight but worthwhile detour from your route – as is the Via Mala gorge, south of Thusis, whose name, meaning 'Bad Path', is as frank an assessment of the difficulty of road-building as you'll find anywhere in the Swiss Alps.

The highest point of the drive lies amid the scree-strewn slopes of the Julier Pass, at 7493ft (2284m). From here, you leave the watershed of the Rhine – everything that follows, including the chain of jewel-blue lakes around Silvaplana, eventually finds its way down the Engadine Valley to the Danube and the Black Sea. St Moritz's lake waters reflect such pioneering icons of Victorian-era Alpine tourism as the Kulm Hotel. In 1879, diners there sat down in the first room in Switzerland lit by electric lamps. Charging your car at journey's end, with a mountain guard of honour on all sides, is not such a big leap after all.

➜ **Distance: 116 miles
(188km)**

➜ **Duration: 4-5 days**

Montreux to Neuchâtel

SWITZERLAND

From Western Europe's biggest lake to the foothills of the Jura Mountains,
this trip is a selection box of Swiss delights, taking in cable cars, chocolate,
cheese, clocks – and Queen.

Few cities have a location quite as spectacular as Montreux, on the waterfront and overlooking the eastern reaches of Lake Geneva (or Lac Léman as it's known locally). This elegant city has been a favourite bohemian hangout for celebrities and the super-rich since the days of Byron: Charlie Chaplin lived out his final years here, and stadium rockers Queen recorded several of their best-known albums at Mountain Studios. Don't miss the rickety cogwheel train up to Rochers de Naye, a natural viewpoint at 6703ft (2043m) offering incredible views over the lake and the Alps; and a boat trip across the water to see the island castle of Château de Chillon, a maze of turrets, courtyards, gardens and armour-filled halls.

Another impressive castle awaits in the town of Gruyères, 26 miles (41km) northeast of Montreux, where nineteen Counts of Gruyère lived in considerable pomp and splendour. The town is best-known for its twin culinary exports: tangy Gruyère cheese and decadent Swiss chocolate. You can taste local *fromage* at farms such as the Fromagerie d'Alpage de Moléson, or take a guided tour of a working chocolate factory in nearby Broc at Maison Cailler, a master *chocolatier* since 1825.

North of Gruyère, track the west side of Lac de la Gruyère in your EV as you travel northwards to Fribourg,

Plan & prepare

Tips for EV drivers

Switzerland currently has around 8000 public chargers, and you should have no trouble finding a place to charge in and around the bigger towns and cities. Evpass (evpass.ch), GOFAST (gofast.swiss) and MOVE (move.ch) all have large networks, while the useful EinfachStromLaden app gives you access to Maingau (maingau-energie.de) chargers.

Where to stay

There's a very wide choice of hotels in Switzerland, from half-timbered heritage to minimalist modern. In Montreux, Hotel Victoria (victoria-glion.ch) is an old-school, 56-room hotel up on the city heights, with views of the lake, lawns and mountains, and a couple of EV chargers for guests' use. In Bern, Hotel Bären (baerenbern.ch) is opposite the Swiss Parliament Building and handy for the city centre. It offers preferential rates at the Bahnhofparking car park, which has ten MOVE chargers.

When to go

Switzerland has two peak seasons to be aware of: summer from July to August, and the main ski season from December to April. Accommodation prices are always much higher at these times of year. For the cheapest rates, come in the low season (October to early December), when hotel rooms can be up to 50% cheaper. Autumn in the mountains is always picturesque, while late spring is best for greenery and wildflowers.

Further info

Drivers must pay an annual one-off charge to use Swiss highways and semi-highways, identified by green signs. The charge is payable at the border (in cash, including euros), Swiss service stations and post offices, and Swiss tourist offices abroad. Upon paying, you'll receive a sticker that must be displayed on the windscreen and is valid for 14 months, from 1 December to 31 January. If you're caught without it, you'll be fined. See www.vignette.ch for more details.

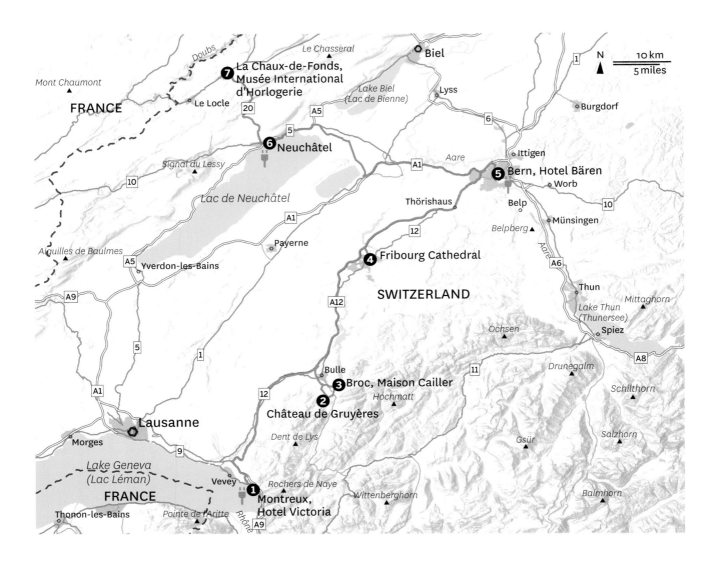

an intriguing city that brings home Switzerland's linguistic divide: residents on the west bank of the river speak French, those on the east speak German. The city's main landmark is the monumental Cathédrale St Nicolas de Myre, a Gothic supertanker whose 243ft-high (74m) tower affords an incredible panorama over town. There are some interesting galleries and museums to visit too: at the endearingly old-fashioned Musée Suisse de la Marionnette, you can catch a traditional puppet show and marvel at the intricate craft involved in making them.

CAPITAL TIME

The Swiss capital, Bern, receives far less attention (and way fewer visitors) than Zürich and Geneva, and its charms are hugely underappreciated. The gorgeous Old Town is a delight to explore on foot, with covered arcades, basement shops, tinkling fountains and cobbled alleys as quaint as any in Switzerland. You can't miss the main

sight here: the Zytglogge, a medieval clock tower where a menagerie of revolving figures twirl at four minutes before the hour. The city's other big-ticket sight is Zentrum Paul Klee. Bern's answer to the Guggenheim, this wave-like structure designed by Renzo Piano houses an exceptional collection of works by the playful, provocative Swiss artist.

After a day or two in the capital, drive west until the great glittering sweep of Lac de Neuchâtel fills the horizon. Its namesake town, Neuchâtel, is another medieval gem, huddled in the foothills of the mighty Jura Mountains and a great spot for some hiking: catch the cable car up to Mt Chaumont and strike out along the mountain trails.

Round the trip off in La Chaux-de-Fonds, a city which (like the rest of Switzerland) tends to run like clockwork. It's famous for watchmaking: several of the most prestigious manufacturers are located here, and you can get a historical overview at the Musée International d'Horlogerie, brimful of ticking, gonging, clanging clocks.

Freddie Mercury & Montreux

Everyone's favourite big-haired, big-riff, big-anthem rockers, Queen had an ongoing love affair with Montreux. Between 1979 and 1993, they owned a recording base in the city, Mountain Studios, where they put down six classic albums – starting with *Jazz* in 1978 and ending with *Made in Heaven* in 1995. Freddie himself settled happily in the city ('if you want peace of mind, come to Montreux', he once said), and various other luminaries recorded at Mountain, including David Bowie, AC/DC, the Rolling Stones, Yes and Iggy Pop – not to mention other Queen members who chose to record solo albums here. The studios have now become a shrine to the band, with costumes, props, band ephemera, recording equipment and handwritten lyrics on display – but for real fans, it's the chance to step into the recording booth that's the greatest draw. Proceeds help fund the Mercury Phoenix Trust, the HIV/AIDS charity set up after Freddie's death. No matter what the time of year, you'll likely see flowers beside the Freddie Mercury statue in front of Montreux's covered market. The dedication – 'lover of life, singer of songs' – sums up the great showman pretty well.

Clockwise from top left:
Bern's medieval Zytglogge clock tower; Freddie Mercury statue, Montreux; Neuchâtel Castle, presiding over the town below

Below: hiking up
Snowdon on the
Llanberis Path
Right: Snowdon
Mountain Railway

➡ **Distance: 77 miles
(124km)**

➡ **Duration: 3-4 days**

Caernarfon to Llangollen

WALES

Plot a wonderful long weekend in North Wales, driving from the castle-guarded coast to the scenic English border via the lakes, mountains and endless outdoor possibilities of Snowdonia National Park.

Driving through Snowdonia is a delight (as long as you don't get stuck behind a tractor). This mountainous, lake-dotted chunk of Wales offers some of the country's most dramatic roads. Bookend it with an atmospheric castle and a gravity-defying canal, and you have quite the little road trip.

SNOWDON BOUND

Guarding the Menai Strait, Unesco-listed Caernarfon Castle is arguably the finest of the 17 bastions that the English king, Edward I, built in Wales in the 13th century. Wander amid its immense walls, murder holes and portcullises, and climb the polygonal towers for excellent views of Caernarfon town's narrow streets.

Then make east for the mountains, squeezing between Llyn Padarn and sheer rocks to reach Llanberis, 10 miles (16km) on. Here, visit the National Slate Museum for insight into the Welsh slate industry – explore the exhibits in the Victorian workshops and watch quarrymen at work.

Nearby is the terminus of the Snowdon Mountain Railway, which has been trundling up Wales' highest peak since 1896. Hop aboard – or hike up to the 3560ft (1085m) summit via the adjacent Llanberis Path. Alternatively, drive up the twisty road for a few miles, past Llyn Peris, to

© Gyuszko / Shutterstock

© Joe Dunckley / Shutterstock

Plan & prepare

Tips for EV drivers

There are charging facilities in Caernarfon but places to top up your EV's charge are not widespread along the route, especially east of Betws-y-Coed, around Llangollen. However, there are clusters of chargers in the nearby towns of Wrexham and Oswestry, as well as at the Pontcysyllte Aqueduct car park. Roads within Snowdonia National Park can be steep and undulating, which can reduce battery range.

Where to stay

The Plas y Brenin National Outdoor Centre (pyb.co.uk) near Capel Curig has simple single and twin rooms, a 16-bed bunkhouse and free parking. The Royal Oak Hotel (royaloakhotel.net) is a 150-year-old former coaching inn overlooking the River Llugwy in Betws-y-Coed, with characterful rooms and a river-view restaurant serving modern Welsh dishes. There are EV chargers on site, too.

When to go

The weather can radically change by the hour in Snowdonia. That said, May to September gives the best chance of sunshine. Note that Snowdon itself, and the surrounding roads and villages, can be heaving in July and August – opt instead for the shoulder months. The area doesn't close for winter, and this can be a spectacular time to visit, but you'll need a guide or expert skills to undertake many outdoor activities.

Further info

The closest international airports are located in Liverpool, Manchester and Birmingham. Snowdonia is a rural area – don't be surprised if you come across tractors or animals on the road. If pulling over to take photos, make sure you do so safely: don't obstruct the road and don't park on verges or block gates. You must pre-book a space to park at Pen-y-Pass (the car park for accessing hikes up Snowdon).

Sleeping with legends

As you drive over the Pen-y-Gwryd pass, you'll notice a lonely old building on the left, sitting above a lake and below Snowdonia's highest peaks: the Pen-Y-Gwryd Hotel (pyg.co.uk). Built in 1810, it was originally a farmhouse. Soon after it was turned into a coaching inn, and became renowned for its hospitality and matchless access to the mountains. In 1898 the Climbers' Club (still going strong) was founded here. The hotel's biggest claim to fame came 50 or so years later. The 1953 Everest expedition trained and tested their oxygen equipment in the surrounding mountains, and used the hotel as their HQ. After becoming the first to successfully conquer the top of the world, Edmund Hillary and co returned here regularly for reunions. The hotel is full of their knickknacks, including Himalayan rocks, tin mugs, crampons and a rope used by Tenzing Norgay and Hillary on the summit. The walls are also hung with signed photos; there's even a signed ceiling. Anyone can pop by for a drink, though most of the Everest memorabilia is in the Resident's Bar. Guest rooms don't have TVs; the idea is to find entertainment outside instead – there's plenty of it.

Above: a snapshot of mountaineering history at Pen-Y-Gwryd Hotel
Right: Pontcysyllte Aqueduct

Pen-y-Pass. At 1178ft (359m) above sea level, this mountain pass is the trailhead for Snowdon's more rugged Pyg Track and Miners' Track routes – a classic 7.5 mile (12km) circuit is to hike up via the former and return via the latter.

OUTDOOR ADVENTURES

Beyond Pen-y-Pass, the road skirts the Glyderau range, crosses Pen-y-Gwryd pass and descends through sheep-grazed hills to the twin lakes of Llynnau Mymbyr and the mountain hub of Capel Curig, 5 miles (8km) on. This is the home of the Plas y Brenin National Outdoor Centre, where you can learn anything from rock climbing to whitewater kayaking to e-biking. There's accommodation on site too.

Betws-y-Coed, 6 miles (10km) east, is the de facto 'capital' of Snowdonia. At the meeting of three valleys, surrounded by Gwydir Forest Park, the village has an almost alpine feel, and is crammed with cafes, outdoor gear shops, art galleries and accommodation (including

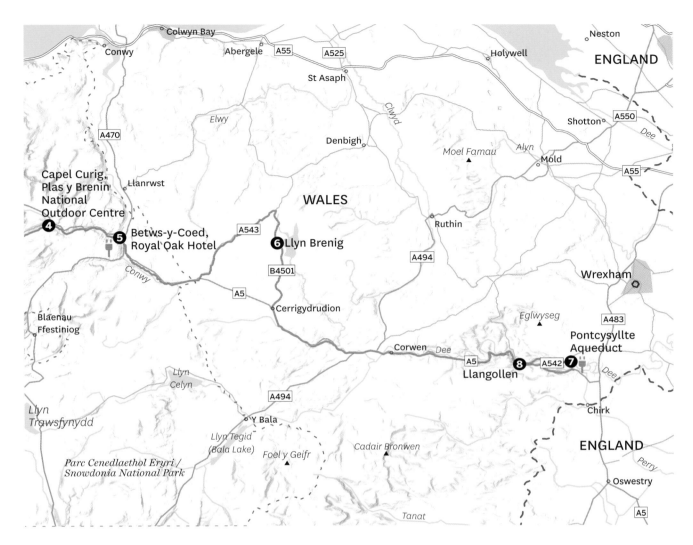

the Royal Oak Hotel). Get ideas for further adventures at the National Park Visitor Centre.

OFF-ROAD, ON WATER

From Betws-y-Coed, the A5 follows the River Conwy southeast out of Snowdonia. For added thrills, veer up the A543 and then down the B4501 to trace the so-called Evo Triangle. This 15-mile (24km) detour of sweeping bends weaves through the unspoilt Denbigh Moors, via Gors Maen Llwyd Nature Reserve and Llyn Brenig reservoir – rent mountain bikes or boats at the visitor centre and cafe.

Rejoining the A5 at Cerrigydrudion, continue for 24 miles (39km) to Pontcysyllte Aqueduct. This engineering marvel, completed in 1805 to carry the Llangollen Canal across the Dee Valley, measures 1007ft (307m) long, 11.2ft (3.4m) wide and 128ft (39m) high – you'll get good views as you drive across the Old Bridge. Park up and walk over the aqueduct, or cross by canoe or barge.

The tiny town of Llangollen is 10 minutes' drive away. As well as having independent shops, pubs and a steam railway, it's a hub for adventures in the Clwydian Range & Dee Valley AONB – hiking, kayaking, rafting, fell running, fishing, gorge walking and more are all possible. But the hike up to hilltop Castell Dinas Bran (purported burial site of the Holy Grail) makes a grand finale.

217

Below: Arthur's Stone, Gower Peninsula
Right: Rhossili Bay and the Worm's Head

➡ **Distance: 118 miles (190km)**   ➡ **Duration: 3-4 days**

Swansea to Pembroke

WALES

On this road trip across striking South Wales, between the country's second-largest city and its western edges, you'll discover Roman heritage, ruined castles, literary legends, mind-blowing beaches and birds galore.

Almost half the population of Wales is crammed into the country's southeast corner. It's where you'll find Cardiff and Swansea, Wales' two biggest cities. So it'll come as a sweet surprise to find the coast to the west – from Gower to Carmarthenshire and into picturesque Pembrokeshire – still feels wonderfully wild.

GOWER GAMBOLING
Swansea isn't gorgeous. But its location on Swansea Bay certainly is, and a large student population lends the city a lively vibe. This is also the birthplace of hard-drinking national poet Dylan Thomas – visit his former home on Cwmdonkin Drive as well as the absorbing Dylan Thomas Centre.

Then follow the bay's curve round to pastel-pretty Mumbles, gateway to the Gower Peninsula. This is a diverse delight of heathland, grassland, marshes, dunes, cliffs, coves and sandy beaches. Book in somewhere secluded like Parc-Le-Breos, 13 miles (21km) from Swansea, and explore the peninsula's narrow, hedge-frilled lanes. Stop for surf at Langland Bay and views at Arthur's Stone. The 3-mile (5km) sweep of Rhossili Bay, at Gower's furthest tip, is unmissable – walk out to Worm's Head (tides permitting) and look for dolphins and seals.

Plan & prepare

Tips for EV drivers

Swansea has a good network of fast chargers in public car parks. However, west of the city, charging points are limited; there are clusters in Llanelli, Carmarthen and Tenby but few outside of these hubs. Facilities are also scarce further along the Pembrokeshire Coast, beyond Pembroke. Some hotels and B&Bs offer charging facilities for guests – check before booking.

Where to stay

Parc-Le-Breos (parc-le-breos.co.uk) is a country-house hotel within an ancient deer park near Penmaen, 7 miles (11km) from Mumbles and a short walk from scenic Three Cliffs Bay. The hotel has an EV charger for residents. Family-run Elm Grove Country House (elmgrovecountryhouse. co.uk), a fine 1850s home in the little village of St Florence, west of Tenby, also has a charger.

When to go

June to September brings the warmest weather – best for beach breaks and camping. You'll need to book accommodation in advance in July and August; expect higher prices too. April and May bring long days and wildflowers. October and November are uncrowded and dappled with autumn colours; this is when the sea is warmest. Winters are relatively mild and quiet – apart from Tenby's raucous Boxing Day Swim. Gower's surf is best over winter too.

Further info

Swansea is around 50 miles (80km) west of Wales' capital, Cardiff, which has an airport. There are no toll roads on this route, and the Severn Bridge, which links England to Wales, has been free to cross since 2018. Road signs are bilingual, with the Welsh language displayed above the English-language translation; for example, 'Abertawe' (the city's Welsh name) will appear above 'Swansea'.

The need for e-speed

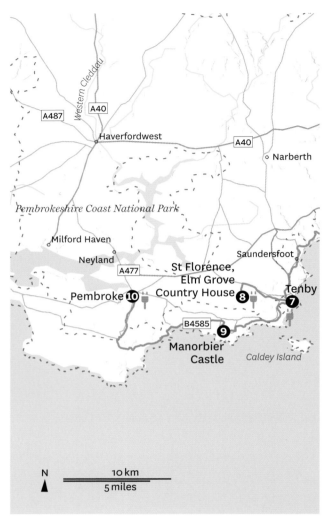

The enormous, dune-backed beach spilling east along Carmarthen Bay from the village of Pendine isn't simply an impressive bit of coastline. It's a piece of motoring history. As world land speed records nudged ever upwards in the early 20th century, road tracks were no longer suitable for such attempts – they simply weren't big enough to allow for the required acceleration and subsequent safe braking. But the flat, firm, smooth 7-mile (11km) beach at Pendine proved ideal. The first attempt here was made by Sir Malcolm Campbell on 25 September 1924. He set a record of 146.16mph (235.22kph) in his 350HP *Sunbeam Bluebird*; the following year he hit 150.87mph (242.8kph) here

– the first person to travel over 150mph. Fast-forward to June 2000, and Pendine was the venue for Don Wales – grandson of Sir Malcolm – setting the UK electric land speed record in *Bluebird Electric*, clocking 137mph (220.5kph). At the time of writing, a new state-of-the-art Pendine Sands Museum of Speed is under construction, which will explore this motoring history. Or explore the sands yourself, in other ways – numerous activities are available, including horse-riding, SUPing, land-yachting and kite buggying.

Above: Don Wales driving the *Bluebird Electric* at Pendine
Right: Dylan Thomas' writing shed, Laugharne

BIRDS & BARDS, COAST & CASTLES
Exit Gower for Carmarthenshire. First stop is Llanelli's WWT Wetland Centre, 20 miles (32km) from Rhossili on the Burry Inlet: its patchwork of lakes, lagoons, streams and marshes support some exotic birds (don't miss the flamingos) and are a haven for waders and wildfowl.

Then head 22 miles (35km) north, following the River Tywi into Carmarthen. The county capital was once the site of Roman Moridunum and alleged home of wizard Merlin – its Welsh name, Caerfyrddin, means Merlin's Fort. The County Museum reveals more local history, as does the Roman amphitheatre, and there's a burgeoning food scene, too – be sure to browse the indoor market.

Lovely Laugharne is 14 miles (23km) southwest, on the Taf Estuary. Dylan Thomas holed up here – explore his writing shed and boathouse, and follow his favourite walk, past the castle and harbour, to Sir John's Hill. Finish in Brown's, Dylan's pub of choice.

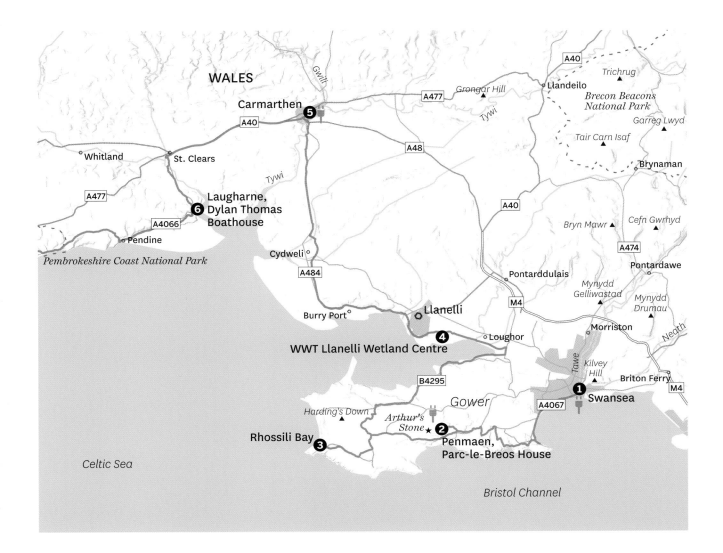

West of Laugharne, the road runs between marshes and wooded hills, kisses the coast at Pendine and then enters Pembrokeshire. After 17 miles (27km) you'll reach Tenby, where a charming harbour and brightly-painted Victorian houses are encircled by 13th-century walls. The beach is a beauty; at low tide, walk to St Catherine's Island. Alternatively, go mackerel fishing or sail to Caldey Island, home to grey seals and Cistercian monks.

Elm Grove Country House, 3 miles (5km) away, is a good base. From here, drive around the dazzling coast, stopping to climb the Norman turrets of Manorbier Castle. At Stackpole, trails lead to Barafundle Bay – possibly the UK's best beach – and Bosherston Lily Ponds, home to otters, dragonflies and a fanfare of water lilies in summer. Take the scenic route to reach Pembroke, 18 miles (29km) on, dominated by its 11th-century castle. Walk the walls and peer into the dungeons, follow Town Trail plaques for more history, and finish with tea and cake on the quayside.

→ **Distance: 219 miles (352km)** → **Duration: 5-10 days**

Cardiff to Conwy

WALES

Explore Wales from bottom to top, on a road trip between the thriving southern capital and the charismatic north coast, via two showstopping national parks and the little-visited mountains in the middle.

Wales is a small place of big space – as you'll discover quickly on a south-to-north drive that crams in the diverse expanses of Snowdonia, the Brecon Beacons and the Cambrian Mountains, a bit of The Valleys, a slice of the coast and, always, a sense of the wild.

CARDIFF & THE BRECON BEACONS

Cardiff has a real buzz. Linger here to visit the Norman-Victorian castle, regenerated Cardiff Bay and, on the outskirts, St Fagans National History Museum, a collection of re-erected historic buildings from across the country. And dive into the city's myriad pubs and restaurants, too.

But the Brecon Beacons beckon. Rising beyond the Valleys – the former heartland of Welsh industry – this national park encompasses sandstone summits, bold ridges, wild moors, waterfalls, lakes, rivers, a sprinkle of villages and properly dark skies. Get orientated at the visitor centre in Libanus, 40 miles (64km) north of Cardiff; it's near 2907ft (886m) Pen y Fan, the highest point in southern Britain and one of the park's most popular hikes. The riverside market town of Brecon, 5 miles (8km) on, is an attractive base, with a remarkable cathedral, streets lined with Georgian houses, and easy walks and cycles along the Monmouthshire & Brecon Canal.

© Simon Thompson / Fiat 500e Passion

Plan & prepare

Tips for EV drivers

Cardiff has several clusters of EV chargers but facilities become scarce as you head north into the less populated interior. Aberystwyth is a useful charging hub. Also look for chargers at visitor centres and attractions (such as the Brecon Beacons and Elan Valley info centres and at the Centre for Alternative Technology in Machynlleth).

Where to stay

The Metropole Hotel and Spa (metropole.co.uk) in Llandrindod Wells has been providing hospitality for 120-plus years. Guests can use the Rock Spa's gym, pool, sauna and steam rooms. It also has chargers. There are two four-star hotels, a range of serviced suites and self-catering cottages in Portmeirion village (portmeirion.wales) – guests can explore the site after daytrippers have departed, and charging facilities are available.

When to go

Spring, with its lambs, daffodils, wildflowers and mild temperatures, is a lovely time to visit. Summer is busier, though many parts of this route remain relatively uncrowded. Autumn is quiet and potentially crisp and misty – good for atmospheric walks. Dark winter nights are excellent for stargazing, though some attractions do close or reduce their operating hours during the low season.

Further info

Phone and internet connection can be poor in the countryside – don't rely on a data signal for directions. Road signs are written in Welsh and English; note, 'Araf' means 'Slow'. High winds can close the M4 Severn Bridge between England and Wales. The alternative is to cross via the M48 Severn Bridge or, if that's closed too, detour north toward Gloucester and cross via the A40.

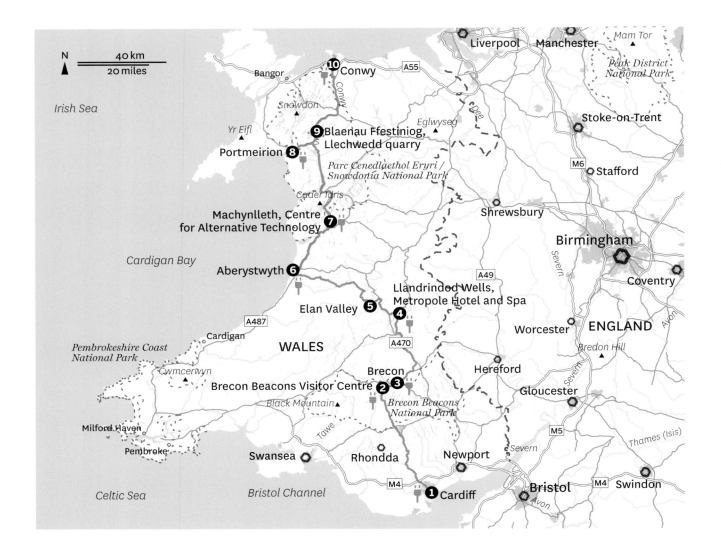

NORTH TOWARD CONWY

Beyond Brecon you're plunging into a rural hinterland where roads are tree-lined, hill-flanked or high-up with views to distant peaks. Follow the winding River Wye to Builth Wells, then continue to Llandrindod Wells, 28 miles (45km) from Brecon. Built around natural mineral springs, this spa town boomed in the mid-19th century – learn more on the self-guided town trail and indulge in some old-school wellness at the Metropole Hotel, where the Rock Spa's pools shimmer beneath a conservatory.

Then veer west for 10 miles (16km), tracing the River Wye to the old crossroads town of Rhayader (stop for shops and tea rooms, and spotting red kites). This is the gateway to the Cambrian Mountains' glorious Elan Valley, where a network of Victorian-era reservoirs has created the setting for one of Wales' most scenic drives. It's also a designated International Dark Sky Park. Drive 4 miles (6.4km) to the Elan Valley Visitor Centre before tracing the mountain

road that weaves around these glittering lakes. Then pick up the narrow, writhing route through the river valley to tiny Cwmystwyth. It continues to Devil's Bridge (allegedly built by the devil himself), where a tiered 300ft-high (91m) waterfall drops into a gorgeous ravine – walking trails lead to the cascade. Though the falls feel far removed from the world, it's only 12 miles (19km) from here to the university town and seaside resort of Aberystwyth. Stroll the prom and Victorian pier, visit the award-winning Arts Centre and the National Library of Wales, and take the cliff funicular up Constitution Hill for super views.

Head northeast for 18 miles (29km), much deeper into the Unesco Dyfi Biosphere Reserve, and you'll reach Machynlleth, a town with strong links to Welsh independence leader Owain Glyndŵr. Just beyond is the Centre for Alternative Technology, an eco-centre dedicated to greener living, where you can learn about everything from organic farming to renewable energy.

The Braveheart of Wales?

Owain Glyndŵr was born in Sycharth Castle in the Welsh Marches around 1359 to a wealthy family of the Anglo-Welsh gentry. But he went on to become the leader of a nationalist rebellion against English rule. Glyndŵr's uprising began in September 1400 in Ruthin, Denbighshire, following a land dispute with a neighbouring lord. To start, Glyndŵr and his followers seized many of the castles that English King Edward I had built a century or so earlier in order to suppress the Welsh. The first to fall was Conwy, in June 1401. The rebellion spread countrywide and by 1404, the castles of Cardiff, Carmarthen, Harlech, Aberystwyth and Caernarfon were all under siege. In the same year a *senedd* (parliament) was held in Machynlleth and Glyndŵr was crowned Prince of Wales. However, over the following years, the tide turned. The English regained their strongholds and Glyndŵr fled to the countryside. He continued to launch raids; the last known sighting of him was in 1412. A medieval townhouse in Machynlleth, thought to stand where the 1404 *senedd* was held, is now the Owain Glyndŵr Centre. The 135-mile (217km) Glyndŵr's Way National Trail, which cuts through the wildest mid-Wales countryside, also passes through the village.

Clockwise from top left:
Constitution Hill funicular, Aberystwyth; Owain Glyndŵr statue, Corwen; Devil's Bridge

Wales on a plate

Wales has upped its culinary game considerably in recent years. In 2022 Ynyshir, near Machynlleth, was named best restaurant in the UK – you'll need to book well in advance to get a table here, but there's plenty more to feast on across the country. Conwy is renowned for its mussels – the merging of the River Conwy's fresh water and the salty waters of the Irish Sea creates excellent conditions for these molluscs; seek them out in season (September to April). Welsh lamb has long had an excellent reputation, and salt-marsh lamb, reared in boggy coastal areas such as around Anglesey and Carmarthenshire, is particularly prized for its sweetness and tenderness. Look out also for laverbread (an intense seaweed puree), cawl (a comforting lamb-and-leek stew), bara brith (a tea-soaked fruit cake) and Glamorgan sausage (a meat-free banger made with cheese, leeks and breadcrumbs).

From left: lamb-and-leek cawl stew; Conwy Castle; working Welsh slate at Llechwedd Quarry

Then shift from the pioneering to the fantastical. Some 27 miles (44km) on, through the spectacular southern reaches of Snowdonia, past mighty mountain Cader Idris, rugged moorland and manmade Trawsfynydd Lake, seaside Portmeirion is a colourful Italianate confection of architectural whimsy. Designed by Sir Clough Williams-Ellis in the early 20th century, the village is brilliantly eccentric – pay a visit or, better, stay overnight.

Plunge back into Snowdonia, veering northeast via the rare Atlantic oak woodland of Coed Felenrhyd & Llennyrch. Around 12 miles (19km) on, you'll reach Blaenau Ffestiniog, a town that impresses and horrifies in equal measure. This was the 'slate capital of Wales' and its slopes are scarred by past industry. But there's now much enjoyment to be had amid all this desolation. First opened in 1846, Llechwedd Quarry has more latterly reinvented itself as the region's hub for white-knuckle thrills: navigate the disused mine by via ferrata, rope bridges and ziplines, tour the mine's darkest depths and bounce on underground trampolines.

The road continues through the mountains, passing lonely Dolwyddelan Castle and, after 11 miles (18km), the outdoorsy village of Betws-y-Coed, a great base for Snowdonia adventures. From here, drive north through the foothills, farms and villages of the verdant Conwy Valley; you'll soon pass Llanrwst, the valley's historic capital and home of Gwydir Castle, a grand Tudor mansion, allegedly haunted by several ghosts.

After 16 miles (26km), the valley leads into Conwy, one of the UK's best-preserved medieval towns, encased in 13th-century walls and dominated by a storybook eight-towered castle. Walk along the walls and down the cobbled alleys, happening upon galleries, bookshops, bakeries and Plas Mawr, an exceptional Elizabethan townhouse. Finish with fish and chips on the quayside, watching boats head out into the Irish Sea.

NORTHERN EUROPE

Below: harbourside
Skuespilhuset theatre,
Copenhagen
Right: the Great Belt
Bridge between
Zealand and Funen

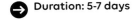

**Distance: 272 miles
(438km)**

Duration: 5-7 days

Copenhagen to Aarhus

DENMARK

Make a happy island-hop by EV, driving from Zealand to Funen to Jutland, encountering Vikings, inventors, fairy-tale-tellers, a toy town, a bog man and a whole lot more.

Frequently voted the world's happiest country, Denmark just seems to get it right. Things tend to work. Society is inclusive. Community spirit is high. Traditions endure. Progression is embraced. It's attractive too, full of sassy cities, cute old towns and rural countryside that's a pleasure to drive.

ZIPPING AROUND ZEALAND

If you're hiring an EV, spend a few days in Copenhagen before you do so. With its world-beating cycling infrastructure, great public transport and cruiseable waterways, the Danish capital isn't a city for driving. Explore hip Vesterbro, hippy Christiania, the uber-cool Designmuseum and the shamelessly fun Tivoli Gardens.

When you're ready, head 20 miles (32km) west to Roskilde to meet Denmark's medieval seafarers. The Viking Ship Museum displays five 11th-century vessels raised from Roskilde Fjord and painstakingly reconstructed; at nearby Museumsø (Museum Island) you can see boat-builders and blacksmiths at work. It's then an 80-mile (129km) drive southwest across pastoral Zealand to Korsør, on the Storebælt strait. Korsør was the main port for ferries plying the Great Belt until the 11-mile-long (18km) Great Belt Bridge made it possible to

Plan & prepare

Tips for EV drivers

The charging network (especially of fast and superchargers) is not as extensive in Denmark as elsewhere in Scandinavia, but is improving rapidly. The main centres (Copenhagen, Odense, Aarhus) have a good number of charging points; there are also chargers near the start of the Great Belt Bridge. Helpfully, the country's flat terrain isn't that draining on battery range.

Where to stay

Hotel Odeon in Odense (hotelodeon.dk) has marked guest spaces in the underground car park below; there are public chargers between some of these spaces. Hindsgavl Slot (hindsgavl.dk), in Middelfart, is an atmospheric castle hotel with a charger on site. Legoland Billund (legoland.dk) has a four-star hotel, a castle hotel and a holiday village with cabins, pirate rooms, tepees and a campsite; chargers are available.

When to go

June to August is the busiest but bonniest time to visit Denmark, with long days (almost 18 hours in mid-June), the most sunshine, the warmest temperatures and the greatest number of festivals. That said, Denmark's cities are year-round destinations, with plenty to enjoy even in winter, from world-class museums and restaurants to hunkering down in a cosy bar for candle-flickered *hygge*.

Further info

Denmark's borders are controlled – if arriving by road, rail or ferry (eg, overland from Germany or across the Øresund Bridge from Sweden), you'll need to show your passport. Denmark doesn't have toll roads but charges are levied on some bridges, including the Great Belt Bridge (Storebælts-forbindelsen; storebaelt.dk) between Zealand and Funen; fees can be paid by cash, card or, if your vehicle is registered, via the automatic BroBizz system (brobizz.com).

Bog on

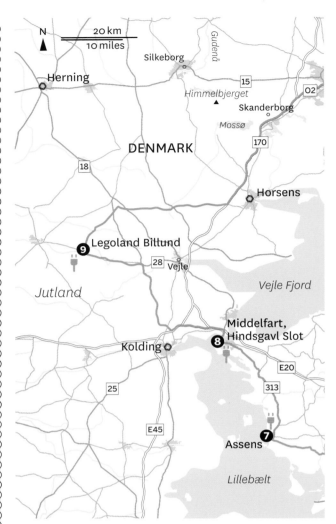

In 1952, peat-cutter Tage Busk Sørensen was digging near the village of Grauballe in central Jutland when his spade smacked into the shoulder of a 2400-year-old man. Freakishly well preserved by the surrounding bog, the naked male, aged around 35 years old, was lying on his stomach; he had smooth skin, a mop of auburn hair, stubble on his chin and a fatal knife wound across his throat. Buried in Nebelgaard Bog, 'Grauballe Man' is thought to have been the victim of an Iron Age sacrifice. He is now on display 25 miles (40km) away at the Moesgaard Museum (moesgaardmuseum.dk) in Højbjerg, a short, scenic drive south along the coast from Aarhus. The striking building has a sloping grassy roof that slides into the surrounding landscape, with views over woodland and the sea; in summer the roof is used as a stage and cycle track, and in winter it's great for sledding. The capacious, modern interior houses exhibits charting the story of humankind, using the latest research and dramatised retellings. Grauballe Man is the star attraction but you can also measure up against ancient hominids, handle a Viking rune stone and wade into an Iron Age battlefield.

Above: Moesgaard Museum, home of Grauballe Man
Right: Copenhagen's Nyhavn in bricks, Legoland

drive over, in around 10 minutes. Before your crossing, learn about pre-bridge days at the tiny Isbådsmuseet, and admire the colossal span stretching across the water.

FUNEN FUN

On the other side lies Nyborg, home to a stocky castle (where Denmark's first constitution was signed in 1282), a handsome main square and the Knudshoved Peninsula, where there are birds, trails and great views back across the strait. Odense, Denmark's delightful third city, is 18 miles (29km) west. Park at Hotel Odeon and walk into the pretty old centre – transformed by a pedestrianisation scheme – to the Hans Christian Andersen House, a unique delve into the life and stories of the writer who was born in Odense in 1805. Then follow a self-guided Andersen town trail, which visits his childhood home and more.

There are 123 castles and manors on Funen. Finest is Egeskov Slot, 20 miles (32km) south, a moated pink-brick

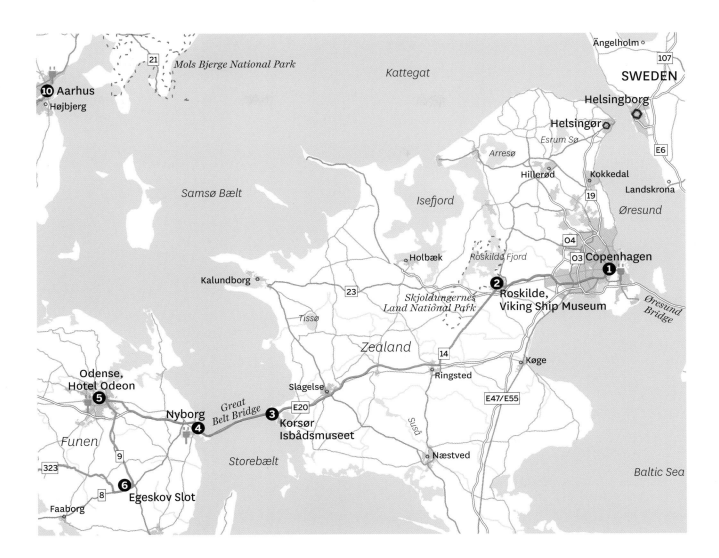

Renaissance pile. Roam its glorious gardens and great halls, and visit the quirky camping museum. You can't stay at Egeskov, but if you continue on through Funen, via lanes lined with thatched cottages and wildflowers, you'll reach Hindsgavl Slot, an 18th-century manor-cum-modern hotel, sitting prettily on the island's northwest tip.

JOURNEY TO JUTLAND

Two links – the Old and New Little Belt (Lillebælt) bridges – span the short gap between Funen and Jutland; the Old Bridge, dating to 1935, can also be conquered by a vertiginous Bridgewalk. Once in Jutland, drive 35 miles (56km) to Billund. Lego was founded here in 1932, and you can indulge in unadulterated Danish fun at the original Legoland, a sprawling theme-park built from a gazillion bricks. Admire the astonishing attention to detail in the models, from a mini Acropolis to a massive Sitting Bull, and enjoy the rides. There's accommodation, too.

Then meander north to Aarhus, the country's student-lively, culture-heavy, sustainability-focused second city. Contrast the half-timbered houses of Den Gamle By open-air museum with the Cubist ARoS art museum (capped by its dazzling rainbow walkway). The city's food scene rivals Copenhagen's – try goodies at the Aarhus Street Food Market or New Nordic cuisine at a Michelin-starred joint.

Below: topping up at one of Denmark's Clever fast-charging stations
Right: Lyngvig Lighthouse

➡ **Distance: 290 miles (467km)**   ➡ **Duration: 4-5 days**

West Jutland

DENMARK

The wild west coast of Jutland is shaped by sand and sea. On this leisurely EV road trip, take in sprawling beaches, lonely lighthouses and epic Viking tales.

akolk Beach, on the island of Rømø, is a jumble of colours and sounds. Gigantic kites flap in the wind, swimmers laugh as they brave the chilly waves and families set up beach chairs right in front of their cars. On this beach, like many others in Denmark, cars are allowed on dedicated areas. It's an exhilarating experience to drive right up to the sea – but be sure to stick to the solid stretches and to follow other vehicles, or risk getting stuck in the sand. If you do get in a jam, don't panic: there's usually a 4WD vehicle around to pull you out. Take care not to park too close to the surf, too, as the tide can come in fast.

Rømø itself is part of the Wadden Sea Unesco World Heritage Site, and on the east side of the island, you'll find rich wetlands where a feast for migrating birds is revealed at low tide. Learn more about the unique ecosystem surrounding the island at Naturcenter Tønnisgård, the starting point of guided activities like mudflat walks or oyster safaris.

RIBE TO THYBORON

After a night at Poppelgaarden B&B, it's time to hit the road: drive east across the causeway connecting Rømø to the mainland and follow the coastline north to Ribe.

© A. Aleksandravicius / Shutterstock

© CloudVisual / Shutterstock

Plan & prepare

Tips for EV drivers

Denmark's charging infrastructure is still limited compared to its neighbouring countries, but charging-station providers like Clever (clever.dk) and E.on (eon.dk) are continuously expanding. A good, general charging card like Shell Recharge (shellservice.dk/lynladning) will give access to nearly all AC chargers along the route, and rapid chargers along motorways – order it well ahead of your trip. For most of the route, you'll have to make do with slower AC chargers; find them via the Shell Recharge app.

Where to stay

With a thatched roof and red-painted walls, Poppelgaarden B&B (poppelgaarden-romo. dk) offers a warm welcome to rural Rømø. In Thyborøn, the Seaside Hotel (seasidehotel. dk) is central and great value for money. Overlooking the dunes, surfer-fiendly Guesthouse Klitmøller (guesthouse-klitmoller.dk) has a sauna and hot tub. Hotel Marie (facebook.com/ hotelmarieskagen) offers tasteful rooms In the middle of Skagen. All these options have public parking, and AC charging stations within walking distance.

When to go

Summer promises the best chance of good weather on Jutland's west coast, but the area is also crowded with holidaymakers at this time. The shoulder seasons are much quieter and often still sunny, but some restaurants and attractions will already be closed. Winter brings lots of *hygge* cosiness and sleepy towns, with places like Ribe's VikingeCenter and Skagen's Blink restaurant closing for the season.

Further info

If you're not bringing your own car, you can rent an EV (via sixt.com) in the nearest metropolis of Hamburg in Germany, which has good connections to most European hubs via rail and air. From Hamburg, it's just under three hours' drive to Rømø and about five-and-a-half hours back from Skagen. Denmark's well-maintained roads make for easy driving. The route includes some hilly sections, so do watch your range, and check the ferry timetable online before driving up. Check visitdenmark.com for more info.

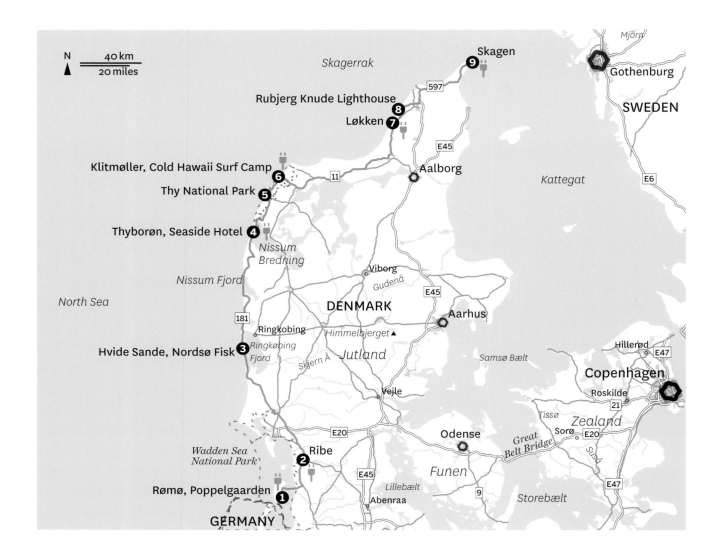

All half-timbered houses and cobbled streets, Ribe is Denmark's oldest town. Head northwest next, past the northern border of the Wadden Sea and onto a strip of land with a well-maintained road between the North Sea on the left and Ringkøbing Fjord on the right. Pause for a pit stop in coastal town Hvide Sande, where you can follow your nose to Nørdso Fisk, a shop selling the winning combination of fresh seafood and local beers. Enjoy a plate of fish and chips at one of the picnic tables outside, or take away a shrimp-loaded bun and drive on, heading further north.

The road borders high dunes that conceal miles of uninterrupted beach, with Lyngvig Lighthouse looking out over it all. To the east, you'll have a clear view of kite-surfers who take advantage of the ideal conditions – steady wind and small waves – on the consecutive fjords. Villages pop up every now and then, mostly made up of holiday homes with thatched or tiled roofs, until

the road ends in Thyboron, a fishing village separated from North Jutland by a small channel, and a good spot to overnight at the Seaside Hotel. Enjoy a stroll around town past the fish restaurants or along the beach to the Sneglehuset, a house completely covered in shells, started by a local fisherman in 1949.

COASTAL HIKES & SURF BREAKS

The next day, take the ferry across the channel and follow the road north, sticking close to the increasingly wild coast. On the beach at Stenbjerg, part of Thy National Park, fishing boats are pulled high onto the sand, out of reach of the churning waves. Get a hiking map at the park's Stenbjerg Visitor Centre and set out through the dunes on a trail to a forest of trees twisted into strange shapes by the ever-present wind. Back on the road, drive north to the small village of Klitmøller, which has been dubbed 'Cold Hawaii'. Even on a rainy

Viking Ribe

In 700 CE, the town of Ribe was founded as a Viking marketplace – making it not only Denmark's oldest town, but also an early hub of the Viking Age, which lasted from the 8th century until the 11th century. During this time, Scandinavian seafarers from Denmark, Sweden and Norway explored far and wide, trading – and raiding – across Western and Eastern Europe. In Ribe, the first marketplace was established on the banks of the Ribe River, where the excellent Museet Ribes Vikinger gives the lowdown on Viking history: permanent and temporary exhibitions cover everything from feats of navigation and intricate jewellery to the Vikings' sages and beliefs. Next, head out of town to the VikingeCenter (just a five-minute drive south) to see Viking history come alive. This living museum is especially great for kids: you can visit a reconstructed longhouse and assembly hall, and meet 'real-life' Vikings (a passionate staff of paid archaeologists, craftspeople and volunteers) for workshops on sword-fighting, archery and minting coins. Every year in May, the VikingeCenter hosts the International Viking Market, set up as a market would have been in Viking times, and with a bevy of crafts on sale and Viking-era activities.

Clockwise from top left: riding the wind on the Rømø coast; replica tools at Ribe's VikingeCenter; Klitmøller surf

Denmark's super seafood

As the coastline is never more than 30 miles (48km) away, wherever you are in Denmark, it's no surprise that the Danes do seafood exceptionally well. From picking oysters with your feet in the mud on Rømø to enjoying fine dining in the shadow of a lighthouse in Skagen, there are many ways to savour the seafood scene along the west coast of Jutland – but be sure to try some of Denmark's typical dishes. Enjoyed here since the Viking Age, *sild* – pickled, marinated herring – is one of the country's most popular seafood options, but it's a bit of an acquired taste. *Fiskefrikadeller* – fried fish cakes – are more of a crowd-pleaser, best enjoyed with a Danish remoulade, the jazzed-up, mayo-based 'national spread'. And you can't go wrong with *smørrebrød* (an open-face, rye-bread sandwich) with toppings like salmon and shrimp.

From left: Danish delicacies at Copenhagen's Torvehallerne Market; WWII bunkers on Løkken Beach, Jutland; Den Tilsandede Kirke, the 'sand-covered church', Skagen

day, you'll see dozens of surfers out in the bay enjoying the constant waves, shaped by a certain curve in the coast that makes them ideal for beginners. If you fancy a go, head to Cold Hawaii Surf Camp, where you can rent a board and wetsuit, or book a lesson. A bed for the night beckons at Guesthouse Klitmøller.

THE HOME STRETCH TO SKAGEN
Back on the road in the morning, head east and then north again to the coastal village of Løkken; you can drive past the beach huts and right onto the beach to take a refreshing dip, or settle down on the white sand and soak up some sun. A short drive north of the village, Rubjerg Knude Lighthouse sits high up on a crumbling cliff. In 2019, the edge of the cliff was getting dangerously close, so the whole brick-built lighthouse was put on rails and moved further inland, where it stands safely – for now.

The final stretch beckons: drive northeast beneath shimmering skies and through an increasingly barren landscape to the Skagen Peninsula, the country's northernmost tip. Skagen town has been drawing painters and writers for years. It overlooks the turquoise waters of the Kattegat, the strait lying between Denmark and Sweden that is typically so much calmer than the North Sea off to the west.

To end your trip on a high note, make a reservation for dinner at Blink. This small, seasonal restaurant in the stables of the old Grey Lighthouse was opened by three young friends wanting a fresh start away from Copenhagen. Begin with a glass of bubbly atop the lighthouse, which presides over the place where the Skagerrak and Kattegat straits meet, then sit down for a fabulous dinner celebrating local produce and seafood, with a view across the ever-present, irresistible sea.

Below: Temppeliaukio interior, Helsinki
Right: looking down on Nuuksio National Park

Distance: 121 miles (195km)

Duration: 2-3 days

Helsinki to Bengtskär

FINLAND

Setting out from Helsinki, this enjoyable road trip takes in the highlights of Finland's southern coast – from pioneering design to peaceful forests, ruined castles and a remote island in the cold northern seas.

Finland is a country of superlative geography – home to about 188,000 lakes, 180,000 islands and some 54 million acres (22 million hectares) of forest. Seeing it all sounds like an exhausting shift at the wheel, but it's very possible to get a long-lasting impression of its landscapes with a leisurely drive along the southern shore – steering from the hubbub of the capital to where a lonely lighthouse sparkles over the Baltic Sea.

INTO THE HINTERLAND FROM HELSINKI

Helsinki is one of Europe's design heavyweights – though no blueprint could ever fully contrive its sublime setting, huddled around a series of islet-studded bays. Architecture is the key draw here. There's the stocky battlements of the Suomenlinna – the fortress guarding the harbour – and the stately neoclassical facades of the Senaatintori square. Most memorable, perhaps, is Temppeliaukio: a space-age 1960s church, its copper dome floating ethereally over a nave of exposed bedrock.

Leaving Helsinki behind, you can very quickly find yourself in the Finnish wilderness. Half an hour from central Helsinki are the boreal forests, shallow valleys and serpentine lake of Nuuksio National Park. Keep your eyes peeled for lumbering elk, leaping squirrels and prowling

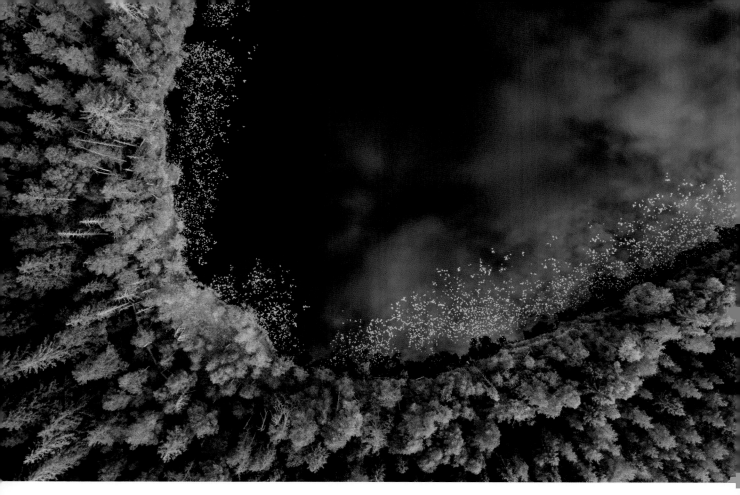

Plan & prepare

Tips for EV drivers

Some EV rentals are available at Helsinki Airport. There are abundant charging stations right across Helsinki; they become somewhat scarcer in rural corners of the south coast, though clusters can be found along Hwy 25 all the way to Hanko. Bear in mind that winter tyres are compulsory if you're driving anywhere in Finland from the beginning of December to the end of February.

Where to stay

Haltia Lake Lodge (haltialakelodge.com) offers a broad range of eco-conscious accommodation at the heart of Nuuksio National Park; staff can arrange canoeing, abseiling and fatbike excursions in the surrounding landscapes. Hanko's Regatta Spa Hotel (regattaspahotel.fl) opened as the Hotel Continental in 1900 – the name has changed but the Jugendstil architecture is as dapper as ever, with guest rooms done up in contemporary decor.

When to go

Finland is best visited in the summer months, when the days are long (or indeed endless), the landscape is blooming and the water temperature is more forgiving in the lakes – Midsummer celebrations in late June are an undisputed highlight. The shoulder seasons also have their appeal, with landscapes thawing in April and May, and russet-red leaves in autumn forests. Unlike Lapland, southern Finland isn't a typical winter destination – though the northern lights can occasionally be seen flaring up in the heavens.

Further info

Elk straying onto the roads is a key hazard of driving in southern Finland – the risk of a collision with these weighty creatures (known as moose in the US) is particularly acute during autumn, especially around dawn and dusk. If you need to swerve to avoid an elk, try to steer well behind its rear legs – they rarely change course once they're on the move.

Home Swede Home

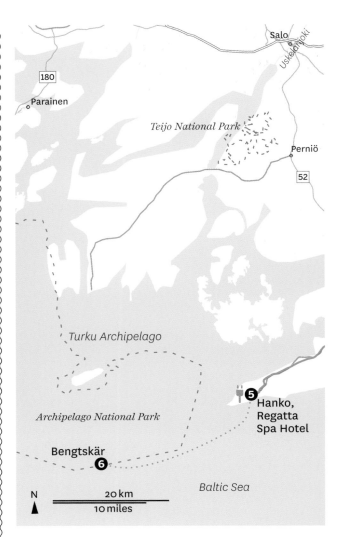

Finnish is a proud language – part of a family entirely distinct from the Indo-European languages that dominate modern Europe and much of the Middle East and South Asia. That said, when travelling along the southern coast you're quite likely to hear local people conversing in another tongue: Swedish. There are around half a million Swedish speakers in Finland. A Swedish presence along this coastline dates back to medieval times and the Northern Crusades – which Swedes allegedly initiated on the (dubious) pretext of converting pagan Finns to Christianity. By the 19th century, language had become intertwined with class politics: Swedish was the language of administration, education

and government in Finland, while Finnish was the language of the peasantry. Only after Finland became fully independent did Finnish complete its 20th-century resurgence: both languages were given equal official status in 1923, a status quo that continues to this day. Today the old linguistic tensions of the past have dissipated and many people along the south coast are happily bilingual. Indeed, many Finnish national heroes were native Swedish speakers – including Tove Jansson, creator of the *Moomins* books, and Jean Sibelius, titan of classical music.

Above: the Sibelius Monument in its namesake Helsinki park
Right: Bengtskär Lighthouse

lynx as you wander the trails; afterwards, hibernate in an elegant glamping pod at Haltia Lake Lodge, perched among pines and with charging stations nearby.

Waking up to birdsong, drive through yet more forests to find Fiskars – a leafy model village beside the Fiskars River that grew from a 17th-century ironworks. Crowned by a stately clock tower, it has evolved into a hub for artisans, with boutiques dedicated to furniture, glassware, ceramics and very sharp kitchen knives. Follow the river on south and you'll soon reconnect with the southern coast, the smell of saltwater wafting in from the Gulf of Finland.

BOUND FOR BENGTSKÄR

Keeping a lonely watch over this stretch of coast is ruined Raseborg Castle – a medieval bastion built when Sweden, the Hanseatic League and Denmark vied for control of the region. The presence of another great power looms further west in Hanko, perched at the end of a narrow peninsula.

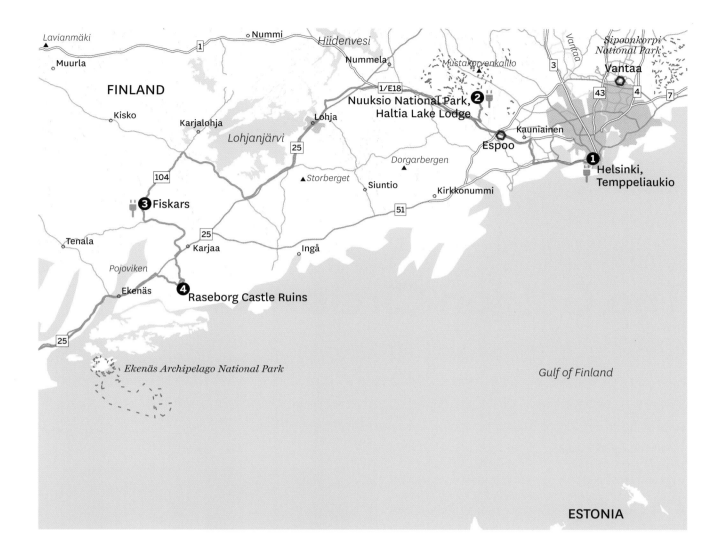

Hanko thrived as a spa resort under Russian control in the 19th century, and today its seafront is lined with Art Nouveau mansions from an era when St Petersburg aristocrats spent their summers by the sea. Among these marvels is the Regatta Hotel – restored to its former glory, with rooms looking out to a sandy beach.

Hanko stands at the southernmost point of mainland Finland – the tarmac runs out at its port, but little crumbs of Finnish territory extend deep into the Baltic Sea. Squint and you'll spot skerries strewn across the horizon. To see them up close, park your EV and buy a ticket to board the MS *Summersea*, which makes daily summer departures from Hanko to the lonely Bengtskär Lighthouse. Built in 1906, it's the tallest lighthouse in the Nordic nations, rising a lofty 171ft (52m) from a wave-lashed lump of granite in the Baltic. During WWII, Finnish forces repelled Soviet gunships that attempted to destroy it, and to this day Bengtskär remains a shining beacon of Finnish identity.

➡ **Distance: 193 miles
(311km)**

➡ **Duration: 4-6 days**

The Golden Circle

ICELAND

Elemental forces collide in a drive around Iceland's most famous landmarks, taking in effortlessly cool Reykjavík, geothermal wonders, thundering waterfalls and an historic park where worlds collide.

A city that punches way above its weight, Reykjavík is small enough to walk around but packed with creative, cosmopolitan people, colourful street art, museums, galleries, live-music venues, edgy bars and legendary nightlife. It's a great place to start and end your trip, its joyfully quirky character immediately obvious as you stroll main drag Laugavegur, make your way up to the towering Hallgrímskirkja, or take in a show at the National Gallery or Nýlistasafnið, the Living Art Museum.

In the evening, settle in for some local specialities at Íslenski Barinn and follow it up by starting the night's partying at the unassuming-looking Kaffibarinn, one of the city's most famous hangouts.

ÞINGVELLIR TO LAUGARVATN

The following morning, take time for any hangover to abate – though the 45-minute drive to Þingvellir National Park will blow final cobwebs away. Here, a snaking walkway leads through a giant rift in the Earth's surface where the Eurasian and North American tectonic plates diverge. In a natural amphitheatre nearby, the world's oldest parliament, the Alþingi, was founded by the Vikings in 930 CE. Walk to the impressive Öxarárfoss to see fissures and lava tubes, then drop into the Hakið Visitor

Plan & prepare

Tips for EV drivers

You can rent EVs at Keflavík Airport, which is about 40 minutes' drive west of Reykjavík. Chargers are plentiful in town but a little more scarce in other areas – though accessible enough to make this route perfectly feasible. It's a good idea to plan well ahead, especially if you're driving in winter: it may take longer to charge your car, and range can be adversely affected by the cold temperatures.

Where to stay

Miðgarður (centerhotels. com) is a slinky-smart hotel at one end of Reykjavík's main shopping street; or opt for artworks and designer furniture at 101 Hotel (101hotel.is). In Laugarvatn, Héraðsskólinn Historic Guesthouse (heradsskolinn. is) is a reimagined 1920s schoolhouse with simple but cosy rooms; further south, Sólheimar Ecovillage (solheimar.is) offers B&B and comfortable apartments. Hveragerði's sleek INNI Boutique Apartments (inniapartments.is) sleep up to four.

When to go

Long days and better weather make May to September the best time to visit. Music lovers should time a visit to coincide with the Secret Solstice Festival in June or Iceland Airwaves in November. Independence Day on June 17th sees festivities across the country, while Reykjavík bursts into action for its Arts Festival in June and again in late August for Culture Night, when there are lots of events and free entry to museums and galleries.

Further info

With good roads (even in some of the most remote stretches of this route) and generally light traffic across the nation, driving in Iceland is far easier than some visitors expect. However, your transport choices may be restricted during winter: roads can close after heavy snowfalls, with mountain passes often cut off until mid-June and some roads only accessible to 4WD vehicles.

Icelandic delicacies

You'd need a strong stomach for some of Iceland's traditional foods, most of which were borne out of necessity in a land where the soil is sparse and the winters long and harsh. Nothing was wasted, and drying, salting, smoking, pickling and fermenting were used to preserve whatever could be gleaned from the land and sea. Although you're unlikely to encounter *svið* (boiled sheep's head), *súrsaðir hrútspungar* (ram's testicles) or *hákarl* (fermented shark) other than at Þorrablót, the Icelandic midwinter feast, you should look out for contemporary fusion foods, especially in Reykjavík. Dill, the city's first Michelin-starred restaurant, serves delicacies such as dung-smoked lamb with pickled angelica shoots, and beef-fat caramel with Arctic thyme. Another option teaming traditional recipes with contemporary thinking is Matur og Drykkur, which is set in a former salt-fish factory and produces dishes like pickled beef tongue with horseradish, and reindeer croquettes with pine emulsion. Kaffi Loki by Hallgrímskirkja offers a more affordable take on home-style dishes such as *plokkfiskur* (pulled fish) and rye-bread ice cream, though possibly best of all is Sægreifinn, a simple shack by the harbour that's renowned for its lobster soup.

Above: head to Sægreifinn in Reykjavík for lobster soup
Right: Strokkur geysir eruption

Center to learn about the folklore, geology and heritage that makes this place so special.

Next, make your way east along Rte 365 towards Laugarvatn (Hot Springs Lake), where you can laze in a geothermal steam bath overlooking two volcanoes. Slide into the warm waters at the Fontana Spa, sit in steam rooms where you can hear natural hot springs boiling below, then cool off with a dip in the lake. Suitably relaxed, check into the Héraðsskólinn Historic Guesthouse, then walk to Lindin to dine on arctic char or reindeer burgers, or drive 10 minutes east to Hlöðuloftið for Icelandic-style farm-to-fork dining.

WONDERFUL WATERS

In the morning, set off through the wilds towards Geysir, the hot-water spout after which all others are named. Although the original geyser here is now considered inactive, its neighbour Strokkur erupts every few minutes

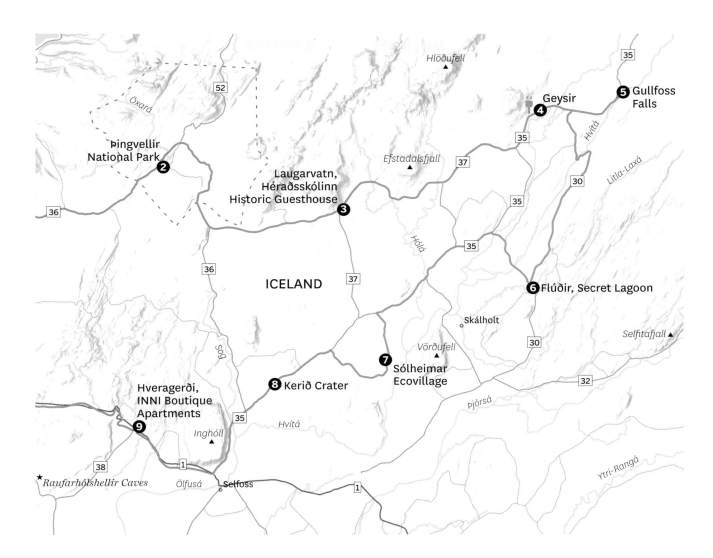

to heights of up to 65ft (20m). Around it are multiple steam vents, colourful hot springs and bubbling mud-pits.

From Geysir, it's a 10-minute drive to Gulfoss, a spectacular cascade thundering down a narrow ravine. Glacial waters from the Hvítá River tumble over a double drop here, and on the approach it appears that the water simply disappears. Walk to the lookout, however, and you'll see a magnificent display – especially on a sunny day, when the spray creates rainbows in the mist.

From the falls, it's a half-hour drive south along Rte 30 to Flúðir, where greenhouses warmed by geothermal activity grow the country's vegetables. Enjoy the spoils of the elemental Earth here with a dip in the Secret Lagoon, Iceland's oldest swimming pool. Low-key and unassuming, it's a glorious place to relax, with three mini-geysers spouting along the edge of the pool. Stop for lunch about 10 minutes' drive away at Friðheimar farm near Reykholt, where you can tour the greenhouses, learn

Diving at Silfra

The only place in the world where you can dive between two tectonic plates, the Silfra fissure in Þingvellir makes the most extraordinary dive site. The fissure is filled with meltwater from the Langjökull glacier, which will have been filtered through lava fields over decades and emerges so clear you can expect visibility of up to 328ft (100m). You'll start by floating through the Big Crack – where you can touch both continents at the same time – then emerge into the widest section of the fissure, Silfra Hall, before descending into the Silfra Cathedral, where the water is deep blue and the steep canyon walls descend to 207ft (63m). The fissure's water hovers just above freezing point year-round, but you'll be given a dry suit and thermals; and if you're not a certified dry-suit diver, you can snorkel instead.

From left: snorkelling Silfra; Kerið crater; hiking along the Varmá River to Reykjadalur

about Icelandic horses and feast on all manner of tomato treats, from fresh soups to tomato beer and schnapps.

Twenty minutes' drive further southwest, you'll arrive at Sólheimar Ecovillage. A visionary project founded in 1930, it's home to about 100 residents as well as a shop, cafe, art gallery, bakery, organic greenhouses and forestry projects. Check in for the night, tour the weaving, carpentry, fine-art and herbal workshops, and pick up some artwork, organic soap or cosmetics made from Icelandic plants.

CLOSING THE CIRCLE

In the morning, stop off at Kerið, a 3000-year-old volcanic crater; steps lead down the steep iron-red banks of the caldera to an emerald lake. It's a good spot for a morning walk before heading to Hveragerði, about 20 minutes' drive away, where more greenhouses dot the landscape. The town is also home to a horticultural college, and thanks to the highly active geothermal field here, you can see bananas and papayas growing. Hveragerði sits right on the Mid-Atlantic Ridge, and mud-pots, hot springs and pools bubble away right in the centre, but a better bet is to hike up the valley to Reykjadalur, where a hot spring feeds the thermal Varmá River: sit in the warm water surrounded by a landscape of lush hills peppered with fumaroles and mud-pits.

Check into the fabulously chic INNI Apartments, then head to Ölverk for pizza and geothermally-brewed beer. From here, it's just a 45-minute drive in your EV back into Reykjavík, but if you have the time and the battery reserves for just one more detour, it's worth nipping south to Raufarhólshellir, one of the longest lava caves in the country. Formed over 5000 years ago during the Leitahraun eruption, the cave extends to 4462ft (1360m); in winter the trapped air creates striking ice formations inside – a sparkling end to one of the world's most impressive routes.

Below: driving through
Berserkjahraun lava
field, Snæfellsnes
Right: Icelandic horses

➜ **Distance: 202 miles
(325km)**

➜ **Duration: 4-5 days**

Reykjavík to the Snæfellsnes Peninsula

ICELAND

Travel through some of Iceland's most extraordinary landscapes, and hear tales of hidden folk and legendary sagas, on this trip from Reykjavík to the country's less-visited western edge.

Reykjavík has more than enough distractions to fill a few days, whether your tastes run to postmodern art or microbreweries – but the west is calling. Ground zero of many of the country's sagas, the Snæfellsnes Peninsula feels a little wilder than the rest of the country. You wouldn't be too surprised to come across a troll on one of its black beaches or find the mythical 'hidden people' known as *huldufólk* rummaging through the luggage in your car boot.

On your way to this fabled land, call into the Settlement Center in Borgarnes, 46 miles (74km) north of the capital. The museum provides a good grounding in the origins of Iceland's sagas, and a fine bowl of fish soup in its restaurant.

ON TO SNÆFELLSNES
It's 60 or so miles (100km) to Snæfellsnes, and you'll experience a slow dropping-away of the world as you travel on, particularly in low season. Cars disappear from the road, settlements start to thin and soon it's just you and the odd field of Icelandic horses, who observe your trundling progress with mild curiosity. You'll find more curious fauna at Ytri Tunga beach – a colony of seals often bask on the rocks here.

© David Noton / Lonely Planet

Tips for EV drivers

The main airport, Keflavik, offers EVs at its rental desks. You should check with the hire company whether it's OK to take the car on Iceland's smaller, rougher F roads; many stipulate against this. There are charge points in cities, towns and popular tourist sites. The Snæfellsnes Peninsula has few settlements, so make sure you know where your next charging point is before setting off.

Where to stay

101 Hotel (101hotel.is) in central Reykjavík has a lovely bar and restaurant, and a plunge-pool in its basement spa. Hotel Búðir (hotelbudir.is) offers stylish accommodation overlooking the church in Búðir; the food is particularly good. Við Hafið Guesthouse, Ólafsvík (booking.com), has private rooms and dorms, and can help book local activities. Converted from a 1930s monastery, Hotel Franciskus (fransiskus.is) in Stykkishólmur has neutrally decorated, eminently comfortable rooms.

When to go

There's a stark beauty to the country in winter (November to March), though bear in mind that days can be very short, with the sun rising at 11am and setting around 3pm. The payoff is that you've plenty of opportunities to see the northern lights. There are many more hours of daylight to play with over summer – the sun never fully sets between May and August. July and August see the most tourists, so avoid Iceland's main sites then if you're averse to crowds. For the best chance to spot whales, come in June or July.

Further info

Car headlights must be turned on at all times. The top speed on highways is 55mph (88kph). Be prepared to change plans if visiting in winter – main roads are quickly cleared of snow, but minor roads may not be. Sign up to safetravel.is for general travel alerts and warnings. Dial 112 in emergencies. The tourist board (visiticeland.com) has tons of info and inspiration.

Snæfellsnes stories

Since it was first settled in the 9th century, Iceland has been a land of myths and legends. A tradition of oral storytelling has been passed down through the centuries – with imaginations fuelled by long, dark winters spent sharing tales round the fire, and perhaps stirred by the country's otherworldly landscapes, too. Many of the stories are rooted in fact, but have been embellished along the way: take Bárður Snæfellsás. The son of a human mother and a half-giant, half-troll father, he is said to have floated to Iceland on a glacier. On landing, he clapped eyes on Snæfellsjökull volcano and was inspired to give the peninsula the name Snæfellsnes ('Snow Mountain Peninsula'). After a family incident that ended with his daughter Helga being pushed onto an iceberg and drifting to Greenland, Bárður retreated into the glacier and was never seen again. He soon became known as the guardian spirit of the peninsula, protecting all who ventured this way. Assuming you don't stumble across him on the glacier, you can come face to face with Bárður at Arnarstapi – there's a giant stone statue of the bearded, hat-wearing legend right by the beach.

Clockwise from top left:
Bárður Snæfellsás statue, Arnarstapi; Búðakirkja, Búðir; basalt cliffs and sea stacks at Lóndrangar

Spend the night at lovely Hotel Búðir, which has a surprisingly urban aesthetic given its rural location; the locally sourced food it serves will likely be a highlight of your trip. Peer out of one of the hotel's south-facing windows to spy Búðir's black wooden Búðakirkja (church), beautiful in its simplicity; look east and you might see Snæfellsjökull, the snow-topped volcano that's said to have inspired Jules Verne's *Journey to the Centre of the Earth*.

Driving on the following morning, leave your EV at Fosshotel Hellnar and take a windswept coastal hike to the old fishing village of Arnarstapi and back, passing the natural rock arch of Gatklettur on your way. You'll

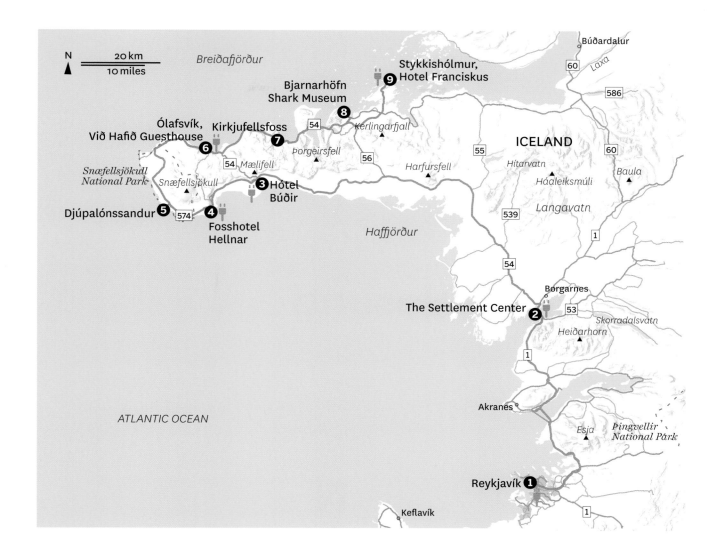

have worked up an appetite by the time you return to the hotel, so stay for lunch. Back behind the wheel again, with Snæfellsjökull a brooding presence to your right, the coastal road around the peninsula takes you to two sites that look lifted straight from a fantasy film: the craggy basalt cliffs and sea stacks at Lóndrangar, and the black lava beach at Djúpalónssandur.

The road continues on through Snæfellsjökull National Park. You'll constantly be hopping in and out of the car to stop at other black-sand beaches and to take photos as the light shifts across the landscape. The car will be glad of a charge at your overnight stop, Við Hafið Guesthouse in Ólafsvík, and you'll be glad of a cuppa at Útgerðin, an art gallery, shop and cafe.

SNÆFELLSNES' NORTHERN COAST

Set the alarm early the next day in order to arrive at Kirkjufellsfoss, 14 miles (23km) east, by sunrise. The waterfall, with the witch-hat-shaped mountain of Kirkjufell behind, is especially magical at dawn. More magic reveals itself on the next stage: the drive through the ethereal lava field of Berserkjahraun to Bjarnarhöfn Shark Museum. Iceland's last producer of *hákarl* (fermented shark), the family-run farm is the place to try the strong, sour taste of the ethically sourced fish. Dishes for less adventurous palates are available in the smart bistro here.

End your trip by driving 15 miles (24km) to Stykkishólmur on the peninsula's northern tip, and trying a different mode of transport. With your EV charging at Hotel Franciskus, hop to a boat and leave the land of the Snæfellsnes Peninsula for a while. Whales pass this way between March and July, and operators in town can take you out to see them.

Below: Hanseatic-era
Bryggen, Bergen
Right: Seven Sisters
Waterfall, Geirangerfjord

➡ **Distance: 396 miles (638km)**   ➡ **Duration: 7-8 days**

Bergen to Ålesund

NORWAY

For most people, Norway is synonymous with its fjords, and this trip takes in some of the mightiest of them – along with three gorgeous National Scenic Routes that climb over sky-high mountain passes.

Norway's west coast is characterised by one feature: fjords. Carved out by glaciers during the last Ice Age, these deep, sheer-sided inlets slash the western seaboard into ribbons, necessitating numerous ferries, bridges and detours to navigate a frustratingly circuitous journey. But while road trips in fjordland definitely take a while, there's an upside: the jaw-dropping scenery that unfurls around every corner. Huge cliffs, glittering waters, cascades, mountain passes, meadows – you'll encounter them all here.

BERGEN TO FLÅM
We begin in Bergen, arguably Norway's most handsome city. An old trading port stacked steeply around seven hills and seven fjords, it's known for its colourful, timber-clad buildings and its long history as a member of the Hanseatic League, the trading network that once extended across northern Europe. Wander around the Unesco World Heritage-listed buildings of Bryggen, visit the KODE galleries and museums, catch the cable car to the top of Mt Fløyen and sample some local seafood at the city's fish market.

From Bergen, take your EV onto the fjordside E16 as it twists and turns inland, offering a fine introduction to

Plan & prepare

Tips for EV drivers

Norway has proportionally more EVs on the road than anywhere else in Europe. There's an extensive nationwide system of public chargers, including at car parks, supermarkets and shopping centres. Of the many providers, major players include Recharge (rechargeinfra.com), Ionity (ionity.eu), Mer (no.mer.eco) and Eviny (eviny.no). At some charge points you pay by credit card; others require the operator's app. Plan charges carefully, as steep mountain roads and cold temperatures drain batteries fast.

Where to stay

Not all hotels in Norway have EV chargers, but there is nearly always somewhere to top up close by. The chateau-esque Hotel Park (hotelpark.no) is in a pretty part of Bergen: the nearest chargers are at GriegsGarajen car park. Fretheim Hotel (fretheim-hotel.com) is a mountain chalet in Flåm, while Fossheim Hotel (fossheimhotel.no) in Lom is a timber-clad inn typical of many in rural Norway. Hotel Brosundet (brosundet.no) in Ålesund makes for a stylish last night, in a renovated waterfront warehouse.

When to go

Since this route traverses three mountain passes, it's only doable in the Norwegian summer. Usually the roads are open between May and September, but this depends on each year's snowmelt: snow could be gone by late April, or linger into July. In most cases there's a workaround via main roads, but you'll be missing out on the sights offered by the Nasjonale Turistveger (National Scenic Routes). You don't have to worry about finding ferries: they run across the fjords pretty much year-round.

Further info

Nearly all major roads in Norway are subject to tolls. These operate on an ANPR (automatic number-plate recognition) system: you are snapped by cameras, and charges are levied according to how far you drive. If you're hiring a car, the cost can come as a shock: you'll only find out the final bill at the end of your rental. Given you'll be driving an electric vehicle, you're in luck: they all qualify for reduced rates.

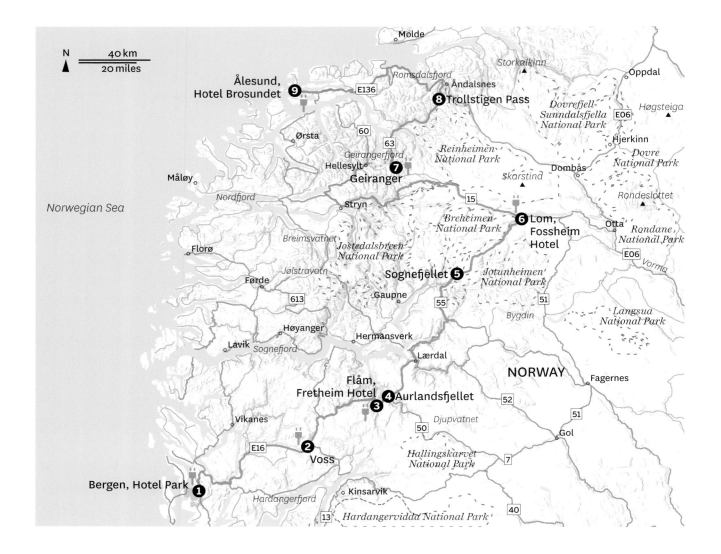

the fjord-filled scenery that awaits. Next stop is Voss, a centre for adventure sports: given a chance, local activity providers will have you rafting, mountain-biking, paragliding and hiking in the hills. You could also simulate a skydive inside the VossVind tunnel: all the fun of freefall with zero chance of turning into a cowpat.

Take an overnight break in Flåm, a small fjordside town that's best-known as the terminus of the Flåmsbana, a miraculous mountain railway that hauls itself up 2841ft (866m) in altitude, via gradients of 1:18 in places, to the top of the snowbound Hardangervidda Plateau. If you have time, it's worth jumping on board for a trip: it only takes an hour or so to reach the summit.

SCENIC ROUTES TO GEIRANGERFJORD

East of Flåm, on the way to Lærdal, is the first of the three Nasjonale Turistveger: Aurlandsfjellet, known locally as the Snøvegen (Snow Road) for fairly self-

explanatory reasons. It climbs precipitously over the mountains via a 4285ft (1306m) pass that's snowbound much of the year: usually it's only passable from June to mid-October. If you decide to brave it, don't miss a pit stop at the striking Stegastein Viewpoint, a curving platform which reaches right out over Sognefjord. If you'd rather stick to the main road, the E16 highway provides a year-round alternative.

From Lærdal, catch the ferry across the still waters of Sognefjord, then turn northeast towards Gaupne, which marks the start of our second Nasjonale Turistveger: Sognefjellet. This is another mind-bogglingly beautiful mountain drive, often billed as 'the road over the roof of Norway'. It climbs up into the heights of Jotunheimen National Park, a stark landscape of plateaus, peaks and lakes that remains snow-dusted well into summer. Near the mountain lodge at Sognefjellshytta, you'll top out at 4705ft (1434m) – officially the highest pass in Northern

Fjord facts

The fjords might appear ancient and unchanging, but they're actually quite young in geological terms. They were formed during the Last Glacial Period, which we colloquially know as the Ice Age. Most of Norway was covered by the great ice cap that stretched over most of the northern hemisphere, in places reaching thicknesses of up to 1.25 miles (2km). For about 100,000 years, from approximately 115,000 to 11,700 years ago, the shifting ice gouged out valleys, sharpened peaks, carved out cliffs and sliced mountain ridges, creating Norway's distinctive topography. Gradually, as temperatures began to warm, the ice sheets retreated and the glaciers melted. This released huge quantities of meltwater that flooded the valleys and submerged large portions of the coastline, creating the fjords as we see them today. Incredibly, it's estimated that sea levels may have risen by as much as 300ft (100m). In total, there are some 1190 fjords scattered around Norway's coast. The longest and deepest is Sognefjord, which runs for 127 miles (204km) and reaches depths of more than 4265ft (1300m). It's often known as the King of the Fjords – and once you've cruised down it, it's hard to disagree.

Clockwise from top left: the Flåmsbana; the Sognefjord's Nærøyfjord arm; the Snøvegen's Stegastein Viewpoint

Norway's National Scenic Routes

The Nasjonal Turistveger (nasjonaleturistveger.no) is a network of 18 roads around Norway, selected for their wondrous scenery. They traverse coast, forests, meadows, plains and plateaus, crisscrossing the country from the southern coastline all the way to the Arctic Ocean. Several are closed by snowfall in winter; others navigate inhospitable terrain that has demanded all kinds of ingenious engineering solutions, showcasing the skill, dedication and ingenuity of the nation's road builders. To enhance the driving experience, teams of architects, designers, landscapers and artists have been commissioned to create artworks and architecture along the routes, ranging from viewing platforms to bird-hides, walkways, bridges and shelters. There surely aren't many roads in the world where the lavatories look more like abstract sculptures than public conveniences – but Norway always does things just a little differently.

Clockwise from top left:
Atlanterhavsvegen National Scenic Route; the Trollstigen; Lom's superb stave church

Europe. The snow sometimes doesn't melt until early July here, although the road is usually open from May to September. No question about it: this is one of Norway's most unforgettable drives.

You might think the scenery can't get any grander, but you'd be wrong. After a night in Lom (notable for its fine stave church), roll west along Rv15 as far as Hornindalsvatnet, then detour back via the Fv60 to Hellesylt. It seems like a bit of a roundabout route, but there's a very good reason for it: it gives you the chance to catch the car ferry along Geirangerfjord, the world-famous, Unesco-listed, ultra-photogenic fjord that makes it into pretty much every Norwegian tourism ad campaign. It really is majestic: sky-high cliffs, sapphire-blue water, waterfalls thundering down from the heights – tick, tick, tick.

THE TROLLSTIGEN

Disembark at Geiranger and follow the twisting Fv63 north to Eidsdal, where you'll cross another fjord before embarking on our last National Scenic Route, the most famous of all: the legendary Trollstigen (Troll's Road). This switchbacking, serpentine road traverses 13 huge loops as it climbs up to Trollstigen Pass at 2789ft (850m). It's the kind of road that really does make you wonder about the sanity of its builders: at several points, waterfalls cascade right over the tarmac, and avalanches are quite common (one smashed into the Trollstigen Cafe in 2022). As well as along the Trollstigen, definitely make sure you stopped for a selfie at the viewpoint at Ørnesvingen, a rust-red steel viewing platform that cantilevers vertiginously out over the valley.

ON TOWARD ÅLESUND

After conquering the Trollstigen, things get less heart-stoppingly steep as you descend towards Romsdalsfjord, turning west at Åndalsnes onto the E136, which provides fjord views all the way to Ålesund. This elegant coastal city has some of the best examples of Jugendstil (Art Nouveau) architecture in Norway. Stretch your legs with the 418-step hike to Kniven Viewpoint, the summit of Aksla Hill, for a knockout panorama over the city and the Norwegian Sea beyond. There's nowhere on the west coast that's better for taking in a sunset.

 **Distance: 390 miles
(628km)**

Duration: 5-6 days

Oslo to Stavanger

NORWAY

Norway's southern shore might lack the fjords, but it has a seaside charm all of its own. Follow the coast from the dynamic capital of Oslo through timber-framed towns and sandy beaches to stylish Stavanger.

© Evikka / Shutterstock

Few travellers take the time to explore Norway's south shore, and that's a pity. This is an ideal area to experience small-town Norwegian life: old fishing harbours, lighthouses, coves, sandy beaches and countless rocky skerries, to which Oslo families flock in summer.

Kick off with a few days in the capital, Oslo – a city as stylish and cosmopolitan as its neighbours Stockholm and Copenhagen, but one that doesn't always receive the same kudos. Essential sights include the Nasjonalgalleriet, home to the nation's foremost art collection (including Munch's original version of *The Scream*); the immersive exhibits at the Fram Polar Exploration Museum; and Viking treasures at the Historisk Museum. Renting a bike is a great way of getting around here, and gives you the chance to tour the city's parks – including Frognerparken and Ekebergparken, with their sculpture trails.

TRACING THE COAST FROM OSLO

Head southwest from the city via Drammen, and out along the shores of Oslofjord. The main E18 highway is fastest, but you can also follow the much more circuitous coast road to reach Risør, a classic seaside town that sets the tone for others along the south shore. Admire the handsome clapboard buildings and perhaps take a boat

Plan & prepare

Tips for EV drivers

The south coast is well stocked with EV chargers, with the main clusters around larger towns and cities. Quiet coastal roads have the best views, but accelerating between twists and turns may drain your battery quicker – and many villages don't have chargers. Oslo is one of the world's most EV-friendly cities: you get discounts of up to 75% on toll roads, and reduced-cost parking at many car parks. EVs are even allowed to drive in the bus lanes.

Where to stay

The south coast has a good selection of hotels, and plenty of cabins and campsites for self-caterers. Hotel Bristol (hotelbristol.no) is a landmark in central Oslo, handy for the Nasjonalgaleriet. Spread over multiple buildings, rooms at Egersund's Grand Hotell (grand-egersund. no) range from timber-clad traditional to functional Scandi-modern. The Sola Strand (solastrandhotel.no) near Stavanger overlooks a dune-backed beach and has a stylish spa. All three options have on-site EV chargers.

When to go

The south coast gets very busy in summer, for obvious reasons. This is one of the sunniest areas of Norway, and in the holiday months of July and August, plenty of families from Oslo, Stavanger and other big cities head for the coast and its many attractive islands. Winter, by contrast, is all but deserted in many areas: outside the towns, the hotels, cafes and seasonal restaurants tend to shut up shop for the winter months.

Further info

Stavanger is a good location for continuing this southern drive up into Norway's fjordland. The E39 runs north from Stavanger along the west coast and past its numerous islands and inlets, but it's not a standard road trip: along the way to Bergen, you'll have to negotiate a number of ferry crossings, including a 24-minute one from Mortavika to Arsvågen and a 50-minute one from Sandvik to Halhjem. The ferries run like clockwork, but you'll have to factor in extra for their cost.

Island time

In summer, the skerries (islets) scattered off Norway's south coast are popular as destinations for sea-and-sun adventure: Oslo families flock here in their droves. There are scores of skerries to choose from; many are little more than rocky islets, far too small for habitation save for by seals and seabirds. A few of the larger ones are served by ferries, but the more remote skerries can only be reached if you have access to your own boat. Out of season, they feel fabulously deserted. Stangholmen is a popular excursion from Risør. Its main feature is an historic lighthouse, dating from 1855 and now housing a pleasant restaurant. Bragdøya lies close to the mainland off Kristiansand,

and is home to a workshop for wooden boats, some of which are available to rent for paddle-powered explorations. Bragdøya also offers gentle wooded walks and has several beautiful places to take a chilly sea dip. In the distance you'll see the lighthouse of Grønningen Fyr, built in 1878. Offshore from Arendal lies tranquil Merdø, which is thought to have been inhabited since at least the 16th century. There are small, sheltered beaches on the harbour-side of the island, and some delightful spots for a picnic.

Above: Stangholmen Island lighthouse
Right: cobblestoned charm in Gamle Stavanger

trip to Stangholmen, a skerry topped by a lighthouse. Further southwest, there are more skerries to visit from Arendal, where the picturesque Tyholmen (Old Town) is full of colourful timbered houses built between the 17th and 19th centuries. Grimstad is worth a stop for its Ibsen connections: the great playwright spent time here as a young man, working in a pharmacy that's now a museum.

Kristiansand is Norway's fifth-largest city, and has some intriguing galleries and museums, as well as excellent restaurants: for New Nordic cuisine, try Bønder i Byen, which sources its produce from local farms and fishers.

Further on, take the coastal roads to pass through pretty small towns, woods, coves, beaches and harbours, with sea vistas filling your windows. Past Mandal, detour to stand beside Lindesnes Lighthouse, officially the southernmost point in Norway. It's a lovely spot on a summer's day, but in winter when the storms roll in, it's a forbidding reminder of the force of the North Sea.

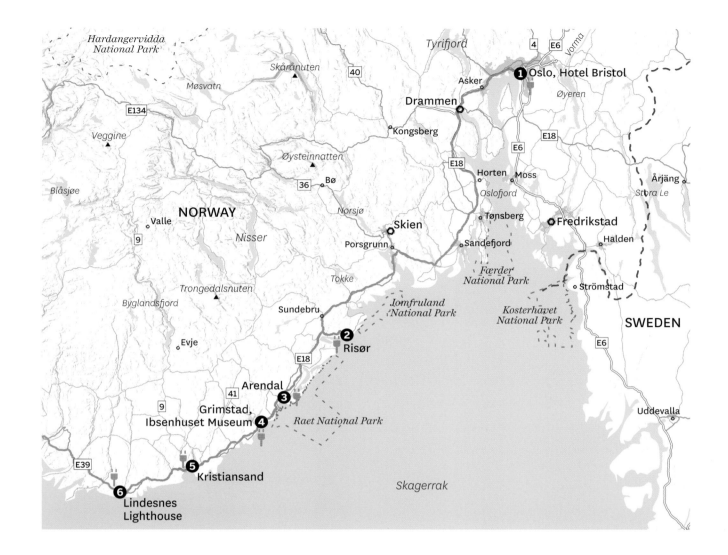

THE JÆREN TURISTVEGEN & STAVANGER

After Flekkefjord begins the most stunning section of the route: the Jæren Turistvegen, one of Norway's National Scenic Routes, a bleakly beautiful sweep of pebbly beaches, rolling coast, sandy dunes and lighthouses – such as the landmark light at Kvassheim, built in 1912. Take your time at magnificent beaches like Orrestranda and Borestranda: vast sweeps of sand framed by endless sea and sky. Soak up the Jæren's charms by checking in for an overnight stay at Egersund's Grand Hotell.

Final stop is the city of Stavanger, a booming hub for the oil and gas industries, yet more appealing than that might suggest. The cobbled Old Town, Gamle Stavanger, is delightful, with some of the best-preserved wooden buildings in Norway, housing traditional cafes, cosy pubs and a handful of top-notch restaurants – like upmarket RE-NAA, overseen by the lauded local chef Sven Erik Renaa, who's known for his love of foraged ingredients.

➡ **Distance: 175 miles (282km)**

➡ **Duration: 4-5 days**

The Bohuslän Coast

SWEDEN

Bohuslän's beautiful coast is dotted with over 8000 islands – hop between them on a West Sweden EV excursion to discover colourful fishing villages, epic water activities and serene spots in which to get away from it all.

Elbil/Concept

A lively port, Sweden's second city is a fitting starting point for a road trip up the coast. Dive into Gothenburg's maritime splendour at the waterfront, replete with historic ships and places to sample succulent, freshly landed seafood. Car enthusiasts can head to the Volvo Museum, giving a complete history of this Swedish automotive icon (bonus points if you spot the early electric concept car).

ISLAND-HOPPING NORTH

Ensconced in your own set of electrically propelled wheels, follow the E6 north out of the city past Kungälv, then on head west through the countryside towards Marstrand, passing the first of many red-painted cottages strewn across green fields. The island of Marstrand is car-free; once over the bridges from the mainland to Koön, park on the east side of its eponymous main town and take the short ferry across to Marstrand. Meander through its cobblestone streets, explore the impressive fortress, then make for the beach to breathe in the fresh sea air and, if you're up for it, to take a dip.

Point your EV back the way you came and at Vävra, head north, meeting up with the E6 again to reach Gustafsberg in about an hour. This quaint town on the banks of the

Plan & prepare

Tips for EV drivers

Download the Vattenfal InCharge app (incharge. vattenfall.se) and link your banking info for access to most of the rapid and AC chargers along this route – including those at the stays mentioned here. As a backup, consider a good, general charging card like Shell Recharge (shellrecharge.com), which will provide access to rapid chargers on the E6 motorway. Along the coast, you'll have to make do with slower AC chargers. Just be sure to top up whenever the possibility presents itself.

Where to stay

Start in style at Hotel Pigalle (hotelpigalle.se), a bang-for-your-buck Gothenburg stay with nearby parking and charging. Gustafsberg Hostel (gustafsberg.se) is a lovingly maintained former bathhouse, with shared and private rooms. In Fiskebäckskil, Gullmarsstrand Hotel (gullmarsstrand.se) is worth the splurge for access to the seaside infinity pool and sauna, plus on-site public chargers. Scandic Laholmen Hotel (scandichotels.com), across from the Kosteröarna ferry dock in Strömstad, is comfortable and convenient.

When to go

Summer is where it's at, with long, sun-soaked days that make for easy driving. The shoulder seasons are less crowded, but many restaurants, tour operators and some hotels will already be closed. Winter means challenging driving (remember that the cold can also impact your EV's range), short days and many closed establishments – but the snow can be quite magical. Just be sure to come appropriately kitted out with winter clothing.

Further info

If you're not bringing your own car, you can rent an EV in Gothenburg and drive it back from Strömstad in just two hours. Gothenburg has good connections to most European hubs via rail and air. West Sweden's excellent roads promise stress-free driving, but as this route includes several hilly sections, do watch your range – and check ferry timetables online before driving up. Both visitsweden. com and vastsverige.com have more tips.

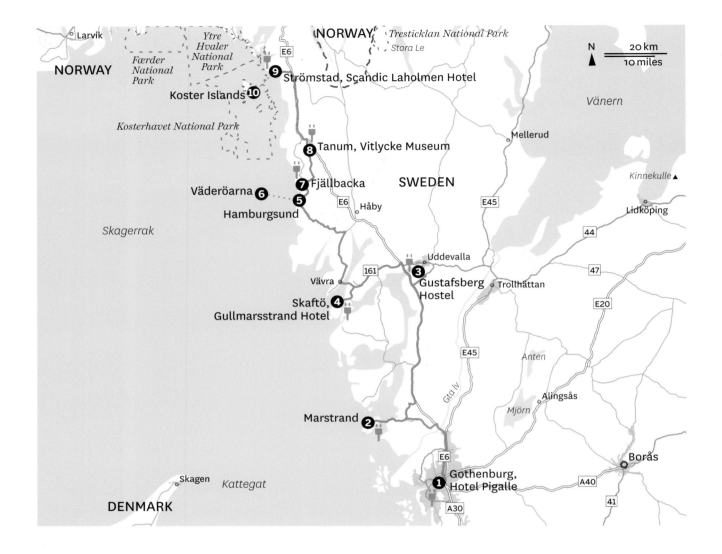

Byfjorden is Sweden's oldest spa resort, with the former bathhouse now serving as the atmospheric Gustafsberg Hostel. A section of the Kuststigen Bohuslän, the coastal path that runs the length of the Bohuslän shore, starts right on the waterfront here.

Next, cross the Uddevalla Bridge and drive west on the 161, then take a detour south and over another bridge to the island of Skaftö, where postcard-perfect fishing villages dot the rocky coast. This is the place to head out on to the water, from sea-kayaking around Grundsund to taking a chilly swim out from the jetty at Fiskebäckskil – followed by a hot sauna with sea views, and a bed for the night, at the Gullmarsstrand Hotel.

FERRIES, FIKA & FINE SNORKELLING
The next day, make the short drive north to board the Skår–Finssbo ferry, then continue onwards through undulating valleys peppered with forests to Hamburgsund. Park here to catch a small-boat ferry out to Väderöarna, the Weather Islands. This archipelago of rocky islets in the Skagerrak lies about 8 miles (13km) west of the mainland. It's a beautiful but barren and windswept place, where you can spot seals and birds on a hike past granite boulders jutting out of crystal-clear seas. Former sea pilots' houses have been turned into an inn offering hearty lunches and hot tubs for soaking sore limbs; there are also simple rooms if you want to extend your stay.

Back to the EV in Hamburgsund, then trace the coastline north to Fjällbacka, a pretty seaside town made famous by Ingrid Bergman, who loved to come here on holiday. Follow in her footsteps by enjoying a *fika* – a coffee-and-cake break. Then, drive inland to Tanum to travel back in time to the Bronze Age: the Vitlycke panel is one of the area's best-preserved rock carvings – get the lowdown at the attached museum. Join up with the E6 again for the final stretch north to Strömstad, gateway

The Tanum petroglyphs

The Vitlycke panel is just one of over 600 petroglyphs that make up the Tanum Unesco World Heritage Site. The best way to travel between the sites is by car – and conveniently for EVers, there are several rapid charging stations nearby at the Tanum shopping centre. Start at the Vitlycke Museum to get your bearings and to join an excellent, free guided tour. You'll learn more about the 3000-year history of the carvings, and how the landscape here has changed (spoiler: at the start of the Bronze Age, the sea reached all the way to Tanum), as well as why thousands of boats – but no dwellings – were etched into the rocks. Take some time, too, to visit the museum's indoor exhibition and the reconstructed Bronze Age farm on site – both are great for kids – then pick a few more rock-art sites in the area to drive to. Fossum is not far (around 10 minutes' drive to the northeast), and has carvings of several different animals as well as the Fossum Woman and a rock with unpainted petroglyphs. While most of the petroglyphs are painted over every few years to make them more visible, it's fascinating to try and make out some of the unpainted designs, which are easiest to see when it's wet or dark (use a torch).

Clockwise from top left:
Fjällbacka; Tanum rock art at the Vitlycke Museum; seaside sunset, Strömstad

to Kosterhavet National Park. Catch a ferry to the two Kosteröarna (North and South Koster Islands), to explore the marine reserve. Whether you go diving among cold-water corals or snorkelling in algae forests, don't miss the sunset back on land, when the islands' granite boulders glow a deep orange and retain the warmth of the day. This is the perfect spot for a final picnic with a view across the sprawling archipelago.

➡ **Distance: 215 miles (345km)**

➡ **Duration: 5-6 days**

Stockholm & around Lake Mälaren

SWEDEN

Cobbled harbour towns, imposing castles, Viking heritage and plenty of mini golf are some of the rewards in store on this leisurely loop around Lake Mälaren from Stockholm.

A city built over 14 islands is a suitable launchpad for this water-based trip. Before you throw your bags in the back of the EV, be sure to spend a few days in Stockholm, wandering between those islands, visiting the open-air museum of Skansen, belting out some ABBA tunes at the band's museum, and sampling as much New Nordic food as you can possibly fit in. Popular Gamla Stan (Old Town) is a particularly pretty place to explore; the neighbourhood of Södermalm will give you a more local flavour.

OUT TOWARDS MARIEFRED
When you're done exploring Stockholm, set off early to Vårby Brygga, 11 miles (18km) west. (Flat-pack fans: note Sweden's largest IKEA on the way out of the city.) Aim to arrive in time to catch the morning boat to Björkö. This island on Lake Mälaren was once the Viking Birka trading centre and is now a living museum, with archaeological sites and reconstructed Viking houses, and demonstrations, feasts and re-enactments on the events calendar. The boat will drop you back at Vårby Brygga by late afternoon, and all you need do for the rest of the day is drive to your accommodation. Gripsholms Värdshus has atmospheric rooms with wooden floors

Plan & prepare

Tips for EV drivers

Sweden has fully embraced electric vehicles. You'll be able to rent one at major car-rental companies and find charging points all along this route; download the Electromaps app (electromaps.com) for locations in Stockholm and beyond. Most chargers use a Type 2 connector. Note that batteries can run down quicker in cold weather; if your EV has it, use eco-mode to extend battery life.

Where to stay

In central Stockholm, Miss Clara (missclarahotel.com) is a boutique pad in an old girls' school. Gripsholms Värdshus in Mariefred (gripsholms-vardshus.se) has antique-filled rooms, a spa and restaurant. Rooms in the castle grounds at Sundbyholms Slott (sundbyholms-slott.se), near Eskilstuna, offer lake views. For something really different, try the über-stylish Steam Hotel (steamhotel.se), in an old power plant in Västerås. In the woods near Sigtuna, Sigtunahöjden (sigtunahojden. se) has modern motel vibes and can organise activities.

When to go

With the sun sparkling on the lake and long days in which to explore, summer is a terrific time to come. It's also the most popular season to visit, particularly with weekenders from Stockholm – book hotels and activities ahead. Note that Swedish school holidays fall between mid-June and mid-August. Winter can be magical, too, particularly when the lake freezes over enough to skate on – but note that some tourist infrastructure and sites will be closed.

Further info

Stockholm's tourist board (visitstockholm.com) has plenty of recommendations for the city, and the national tourist board (visitsweden. com) has suggestions for Lake Mälaren. Alcohol limits when driving in Sweden are some of the strictest in Europe – it's safest to avoid alcohol altogether if getting behind the wheel. You must have winter tyres fitted between December and March, and your headlights on at all times throughout the year, day and night.

Gorgeous Gamla Stan

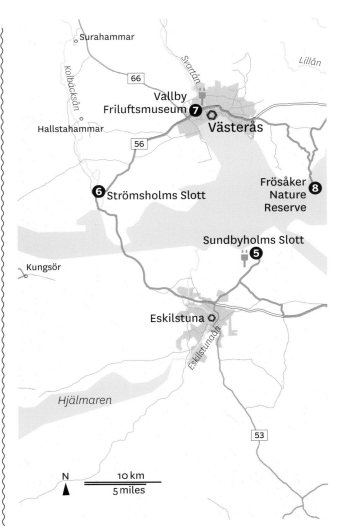

Gamla Stan is one of Sweden's most popular and atmospheric places to visit. Stockholm's beautifully preserved Old Town sits on its own island and is almost too picturesque to be real. Labyrinthine alleys lit by gas lanterns lead to cobblestone squares lined with old merchants' houses. Squirrelled away inside those handsome ochre- and ruby-coloured buildings are restaurants, coffeeshops and high-end boutiques. But it wasn't always this way. Established in the 13th century, Gamla Stan was an important trading post for centuries, with easy access to Sweden's waterways helping to establish it as a commercial hub. By the mid-1800s, however, it had deteriorated into a crime-ridden slum. Its wealthier residents were turned off by the overcrowding, poor sanitation and crumbling, hemmed-in streets, and moved further out of the city to find more space and larger, modern dwellings. Plans were put in place to raze the entire neighbourhood to the ground and start again – it was saved only because the demolition costs were too high. To learn more of this very close call, and of Gamla Stan's fascinating history, take a guided walk through the district with Story Tours (storytours.eu).

Above: Stockholm's Gamla Stan, mostly dating from the 18th to 19th century
Right: afternoon sun over Strängnäs

and beamed ceilings. The restaurant is a fine choice for dinner, serving Swedish classics such as salmon, char and elk. The inn is in the pretty town of Mariefred; crammed with traditional Swedish wooden houses, it's a lovely spot for a post-dinner meander.

Leaving the hotel the following morning, you'll clearly see Gripsholm Slott across the water. The sturdy Renaissance castle, complete with massive circular towers, is now a museum and houses the country's State Portrait Collection. It has an impressive theatre, too. Once you've done exploring, a sandwich at Anna's Hembageri in Mariefred, voted one of Sweden's best cafes, will fill you up for the afternoon.

If you'd like to linger longer, you could take an outing across the lake on the S/S *Mariefred* steamboat, but otherwise continue the drive west. The Swedish love of mini-golf soon becomes all too apparent, with courses popping up every few miles. Consider making it a

© Marco Bottigelli / Getty Images

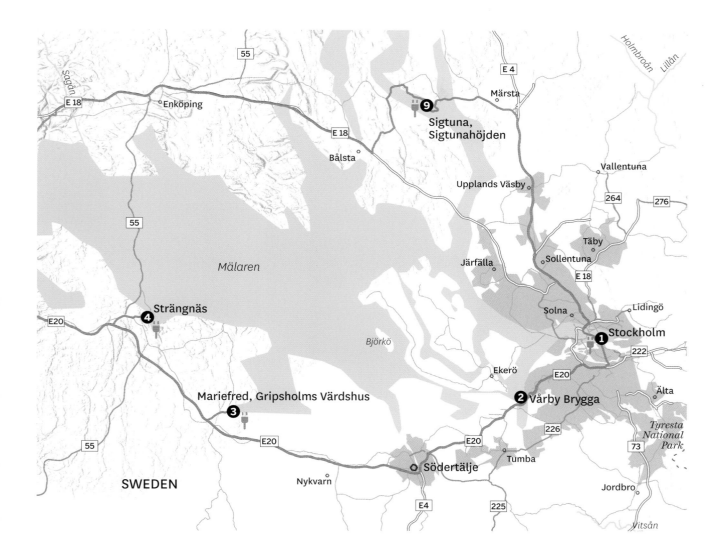

mission to stop at every one and declare a Mälaren Mini-Golf Champion at the finish of your trip.

CASTLE COMFORTS

The next stop is the town of Strängnäs. It's a handsome place, with a medieval cathedral, cobbled streets lined with traditional red-painted houses, and a lively harbour. Grab an ice-cream and spend some time poking around its small shops, walking up to the windmill, and strolling around Ulvhälls, a park displaying contemporary art over the summer.

You spent the morning roaming around a castle, so how about having dinner in one? Further around the lake and just outside Eskilstuna, Sundbyholms Slott was built in 1648, and its restaurant occupies a series of rooms on the ground floor. You won't have far to travel to bed once you've had your fill: hotel suites are in buildings scattered around the castle grounds.

After breakfast, take Hwy 56 towards Västerås, crossing over to Lake Mälaren's north side. It's well worth stopping to explore the interiors and gardens of Strömsholms Slott. The beautiful, pale-yellow baroque palace was a wedding present from King Gustav III to his new wife, Queen Sofia Magdalena, in 1772.

Unique retreats

On this trip, you can't fail to notice Sweden's traditional houses – cute little wooden cottages painted red or yellow, with white window frames and doors. You might not expect to see these same houses floating on the middle of the lake or hitched up a tree. Swedish artist Mikael Genberg has recreated the form in three unique properties: Hotell Hackspett (Hotel Woodpecker), a one-person lodge 43ft (13m) up a tree; Utter Inn (Otter Inn), a two-bed place 10ft (3m) beneath the surface of Lake Mälaren; and the Ooops Hotel, an apparently half-submerged pad sleeping two, also on the lake. Genberg aimed to be the first person to put an artwork on the Moon, but his ambitious plans to land a little red house there stalled due to lack of funding. For now, you'll just have to make do with his earthbound creations (visitvasteras.se/botips-unika-boenden).

From left: a Mikael Genberg creation finds a temporary home atop Stockholm's Avicii Arena; Sigtuna's historic Rådhus (Town Hall); Lake Mälaren sunset

EAST TO STOCKHOLM

From this point on, you're circling back towards Stockholm, but there are many more distractions before you return to your starting point. Vallby Friluftsmuseum is one of them. This living museum showcases traditional rural life in Västmanland, with a collection of 50 historic buildings scooped up from across the region and spread through the site's 37 acres (15 hectares).

There's architectural heritage of a very different kind at your digs for the night. The Steam Hotel in Västerås occupies the town's old power station – you can't miss the red-brick building towering over the harbour. It's very much a destination hotel, with two restaurants, four bars, a cinema, spa and pool; you'll struggle to find a reason to leave once you're settled in.

When you finally emerge, you're heading to Frösåker. The nature reserve here has several looping walking trails that lead through the forest along the lake, giving you terrific views across the water. You'll want to grab lunch at the nearby Viking Bay Hotel before rejoining the road towards Sigtuna, your final Mälaren stop. The town dates to the 10th century, and was once the Swedish capital. You get a sense of its history on spruced-up Stora Gatan, the country's oldest street – its charming wooden buildings now contain a mix of gift shops and cafes.

While you're still on the lake, don't miss the opportunity to enjoy some more natural pursuits. Set in woodland close to town, Sigtunahöjden Hotel makes for a revitalising destination for a pre-Stockholm overnight and can arrange various activities, from mountain-biking to kayaking. Fully energised, you'll be ready to return to Stockholm and indulge in a few more urban diversions before it's time to pack your bags and say goodbye to Sweden.

EASTERN EUROPE

Below: Pula's Roman amphitheatre
Right: Motovun

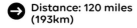 **Distance: 120 miles (193km)**

 **Duration: 5-6 days**

The Istrian Peninsula

CROATIA

Vineyard-dotted hills, truffle-filled forests and rocky mountains sweep down to crystal-clear seas in a region littered with Roman ruins, medieval villages, Venetian palazzi and stately Belle Époque villas.

Roll down your EV's windows, slip on your shades and cruise along snaking backcountry roads through a landscape of rippling mountains, woods and vineyards on the Istrian Peninsula, a region dubbed the 'Croatian Tuscany'.

Start your trip in Opatija, once a fashionable getaway for the Austro-Hungarian elite. Royalty, aristocrats, tsars and the merely monied flocked here in the 19th century, building ever-more elaborate villas by the sea. Make a base at the Hotel Sverti Jacov, then stroll the waterfront for views of the Kvarner Gulf and Opatija's magnificent neoclassical architecture.

HIKES & HILLTOP TOWNS

From here, it's a half-hour drive west to Učka Nature Park, where you can hike to the Istrian Peninsula's highest point, Vojak (4596ft/1401m), for panoramic views of the Julian Alps, the Gulf of Trieste and the Istrian islands.

Continue on for another half an hour through a landscape of rolling hills, meadows, woodlands and vineyards to tiny Roč. Encircled by 15th-century walls, the honey-coloured cobbled lanes lead to Roman monuments, a Romanesque church and Renaissance-

Plan & prepare

Tips for EV drivers

Low-cost air carriers fly into Pula, where electric vehicles are available to rent (albeit in limited numbers at the time of writing). The closest major international airports are in Croatia's capital, Zagreb; and in Slovenia's capital, Ljubljana. EV chargers can be found in all the major towns in Istria, often at high-end hotels or in main car parks.

Where to stay

Savour splendid Opatija at Hotel Sveti Jacov (amadriapark.com), in an Austro-Hungarian villa; or Empire-style Hotel Palace Bellevue (liburnia.hr), with a heated seawater pool. For sleek sophistication and fine food and wine, try Motovun's Roxanich Winery & Design Hotel (roxanich. com). In Rovinj, waterfront Hotel Lone (maistra.com) is effortlessly elegant despite its size; Pula's La Preziosa Rooms (la-preziosa-rooms. pula-hotels.org) is a steal, with contemporary decor and rooms with private balconies.

When to go

Istria is at its finest between the months of May and September. Consider a trip in May to catch the Vinistria Wine Festival and the open-cellar day for tastings and tours. Pula's Days of Antiquity in mid-June sees festivities celebrating the town's history, while in autumn, you'll find festivals dedicated to truffles and chestnuts across the region.

Further info

The narrow, winding country roads of Istria's interior are wonderfully scenic, but quite a challenge to drive – and note that the steep inclines will tax your battery range, so be sure of the location for your next charge-point before setting out. Istria is also a popular cycling destination, so watch out for road cyclists, particularly as you head around bends on narrow mountain roads.

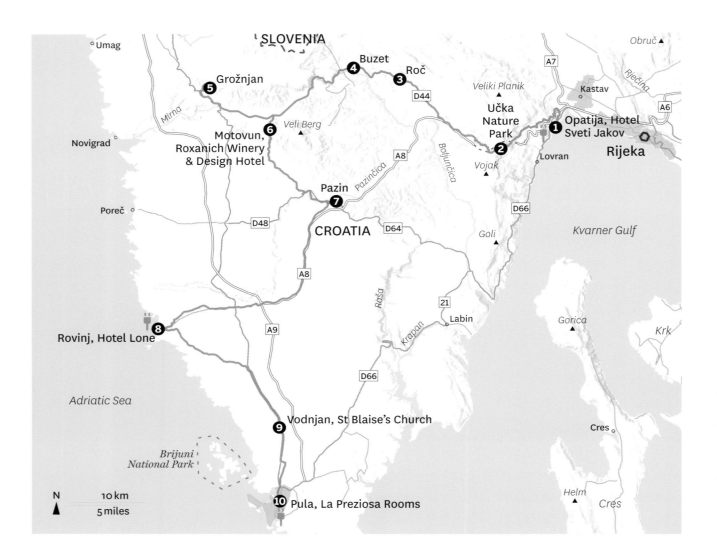

era townhouses. Stop for a lunch of *fuši* (homemade Istrian sausages) or pasta with truffles at Ročka Konoba before heading for nearby Buzet, where the Venetians lined the narrow streets with handsome palazzi in the 16th and 17th centuries.

Bed down for the night at the Roxanich Winery & Design Hotel in Motovun, 20 minutes' drive on. An artisan winery with chic rooms and an excellent restaurant serving Istrian cuisine made with organic produce, it makes a great base for exploring this enchanting little hill-town, with its Romanesque and Gothic townhouses, ornate church and glorious views down over vineyards, forests and the Mirna River below.

About half an hour northwest of Motovun, another gorgeous hilltop town, Grožnjan, is worth a detour. A strategic Venetian fortress in the 14th century, it fell into serious decline before its handsome medieval houses were rescued by an influx of artists and

musicians, who today run a host of galleries, craft workshops and studios here.

PAZIN TO PULA VIA ROVINJ

Next, drive south to Pazin, where the Pazinčica River has cut a chasm 328ft (100m) deep into the limestone. A medieval castle lords over the canyon and a trail leads down into the abyss, where the river disappears underground – the wild scenery inspired fantasy writer Jules Verne, who set his novel *Mathias Sandorf* here.

It's a 40-minute drive on to ever-popular Rovinj, where a charismatic jumble of Renaissance, Gothic, baroque and neoclassical buildings crowd the narrow streets around the hilltop church of St Euphemia. Browse the many galleries, stop for a gelato by the waterfront or hop on a boat to one of the nearby islands. In the morning, head off to St Blaise's Church in Vodnjan, half an hour away, home to a set of saintly

Istria's liquid gold

mummies said to have miraculous powers, and a bizarre collection of relics that include various body parts – there's also a fragment said to be from Jesus's cross and a thorn from his crown.

Roll on for another 20 minutes to the Roman glories of Pula. Take in a show at the well-preserved amphitheatre, built between 27 BCE and 68 CE; stroll through the Triumphal Arch of the Sergii; and sip coffee by the Temple of Augustus. Finish the day watching the colourful light-show at the Uljanik shipyard, where the cranes seem to dance in the night.

With a growing reputation for its fine wine, truffles, seafood, chestnuts and wild game, plus prosciutto delicate enough to rival anything from across the border in Italy, Istria is becoming something of an epicurean hotspot. Its most glorified export, however, is its olive oil – in Flos Olei's annual ratings, Istria has been crowned the best extra-virgin-olive-oil region in the world for seven years in a row. Production here is small-scale, with family farms championing quality over quantity. Many makers here offer guided tastings, and Istria's Olive Oil Roads trail highlights growers open to visits; pick up a map at tourist offices or search istra.hr for more info. Near Motovun, Ipša offers

memorable views from its tasting room, while Meloto, near Vodnjan, produces some of the most lauded oils in the region. You can see the whole process in action at the Chiavalon Olive Oil Centre in Vodnjan, while the House of Istrian Olive Oil in Pula runs you through the history and development of production, explaining everything from Venetian tax systems to traditional milling. If you can, time a visit to coincide with the November harvest to meet producers and try freshly-pressed oils at Vodnjan's Olive Oil Festival.

Clockwise from top left: eggs with Istrian truffles; olive-oil tasting at Ipša, near Motovun; Pazinčica River canyon, Pazin

Below: Split's
Diocletian's Palace
Right: Cetina River
Canyon, Omiš

→ **Distance: 145 miles (233km)**

→ **Duration: 3-5 days**

The Dalmatian Coast

CROATIA

Antiquities, imperial riches, gourmet food, fine wines and glittering beaches lapped by pellucid waters combine to make this gorgeous stretch of coastline ideal for a leisurely EV drive.

Grab sunnies, swimsuit and photo-taking device of choice for an electric drive between two of the most remarkable cities on the Adriatic, along a coastline flanked by high mountains and glittering turquoise waters. Start in the wonderfully exuberant Split, a jewel of a place where an imperial palace built by a Roman emperor is still in use today.

Constructed in 295 CE, Split's Diocletian's Palace remains at the heart of city life, its smooth white streets home to shops, restaurants, bars and clubs, its temples and squares simply repurposed for modern use. Visit the octagonal Cathedral of St Domnius, originally the Roman emperor Diocletian's mausoleum; and the Temple of Jupiter, now the cathedral's baptistry. Stroll through the Renaissance Republic Square to the Riva, the city's lively waterfront promenade, and soak up the unique mix of history and modern life here.

FROM CANYON TO BEACH

From Split, drive your EV south out of the city towards Omiš to reach the limestone cliffs of the Cetina River Canyon. With walls that reach up to 650ft (200m) high, plus churning waterfalls, rapids and plenty of history, it's a great spot to try rafting, canyoning, river-tubing, ziplining

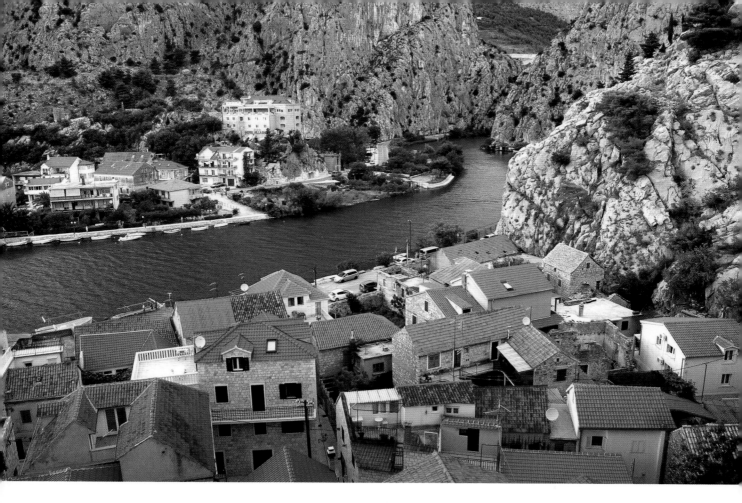

Plan & prepare

Tips for EV drivers

Both Split and Dubrovnik have busy international airports; you can rent an electric vehicle at either location, although note that picking up at one airport and dropping off at the other usually incurs an additional fee. Both cities have pedestrianised areas and resident-only parking zones in their centres, so watch out for the signs; in Dubrovnik, an EV-only zone has been considered (though not yet realised).

Where to stay

In Split, Heritage Hotel 19 (heritagehotel19.com) has a quiet location and parking near Diocletian's Palace. A palazzo turned boutique hotel, Heritage Hotel Porin in Makaraska (hotel-porin.hr) lords it over the promenade. In Mali Ston, the Hotel Ostrea (ostrea.hr) has simple rooms on the waterfront. In Dubrovnik, Heritage Villa Nobile (hotel-marcopolo. com) channels the spirit of 19th-century intellectuals, and has a garden and parking; Villa Anica (villaanica.com) is more affordable, with plenty of rustic charm.

When to go

Visit in May, June or September for the best weather and a chance to wander the handsome streets of Split and Dubrovnik without the summer crowds. Carnival in February is also an excellent time to visit, and if you arrive in mid-May, you'll catch the Festival of Oysters in Ston on the Pelješac Peninsula, a jubilant celebration of fine foods, wine and traditional singing and dancing.

Further info

When driving in Croatia, note that you are required by law to carry a reflective jacket, warning triangle and first-aid kit – be sure to check that these are included with any rental car. Parking in Split or Dubrovnik in high season is challenging: look for a hotel with private parking or consider staying a little bit out from the centre.

Dalmatian Coast islands

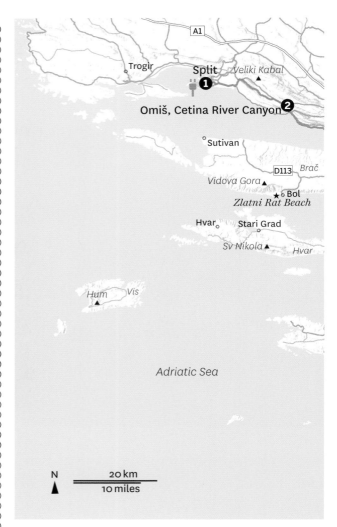

Adriatic Sea

N
20 km
10 miles

Rather than sticking to the coast road between Split and Dubrovnik, you could also indulge in some island-hopping, visiting sun-soaked Brač, glitzy Hvar or tranquil Korčula along the way. Car-ferries run from Split to each of the islands year-round, so you can explore at your own pace before rejoining the main route. Choose Brač to laze on the smooth white pebbles of Zlatni Rat (one of Croatia's prettiest beaches), see Sutivan's palaces and baroque summerhouses and explore the interior's karst uplands, before crossing back to Makarska on the mainland. Alternatively, head for Stari Grad on Hvar, a stunner of a town set on a horseshoe bay. Visit the ancient agricultural terraces of Unesco-listed Stari Grad

Plain and the Gothic and Renaissance palaces of jet-setting Hvar Town before driving along the coastline to Sućuraj, for the ferry back to Drvenik on the mainland. For traditional culture, olive groves and small-scale vineyards producing quality white wines, choose Korčula, where you'll also find Venetian palaces, grand squares and medieval churches in the main town. From there, you can take the car ferry to Orebić on the Pelješac Peninsula, an hour's drive from Mali Ston and the main route of this EV excursion.

Above: Hvar Town harbour
Right: Pelješac Bridge between mainland Croatia and the Pelješac Peninsula

or hiking. Recover on one of Omiš' sandy beaches before continuing south along the coast, past pebbled beaches whose crystalline waters demand a quick dip or snorkel.

With stark mountains on one side and the ever-blue Adriatic on the other, the drive is dramatic as you head towards Makarska, a popular resort set on a small bay between two headlands. Fought over by the Romans, Ottomans, Venetians, French and Viennese through the centuries, the town has a rich architectural legacy and many of its fine buildings now house grand hotels. Base yourself at Heritage Hotel Porin on the busy promenade, then enjoy an evening waterfront stroll, a cocktail overlooking the sea and a feast of local fish and seafood.

THE PELJEŠAC PENINSULA

With the car freshly charged, it's time to head south again the next day, perhaps stopping off for a morning swim at Nugal Beach, where high cliffs cradle a beautiful cove.

© DaLu / Shutterstock

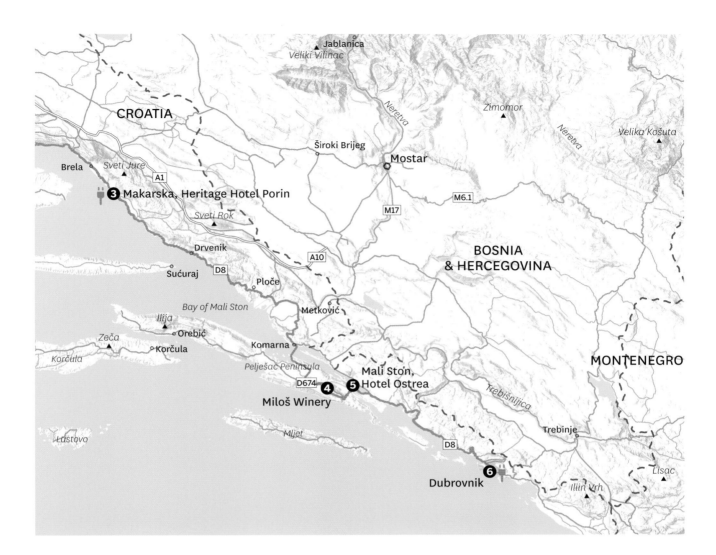

Continue on, soaking up the views of the meandering coastline, stopping off at roadside stalls to pick up local honey, orange juice and fresh produce before crossing over the Bay of Mali Ston near Komarna, via the shiny new Pelješac Bridge, to reach the Pelješac Peninsula.

A gourmet hub known for its fine red wines, excellent seafood and top-quality olive oil, the mountainous Pelješac has a quiet, rustic character. It's around 20 minutes' drive south along the peninsula to Miloš Winery, a family-run organic vineyard. Take a tour to learn about the history and cultivation of the Plavac Mali grape here, and the labour-intensive farming methods used on the steep terraced slopes. With a designated driver volunteered, finish your visit off with a tasting of the estate's award-winning dry reds, rosés and dessert wines.

Hop in the EV for the 15-minute drive to Ston, a handsome town once part of the Republic of Dubrovnik. A key producer of salt, set in a strategic position at the

Game of Thrones locations

Few special effects were needed to transform the Dalmatian Coast's remarkable cities into settings for HBO's mega-hit *Game of Thrones*. In Split, the basement rooms and echoing tunnels of Diocletian's Palace were where Daenerys had her throne room, and kept and trained her dragons, while the dramatic Klis Fortress to the northeast doubled as the city of Mereen. Dubrovnik's medieval fortresses and streets provided the perfect backdrop for series city, King's Landing: Lovrijenac Fort, which sits on a rocky outcrop near Pile Gate, served as the Red Keep, seat of power of the rulers of Westeros. The harbour below became Blackwater Bay; Minčeta Tower, the Old Town's highest point, was Qarth's House of the Undying. Possibly the most memorable location, however, is the Jesuit Stairs near St Ignatius Church, where Queen Cersei's 'walk of shame' was filmed.

From left: Dubrovnik, stand-in for *Game of Thrones'* King's Landing; Nugal Beach, Pelješac Peninsula; fresh Mali Ston oysters

head of a narrow bay, the town was fortified in the 14th century. Ston's protective walls survive largely intact and sweep around the medieval town and up the steep hill behind it. Climb the many steps past the lookout towers for far-reaching views over the peninsula and islands.

Down in Ston town, the narrow winding streets are flanked by honey-coloured townhouses, and a bumper crop of cafes, bars and restaurants serve excellent local seafood. Ston and its harbour village Mali Ston, just to the northeast, are particularly renowned for their oysters, with the mix of fresh- and salt-water at the Mali Ston oyster beds providing ideal conditions for the molluscs to thrive. Check in to the Hotel Ostrea in Mali Ston, tour the oyster beds and salt pans, and then set yourself up for a gastro feast at Ston's family-run Stagnum.

DOWN TO DUBROVNIK

Relaxed, restored and well fed, make the final hour-long drive into Dubrovnik in the morning. In this fairy-tale city contained within 9th-century walls, it's best to ditch the car on arrival and head into the Old Town on foot. You'll quickly see what five centuries of peace enabled a prosperous merchant city to achieve during the Middle Ages: the elegant streets are lined with an enviable tangle of baroque palaces, ornate churches and lavish fountains, plus monasteries and museums, chapels and towers. Whatever route you take, you'll inevitably end up at the old port, its turquoise waters washing up against the golden-stone walls.

After a day spent exploring Dubrovnik's delights, walk the city walls at sunset to soak up the view before creeping through a hole in the ramparts to the hidden Buža Bar, for a cocktail overlooking the Adriatic. With the lights twinkling over the port, make your way to the hulking Fort St John for an exceptional final meal at the Michelin-starred Restaurant 360.

Below: a flash
of frescoed
colour in Prague
Right: Malá Strana
district, Prague, from
medieval Charles Bridge

➡ **Distance: 385 miles
(620km)**

➡ **Duration: 4-5 days**

Prague to Karlovy Vary

CZECH REPUBLIC

Drive out beyond Prague's atmospheric streets to explore castles, taste crisply clean lager in its place of origin and wander through medieval towns set among the green landscapes of Bohemia.

Prague's architectural beauty rivals that of Paris, and seems all the more magical for having escaped the destruction of the two World Wars. Watched over by Prague Castle – with its collection of museums and galleries – the city is steeped in the presence of the past: medieval churches bear bullet scars, and historic squares echo with the ghosts of revolutionary protest.

SOUTH & NORTH TO KARLOVY VARY

A winding 40-minute drive southwest from Prague shifts the scene to verdant countryside and Karlštejn Castle. Built to secure the crown jewels hoarded by Holy Roman Emperor Charles IV, Karlštejn looks straight out of a Gothic fairy tale, never more so than when draped in mist.

It's 58 miles (93km) from Karlštejn to pretty Kutná Hora – leave your EV charging at the Kolin bus station and take a 20-minute bus ride into town to explore on foot. Admire the 15th-century frescoes at the Gothic Cathedral of St Barbara; the building's oft-interrupted construction began in 1380 and was finally completed in the late 19th century – it's now a Unesco World Heritage Site. Drive on south through farmland towards Hotel Nautilus in Tábor, your stop for the night. About halfway, a short detour towards Benešov takes you to Konopiště Chateau, former home of

© Matt Munro / Lonelyp Planet

© TomasSereda / Getty Images

Plan & prepare

Tips for EV drivers

To use ČEZ Group charging stations, register in advance (at elektromobilita.cz) and either pay via its app or an RFID charging card. The ORLEN Charge app (orlen. pl) lets you use PKN ORLEN's charging points. EVs are exempt from tolls and can use all roads without the vignette required by standard vehicles. There are some dedicated parking spaces for EVs (with charging points) in Prague, Plzeň and other large towns and cities.

Where to stay

Le Palais (lepalaishotel. eu) is a luxury hotel in a beautifully restored Belle Époque building, with views of Prague's Vyšehrad fortress. Hotel Nautilus in Tábor (hotelnautilus.cz) has effortless style and a prime position on the main square. Český Krumlov's Monastery Garden Hotel (monasterygarden.cz) has Scandi-style rooms in a 16th-century former monastery. Karlovy Vary's Hotel Romance (hotelromance.cz) is an excellent mid-range option, located just across from the Hot Spring Colonnade.

When to go

High season in Prague generally means April to June (plus the Christmas and New Year holidays), but visitor numbers across the nation swell in the hottest months of July and August. Autumn is particularly beautiful as Bohemia's many trees start to turn, adding colour to its landscape. Spring is mid-March until mid-June, and this is when Prague comes to life with some of its best events, including the Prague Food Festival.

Further info

Prague's old town is largely pedestrianised, but a number of hotels (including Le Palais) allow you to park and charge your car. Even better, pick up your rental car as you leave the city, to reduce hire and parking costs. The Prague-specific Citymove app (citymove.app) allows users to compare different city routes, as well as pay for parking, public transport and even scooter rental.

Clockwise from top left: wetlands
en route to Třeboň; lynx in Šumava
National Park; Konopiště Chateau

Šumava National Park

As you leave Český Krumlov, you'll notice the road passes dense patches of forest: these are the furthest edges of the Šumava National Park (npsumava.cz/en), on the Czech-Bavarian border and known in Germany as the Bavarian Forest National Park (nationalpark-bayerischer-wald.bayern.de). Take a detour into the Šumava to explore the largest forested area in Central Europe. Old-growth woodlands and stands of spruce are interspersed with peat bogs and glacial lakes to create a rich habitat for more than 10,000 animal species, including populations of lynx, European wildcats, wolves, otters and elk. Notable birds include Ural and pygmy owls, corncrakes and red-billed black storks. Clustered along the Czech border, a scattering of derelict villages are the remnants of settlements abandoned at the end of WWII, after the Czech government expelled the ethnic German population. Some of the ruins are marked by Czech or German signs and lie close to hiking routes and roads, but plenty are hard to spot, especially when vegetation is thickest in summer. Until the fall of the Iron Curtain in 1989, an electric fence separated the then-Czechoslovakia from Bavarian Germany, and few people ventured into the region. Fascinatingly, studies have found that red deer here still keep to the sides of the park that their ancestors were raised in.

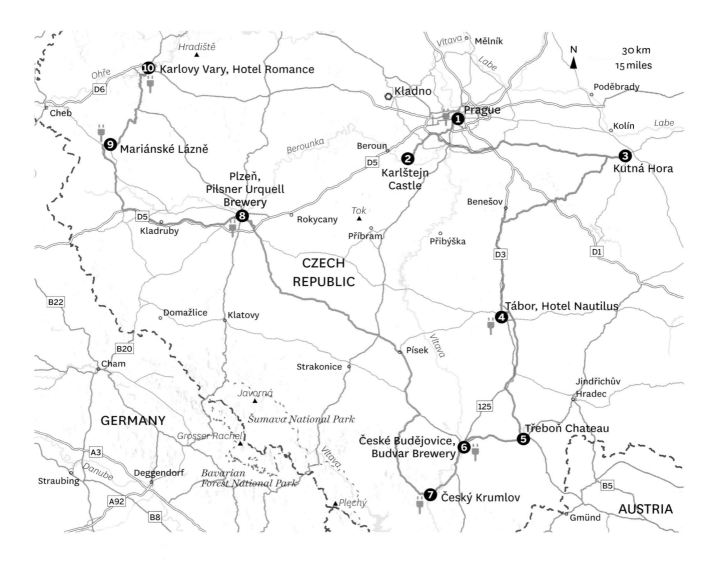

Austria's Archduke Franz Ferdinand, whose assassination in 1914 sparked WWI. Once in Tábor, leave your EV charging at the Čsl. Armády car park while you stroll the medieval Old Town and enjoy dinner by the main square at Nautilus' elegant restaurant. The next morning, it's only 40 minutes' drive to Třeboň, through sparkling wetlands and past lakes cradling tiny islands. An attractive spa town with a Renaissance castle to visit, Třeboň sits on the shore of the Svět artificial lake, created in the 16th century – like others hereabouts – to develop the region's carp fisheries.

It's just a 30-minute hop on to České Budějovice, for a pilgrimage to the Budvar brewery. There are chargers here, but you could drive on and top up in castle-topped Český Krumlov, with a charismatic riverside location and a mix of Renaissance and baroque architecture; its crowds of young backpackers and busy bars are reminiscent of Prague, but on a more accessible scale. Stay over in one of the cosy rooms at the Monastery Garden Hotel.

From Český Krumlov you'll leave southern Bohemia and drive north for 98 miles (158km) along forest-lined roads through Písek, whose 13th-century bridge is the country's oldest. Pass a succession of well-preserved towns and pause at Plzeň, home of the open-for-visits Pilsner Urquell Brewery; but don't miss the Underground Plzeň tour, through passageways that date back to the 14th century.

Heading west, you'll drive past Kladruby's domed baroque church before pivoting north, through forested countryside, towards the spa town of Mariánské Lázně. The manicured parks here offer a pleasant place to stretch your legs. Then it's a further 50 minutes' drive to Karlovy Vary, the final stop on your EV road trip. This colourful spa town's imposing 19th-century buildings are embedded in forest, set against the soundtrack of splashing fountains. The Art Nouveau Hotel Romance is the perfect place to find rest and revitalisation – as many decades of travellers here have done before you.

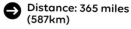

Distance: 365 miles (587km)

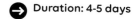

Duration: 4-5 days

Wrocław to Blizne

POLAND

A drive through Poland's history – equal parts majestic and solemn – this southern route takes in two cities with dramatic heritage, and the site of the nation's greatest tragedy.

Wrocław is a distinguished university city, with a youthful population and nightlife to match. Controlled during stages of its eventful history by Austria, Prussia, Hungary and Bohemia, it has absorbed influences from each. It is flush with religious monuments and museums, such as Wrocław University's baroque-rococo Church of the Holy Name of Jesus and the superbly curated National Museum. The grand Rynek (market square) surrounds this attractive city's defining sight: the astonishingly elaborate Old Town Hall, a Gothic marvel built between the 13th and 16th centuries.

Just over an hour's drive southeast is the quieter city of Opole – founded, like Wrocław, in the 9th century. This is home to the National Festival of Polish Song, with modern outskirts wrapping around an Old Town that has remnants of medieval defences and the 14th-century red-brick Franciscan Church of the Holy Trinity. If you're a lover of smoked fish, stock up at the Rybex delicatessen.

A couple of hours further southwest, Pszczyna is one of Poland's most beautiful castles. This 17th-century ducal palace overlays a 13th-century Gothic original, with landscaped grounds, period rooms and themed displays.

Due north, via forests and wildlife reserves, lies the sprawling industrial city of Katowice. Ravished in WWII

Plan & prepare

Tips for EV drivers

Major car-rental companies operate at Wrocław Airport, 30 minutes' drive east of town, and can pre-book you an EV. Chargers can be found in several clusters along this route, although there are few in Oświęcim – so charge up in Katowice, and again as you approach Kraków. Rzeszów to Blizne is a barren stretch – get a full charge in Rzeszów, where you should also consider staying overnight.

Where to stay

In Wrocław's Old Town, Hotel Monopol (monopolwroclaw. hotel.com.pl) was built over a ruined priory in 1892, and has hosted Pablo Picasso, Marlene Dietrich and Charles de Gaulle in its distinguished history. Kraków's Hotel Stary (stary.hotel.com.pl) is set in an 18th-century mansion right in the centre. In Tarnów opt for the central, Art Nouveau charmer that is Hotel Gal (hotelgaltarnow. pl). Blizne has fewer choices for accommodation, so head back to Rzeszów and the Grand Hotel (grand-hotel.pl), one of Poland's best.

When to go

April to September promises the best weather, without the snows of a Central European winter. Four May days in Kraków are dedicated to Juwenalia (juwenalia. krakow.pl), a joyful, student-led carnival of live music, outdoor dancing, parades and masquerades. Notable dates include Constitution Day (3 May) and the Assumption of Mary (15 August); both are national holidays, when most businesses close.

Further info

Competition and prices for accommodation in Kraków and Wrocław peak during the summer holidays, so be sure to pre-book; in summer it's also advisable to pre-book for the most popular attractions, such as Rynek Underground in Kraków. Outside this busy period, you can afford to be reasonably relaxed about encountering crowds and gaining access to sights, bars and restaurants.

Zalipie, the 'painted village'

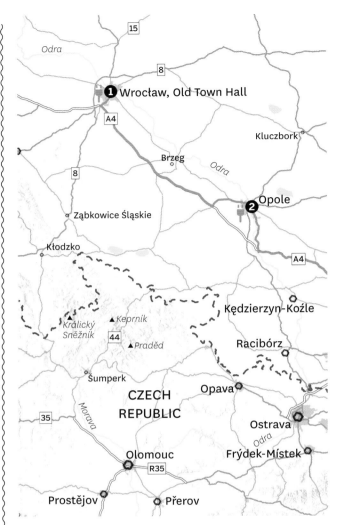

Set in the countryside 40 minutes' drive north of Tarnów is the 'painted village' of Zalipie. This tiny hamlet's photogenic fame comes from the profusion of intricate floral designs that cover more than 30 of its houses, inside and out. The complex, painstakingly rendered patterns are quite spectacular, and can also be seen adorning barns, fences, wells and even buckets. The tradition is understood to have begun in the 18th century, when Zalipie's women whitewashed begrimed surfaces, then decided to beautify them with floral embellishments using, originally, paints made from a mixture of powdered dye and milk. As each self-taught artist gained her own style, no two houses shared

the same designs, and no specific (or even, necessarily, naturally occurring) flowers predominated. The most famous of Zalipie's artists, Felicja Curyłowa (1904–1974) tirelessly painted her three-room farmhouse with flamboyant floral patterns. It's now the Felicja Curyłowa Farmstead Museum, where her work also appears on dishes, clothing and most surfaces of this extraordinary space. Grab a map of the village's best-painted houses at Zalipie's House of Painters (dommalarek.pl), a unique little gallery displaying the work of local artists.

Above: floral adornments in Zalipie
Right: displays at Oshpitzin Jewish Museum

and rebuilt in Communist times, it's not elegant, but it does have a modest urban buzz and some top-notch museums: overnight at grand Hotel Monopol to peruse the Museum of Katowice History and artwork at the Silesian.

OŚWIĘCIM TO BLIZNE

Oświęcim, 40 minutes south, is better known by its German name: Auschwitz. The extermination camps of Auschwitz-Birkenau are preserved much as they were at the moment of liberation by Soviet Red Army troops on 27 January 1945 (now International Holocaust Memorial Day), and stand as monuments to the 1.1 million people murdered here by the Nazis. Oświęcim's synagogue doubles as the Oshpitzin Jewish Museum, documenting a population established here in the 16th century.

An hour's drive east, with the Tenczyński forests visible immediately north, is Kraków, Poland's second-largest city and arguably its most handsome. Founded in the 7th

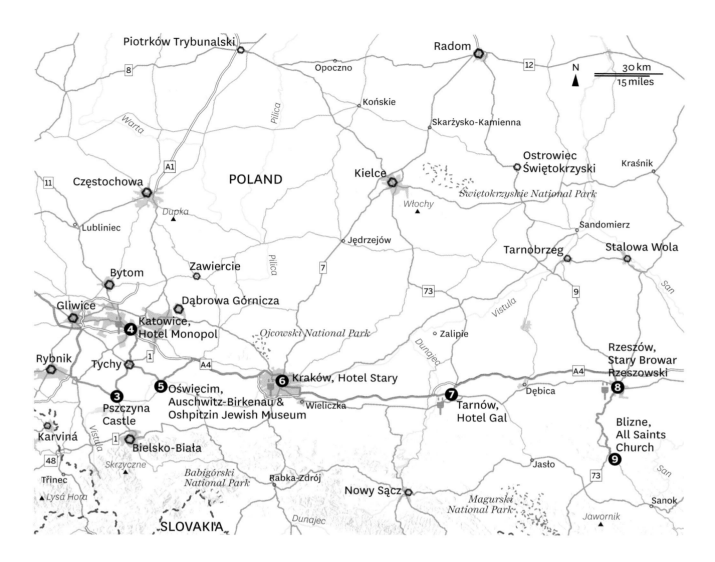

century and once the nation's capital, it has an Old Town bursting with historical sights – stay over at the Hotel Stary and you'll be steps away from treasures like the Jagiellonian University's 15th-century Collegium Maius; and the Rynek Underground, an excavated subterranean warren of ancient tunnels and chambers.

Another hour east and you're in Tarnów, its dignified Old Town pierced by tenement-lined 16th-century streets that radiate from the Rynek, with its arresting 15th-century Gothic Town Hall. Then head east to the 13th-century university town of Rzeszów. Stary Browar Rzeszowski is the best of the microbreweries that line its Rynek, where there's another impressive Gothic town hall. As in Kraków, Rzeszów's buried medieval streets have been excavated and opened up. Journey's end is just south through farmland at Blizne, home to the wonderfully preserved 15th-century All Saints Church, one of the region's six Unesco World Heritage wooden churches.

Below: a slice of Bled
cream cake, Ljubljana
Right: Istrian coastline
around Koper

➡ **Distance: 188 miles
(302km)** ➡ **Duration: 5-7 days**

Ljubljana to Piran

SLOVENIA

Green, glorious, tree–cloaked and compact, Slovenia is an engaging choice for an electric drive – spend a week connecting the capital and the coast, via magical lakes and flourishing vineyards.

Slovenia knows a thing or two about exploring in a more environmentally friendly fashion. International organisation Green Destinations declared it 'the first green country in the world', and 100-plus accommodation providers and attractions nationwide are signed up to the tourist board's Slovenia Green scheme. This omnipresent eco-ethos makes it increasingly easy for conscientious travellers to make more sustainable choices here. And, Slovenia is simply drop-dead gorgeous. The nation is 70% hills and mountains and 60% swathed in trees, with fertile plains, cave-riddled karst and a short-but-sweet Adriatic coast – together perfect for a varied, scenic drive.

LJUBLJANA TO THE LAKES
Start in Ljubljana. Crowned Europe's Green Capital in 2016, this petite city offers free public transport, a pedestrianised centre and heaps of leafy outdoor spaces. It also has a hilltop castle, a medieval and baroque Old Town that's perfect for strolling, plus elegant Italianate and Secessionist architecture, an emerald-hued river and plentiful pavement cafes. Pop into the National Museum of Slovenia, and take a food tour for local insight and sustenance.

© AAR Studio / Shutterstock

Plan & prepare

Tips for EV drivers

Slovenia is wholeheartedly embracing EVs. The network of chargers is swiftly growing with proportionately more fast-charging points being introduced and more accommodation providers installing chargers for guests. Also, the country is compact, so distances between chargers are never too great, although the terrain can be hilly. Capital Ljubljana has a high number of charging points.

Where to stay

The Bohinj ECO Hotel in Bohinjska Bistrica (bohinj-eco-hotel.si) is a properly green base: it has its own energy cogeneration station and underground heat-pumps (used to warm its rooms and aquapark), and has easy access to EV chargers. In the Vipava Valley, Domačija Majerija (majerija.si) has 10 modern rooms built under the herb garden of a converted 18th-century estate house; there's an excellent restaurant and on-site chargers.

When to go

July and August are warm and sunny but extremely busy, especially around Bled. Better to opt for May to June or September, when the mountains and rivers are open for activities but there are fewer people. September into November brings wine harvests and autumn colours; winter is great for snowsports and warming up in the county's many spas and hot springs. Ljubljana is appealing year-round.

Further info

A vignette is required to drive on most toll motorways and expressways, including the A2 northwest from Ljubljana to Jesenice (for Bled) and the A1 southwest towards Koper. Slovenian e-vignettes, valid for a week, month, six months or year, can be purchased online via the official website (evinjeta. dars.si). Rental cars usually come with a vignette – check it is valid.

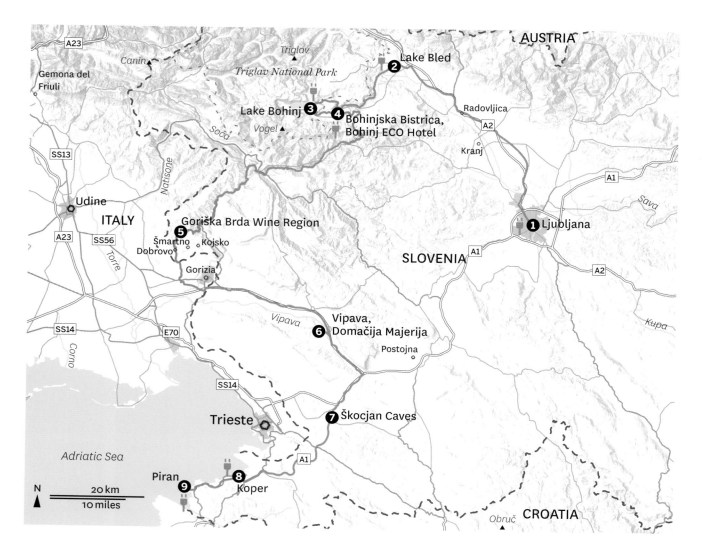

Once you've had your fill, hit the highway northwest, bound for the mountains. If you keep going, you'll soon be in Austria. But do stop: first, after 30 miles (48km), at medieval Radovljica, Slovenia's beekeeping and honeybread hub; and then, just beyond, at fairy-tale Lake Bled. Here, a crag-top medieval castle looms beside a mirror-calm lake, from which a bell tower rises on a tiny isle, all against a backdrop of green foothills and snowcapped peaks. Photo perfection. Visit the castle museum, take a wooden *pletna* boat across to the island (it'll be busy, but the ice cream is excellent) and hike into one of the nearby gorges, such as waterfall-splished Vintgar or lush and narrow Pokljuka, where Nazi-fighting partisans hid during WWII.

Then drive on for 16 miles (26km), winding around the eastern edge of the majestic Julian Alps to reach Lake Bohinj, Bled's wilder, undeveloped sister. Pooled in a deep glacial valley and flanked by sheer slopes on all but one

side, it's a secretive-feeling spot. Go for a swim, hire an SUP, hike the 7.5-mile (12km) trail around the water's edge and ride the cable car from Ukanc up to Vogel – in winter, there's good skiing here. The Bohinj ECO Hotel, 4 miles (6km) away in Bohinjska Bistrica, makes a great base.

RAISE A GLASS
Next, leave Bohinj behind for wine country. Hemmed in by mountains and dubbed 'Tuscany in Slovenia' for its undulating terrain, hilltop villages and endless rows of vines, Goriška Brda, around 50 miles (80km) southwest, is one of Slovenia's key wine-producing regions. It's renowned for its Merlot, Chardonnay and Rebula, an ancient white grape that produces lively but complex wines; its (often unfiltered) orange wines are growing in popularity too. Visit the vineyards and wend between the fortified medieval village of Šmartno, Dobrovo's Renaissance castle-museum, and Kojsko's Gothic church.

Food for thought

Slovenia's menu is a mix of Italian flair, Balkan roots, Hungarian plains, Austrian mountains and Slovene originality – washed down with a lot of schnapps. Lately, it has garnered international acclaim: in 2022, Hiša Franko, in the Soča Valley, was ranked 21st on the World's 50 Best Restaurants list. There are plenty of dishes you should seek out. The most typical Slovenian dessert, served at Easter and Christmas, is *potica*, a folded leavened-dough cake, commonly filled with walnut paste. *Gibanica* is a creamier pastry-cake from the eastern Prekmurje region, layered with apple, walnuts, curd cheese and poppy seeds. Also from the east is *bučno* (pumpkin-seed oil), which has an unctuous nuttiness and is delicious dribbled on everything from salad to ice cream. *Kranjska klobasa* is a sausage from Carniola made with pork and bacon plus salt, garlic and black pepper. Another hearty option is *štruklji*, dumplings with either sweet or savoury fillings, found in central Slovenia. Around Bohinj, look for farms making *mohant*, a semi-soft cheese with a musty smell and a bitter, tangy flavour. When in the Karst, look for *Kraški pršut*, prosciutto dry-cured by the chilly northeasterly wind that blows across the region.

Clockwise from top left:
wine-tasting in Goriška Brda; Slovenian *potica*, a walnut-paste-filled cake baked at Easter and Christmas; onto the water at Lake Bohinj

Apicultural epicentre

Bees are big in Slovenia. The country is said to have more beekeepers per capita than anywhere else, while the Carniolan honey bee, a native subspecies, is one of the most widespread across the world. Slovenia was also the home of Anton Janša, widely regarded as the father of modern beekeeping. Janša was born in Breznica, near Bled, in 1734, and taught his innovative apiculture methods at the Habsburg court in Vienna. Now, World Bee Day – an initiative spearheaded by Slovenia to celebrate these vital insects – is held annually on 20 May, Janša's birthday. You can visit Janša's beautiful original beehive in Breznica and learn more in Radovljica's Museum of Apiculture, which houses a fascinating collection of antique painted beehive panels. Also look for places offering medicinal apitherapy, including treatments that involve honey, beeswax, royal jelly and even lying above hives in special 'bee houses'.

From left: tending Slovenia's native Carnolian bees; Lake Bled; the Karst region's Škocjan Caves

The Vipava Valley, 30 miles (48km) further south, is arguably Slovenia's most dynamic wine region. Progressive vintners are using organic and biodynamic methods to create exciting, mainly white wines, with old indigenous grape varieties such as spicy Zelèn and floral Pinela. Stay somewhere atmospheric like Domačija Majerija, where guest rooms sit amid orchards and vines.

The Vipava extends south to the Karst, also a wine-growing region but better known for what's going on underground. This limestone plateau is riddled with tunnels and caves, and its name is the descriptor for such karstic landscapes worldwide. Drive south for 16 miles (26km) to Unesco-listed Škocjan Caves, one of the most astonishing examples of this subterranean splendour. You can tour miles of underground chambers bedecked with stalactites, stalagmites, flowstones and dripstones, culminating in the Great Hall, a cavern measuring around 100ft (30m) high and 400ft (120m) wide.

ADRIATIC ENDING

Continue into the sunny southern province of Istria and you'll start to sniff the sea. Slovenia has only 30 miles (48km) of coast, but it's well worth exploring. Drive 21 miles (34km) southwest, via limestone outcrops, olive groves and Socerb Castle, to reach Koper. This big port has a comely historic core, centred on Titov trg (Tito Square), with its 15th-century Praetorian Palace and the Cathedral of the Assumption – climb 204 steps up the cathedral's tower for splendid views. Then continue around the coast for 10 miles (16km) to journey's end, Piran. A preposterously pretty tangle of Venetian-Gothic alleyways wending around the tip of the Piranese Peninsula, it makes an enchanting finale. Walk the city walls, gen up on local history at interactive Mediadom Pyrhani museum, and delve into Piran's centuries-old salt harvesting traditions by becoming a salt-panner for the day.

INDEX

Electric Vehicle Road Trips Europe
May 2023
Published by Lonely Planet Global Limited
www.lonelyplanet.com
10 9 8 7 6 5 4 3 2 1

Printed in China
ISBN 978 1 83869 994 9
Text & maps © Lonely Planet 2022
Photos © as indicated 2022

General Manager, Publishing Piers Pickard
Associate Publisher Robin Barton
Commissioning Editor Peter Grunert
Designer Kristina Juodenas
Picture Research Claire Guest
Editor Polly Thomas
Index Bridget Blair
Cartographers Katerina Pavkova, Bohumil Ptáček
Print Production Nigel Longuet

Data sources
© Lonely Planet
© OpenStreetMap contributors
NASA/METI/AIST/Japan Space Systems, and US/Japan ASTER Science Team (2019). ASTER Global Digital Elevation Model V003
NASA JPL (2013). NASA Shuttle Radar Topography Mission Global 1 arc second
British Oceanographic Data Centre(2015). The GEBCO_2014 Grid

STAY IN TOUCH lonelyplanet.com/contact

Lonely Planet Global Limited

Digital Depot, Roe Lane (off Thomas St), Digital Hub, Dublin 8, D08 TCV4, IRELAND

Writers Alexis Averbuck, Sarah Baxter, Oliver Berry, Amanda Canning, Joanna Cooke, Rory Goulding, Hugh McNaughtan, Etain O'Carroll, James Smart, Oliver Smith, Orla Thomas, Sara van Geloven, Ryan Ver Berkmoes
Thanks to Felix Hamer (electricfelix.com)
Cover image © AerialVision_it / Shutterstock